Profits *with* Principles

Profits *with* Principles

Seven Strategies for Delivering Value with Values

Ira A. Jackson *and* Jane Nelson

Currency  **Doubleday**

New York / London / Toronto / Sydney / Auckland

A CURRENCY BOOK
PUBLISHED BY DOUBLEDAY
a division of Random House, Inc.

CURRENCY is a trademark of Random House, Inc., and DOUBLEDAY is a
registered trademark of Random House, Inc.

Book design by Laurie Jewell

Library of Congress Cataloging-in-Publication Data
Jackson, Ira A.
Profits with principles : seven strategies for delivering value with values /
Ira A. Jackson and Jane Nelson.
p. cm.
Includes bibliographical references.
1. Business ethics. 2. Social responsibility of business. 3. Corporate
profits—Moral and ethical aspects. 4. Corporations—Moral and ethical aspects.
5. International business enterprises—Moral and ethical aspects. 6. Corporate
governance. 7. Values. I. Nelson, Jane, 1960– II. Title.
HF5387.J2946 2004
658.4'08—dc22   2003068849

ISBN 0-385-50163-3
PRINTED IN THE UNITED STATES OF AMERICA
First Edition: June 2004

SPECIAL SALES
Currency Books are available at special discounts for bulk purchases for sales
promotions or premiums. Special editions, including personalized covers, excerpts
of existing books, and corporate imprints, can be created in large quantities for
special needs. For more information, write to Special Markets, Currency Books,
specialmarkets@randomhouse.com

1 3 5 7 9 10 8 6 4 2

To our families
and to the corporate pioneers
who are paving a new path
toward capitalism with a conscience

Contents

Preface

This book offers companies a framework for delivering profits and long-term value for shareholders while rebuilding trust and providing value for society. It identifies seven principles for achieving a new level of excellence and leadership that is required for business to succeed and society to prosper in the twenty-first century. The book draws upon the experiences of successful companies from around the world that are navigating relentless competitive pressures, increased political and economic uncertainty, changing societal expectations, and public demands for better governance, transparency, and accountability. These companies are demonstrating a qualitatively new form of corporate leadership and new types of partnership at a time of immense complexity and challenge.

Profits with Principles is aimed at business managers who care about the future of their company, whether they manage on the factory floor, in distant foreign subsidiaries, through corporate functions, or at the boardroom table. It is written for those who lead companies and business units today and for those who aspire to lead in the future. It provides relevant models and case studies useful to board directors, general managers, accountants, strategic planners, heads of R&D, marketing and sales, procurement, human resources, and product specialists, corporate responsibility and public affairs managers, business consultants, and trainers. It is aimed, as well, at leaders in government, academia, activist movements, and civic organizations who have a stake in the performance of the private sector and in leveraging its potential to shape a more sustainable and prosperous future.

We have written the book from the perspective of two practitioners who have worked in and with companies around the world, as well as in the public, academic, and nonprofit sectors. Between us, we have worked in two of the world's oldest and most successful banks, Citibank (now Citigroup) and BankBoston (soon to be Bank of America) and have lived in some of its great commercial cities, from New York, Boston, and Atlanta to Tokyo, Hong Kong, and London. Our work brings us into regular contact with leaders in business, government, and civic organizations, and we have participated in building new types of cross-sector partnerships, from community-level projects to global alliances.

We share a strong belief, backed by growing empirical evidence, that tomorrow's most successful and competitive companies will be those that combine a commitment to profitability with an explicit commitment to advancing the public interest. We illustrate this argument through examples from a wide range of companies that are pursuing profits with principles by publicly stating their values, setting clear targets and management metrics, and implementing against plan in all their areas of performance—ethical, social, and environmental, as well as financial.

We share a strong belief that capitalism and the private entrepreneurs and enterprises that drive it offer great promise for achieving a more prosperous and sustainable world. We believe that efficient markets embedded in democratic, well-governed societies provide enormous opportunities to drive innovation, spread wealth creation, raise living standards, and improve the quality of life for millions of people in America and around the globe. We agree with the Secretary-General of the United Nations, Kofi Annan, and others who have commented that "globalization, so far from being the cause of poverty and other social ills, offers the best hope of overcoming them."[1] Today, however, as he and others are arguing, there is an urgent need for leaders in the public and the private sectors to address the low levels of trust, high levels of inequality, and rising levels of environmental damage that challenge globalization. In the case of corporate leaders, there is a need to address these challenges head on, with the courage and vision to go "beyond business as usual" by deliberately choosing a strategy of profits with principles.

We are convinced that the companies playing a leadership role in addressing these challenges will reap sound business benefits in terms of long-term competitive advantage, better risk management, and new market opportunities. At the same time, in a world where the private sector is increasingly powerful and influential, taking on a greater leadership role is simply the responsible and right thing to do. This leadership role is about value and also about values; about competition and also about collaboration; about economics and also about ethics; about compliance and also about character; about institutions and also about individuals. It is about business leaders recognizing that successful and sustainable companies need the existence of prosperous and just societies and playing a role to help build such societies, through their own companies and in partnership with others.

In the pages that follow we lay out the case for how companies can benefit from creating value for both shareholders and society alike and how society can benefit from a greater alignment between private initiative and the public interest. We write with the strong conviction that principled business leaders, at all levels of a company, can build great companies while also contributing to more prosperous countries and communities. Our hope is that this book will challenge and inspire many others to follow their lead.

Jane Nelson and Ira A. Jackson
London and Boston
February 2004

Profits *with* Principles

Introduction

Is big business bad business?

NEWSWEEK

Kapow! American capitalism takes a beating.

THE ECONOMIST

System failure—Corporate America has lost its way.

FORTUNE

Can trust be rebuilt?

BUSINESS WEEK

The idea of making a reputation for corporate responsibility an investable theme is one of the best new ideas in Corporate America today.

BUSINESS WEEK

Some of America's biggest corporations believe that the best way to make money is by saving the world. And guess what? They just might be right.

FORTUNE

Corporations in America and around the world stand poised at the dawn of a major transformation. Not since the days of the Great Depression has there been such a severe decline of public trust and investor confidence in big business and in our economic system—nor has there been a better opportunity to build a new era of business-led excellence and leadership: an era in which business excellence is measured not only in terms of product, process, and financial performance, although no company can succeed without these, but also in terms of ethical, social, and environmental performance; an era in which corporate leadership is judged not only in terms of profit delivered, although this remains more important than ever, but also in terms of principles lived.

This book describes some of the global trends, competitive pressures, and changing societal expectations that are reshaping the rules of the game for running a profitable and principled business. Within this context, the book offers companies a framework for mastering these new rules of the game, by realigning their business practices in a way that restores trust while continuing to build competitive advantage and long-term opportunities for growth.

Although written in the context of daily headlines about corporate malpractice and malfeasance, this book is unabashedly positive and hopeful. It focuses on companies and businesspeople who are already delivering both private profits and public benefits, not on wishful thinking or good intentions. We profile real companies delivering measurable performance and concrete solutions for their stakeholders in an increasingly complex and difficult operating environment.

None of the companies we profile gets it right all the time. Almost every company has faced financial or reputation crises. Some have stumbled in the past; others undoubtedly will trip or be found wanting in the future; and a few face major leadership challenges today. While their experiences represent a cautionary tale of how complicated today's terrain is to navigate, they illustrate a constructive new approach to doing business. This is an approach that we believe is creating a new competitive context for the twenty-first century and will increasingly become a requirement for future corporate success, perhaps even survival.

We identify seven principles that can serve as a framework for any company or businessperson who aspires to contribute to a better world, while delivering long-term value and profitability under the new rules of the game.

Principle #1: Harness Innovation for Public Good

Innovation that anticipates or responds to changing consumer needs and societal trends is the lifeblood of sustainable and profitable business. It is also vital for building national competitiveness and social progress. Great companies understand the immense opportunities and responsibilities of innovation. They explicitly and systematically integrate ethical, social, and environmental considerations into their innovation and research-and-development (R&D) efforts. This includes efforts to develop new products and services, improve operational processes, and develop new business models that address social and environmental needs while still delivering profitable customer solutions. Harnessing innovation for the public good also requires the application of rigorous due diligence procedures to minimize any negative impacts that may arise from a company's R&D activities and its operations and products.

Principle #2: Put People at the Center

The quality of relationships that a company has with its employees and other key stakeholders along its value chain—customers, investors, suppliers, public officials, activists, and host communities—is crucial to its success and its ability to anticipate or respond to changing competitive conditions and societal expectations. It is the ideas, interests, and energy of people who work in and interact with a business that underpin innovation and transformation. Leading companies ensure that they have a clear understanding of who their stakeholders are and what matters to them. They work to ensure that there is regular communication and consultation with these people. They aim to build relationships that are based on mutual benefit, learning, accountability, transparency, and trust.

Principle #3: Spread Economic Opportunity

Great companies create wealth and increase economic opportunity. They make systematic efforts to spread economic opportunity as widely as possible, not only to their owners but also in the workplace, along the supply chain, and in local communities. They do so in the knowledge that this will help to enhance the prosperity and loyalty of their employees, business partners, and local neighbors, and may also help to build future markets and business relationships for the company. Efforts to spread economic opportunity include making a commitment to employee diversity, investing in local economic development, building business linkages with small and microenterprises, and supporting programs to increase access to information technology, education, and training.

Principle #4: Engage in New Alliances

There is a growing need and potential for companies to build cross-boundary alliances, often with nontraditional allies beyond the business sector. Successful companies are creating such alliances for a variety of purposes. They are collaborating to enhance their core business proposition and performance. They are building new types of partnership to increase the leverage and effectiveness of their philanthropic and community investment efforts. And they are undertaking joint efforts with other companies, as well as nongovernmental organizations and government bodies, to build more progressive public policy frameworks, more legitimate governance institutions, and more equitable market mechanisms.

Principle #5: Be Performance-Driven in Everything

A growing number of the world's most successful companies publicly commit to explicit targets for their ethical, social, and environmental performance, in addition to their financial and commercial performance. They establish management systems, incentive structures, training programs, and compliance processes to create the performance-driven culture that is necessary to strive toward the achievement of these targets. They report publicly on their progress, acknowledging failure and celebrating success, while continuously learning and adapting as they proceed.

Principle #6: Practice Superior Governance

The most visionary companies have a good understanding of the emerging governance agenda for business, and they are actively responding to and shaping this agenda. They recognize that practicing superior governance in today's world calls not only for more rigorous approaches to corporate governance, but also sustainability governance—namely, greater accountability, transparency, and independent overview of all the company's key areas of performance, not only its financial performance.[1] They also see the importance of supporting more transparent and noncorrupt interaction between business and governments—what we have termed public governance.

Principle #7: Pursue Purpose Beyond Profit

Sustained, long-term business leadership is built upon clarity of purpose, principles, and values. These are what a great company stands for, and would stand by, even if adhering to them results in a competitive disadvantage, missed opportunity, or increased costs. The best leaders recognize that embedding principles and values in the company's day-to-day operations requires a systematic, rigorous, and ongoing effort that reaches far beyond vision statements and fine words. In order to align words with action, they actively engage their employees, consult with external stakeholders, invest in training and accountability systems, act as role models in the workplace and beyond, and emphasize the centrality of purpose and values even more in tough times than in prosperous ones.

These seven principles offer no quick fixes or "off-the-shelf" solutions. The issues, management dilemmas, and business opportunities that they cover are complex. In most companies they call for difficult strategic choices and often organizational and cultural change. This is challenging, especially during a period of economic upheaval, geopolitical uncertainty, and relentless competitive pressure. But it is possible—we would argue, essential. And, as we will show, it can also be profitable.

We describe over sixty examples of companies from around the world that illustrate one or more of these principles in practice. We illustrate the benefits that principled companies can offer to society and the potential that sound principles can offer to business for delivering profitable and sustainable growth. This potential includes opportunities to transform operational processes; deliver better quality and value to customers; motivate employees; develop new products; enter new markets; build new business models; and achieve a greater competitive edge. In many cases companies practicing these principles have also been able to lower costs; enhance reputation; raise quality; improve risk management; increase access to capital; decrease their cost of capital; and attract and retain the best talent. They have been able to make a profit *and* make a positive impact on society.

Part One of this book establishes the context for doing business in a turbulent world. The first chapter outlines some of the events that have led to or exacerbated the current low levels of trust and high levels of inequality in America and globally. It argues that relentless competitive pressures and economic downturn, corporate governance crises and ethics scandals, and geopolitical uncertainty and ongoing environmental decline have combined to create the equivalent of a "perfect storm" for the private sector. The chapter concludes with some key messages as to what these trends mean for business in terms of rising societal expectations and new leadership challenges.

The second chapter looks in more detail at the context in which competitive advantage is formulated. It reviews how emerging societal expectations and demographic, economic, and political trends are influencing values and changing the rules of the game for business. It highlights some of the key business risks and opportunities created by these changing rules of the game. And it outlines the direction that leading companies are starting to move in to deliver value for both their shareholders and society within this new context. This is the direction that we predict will differentiate the successful companies of the future.

Part Two demonstrates how some of the world's leading companies are mastering the new rules of the game. Using our framework of seven principles, we describe how different companies are putting these principles into practice and we highlight key lessons that are relevant to others.

We focus on large companies, as they are the businesses that we work with and know best. We believe, however, that the seven principles and the practical ideas that we offer have relevance for all companies and business leaders, regardless of their size, industry sector, or country of origin.

Most of the companies we profile face, or have faced, major financial or reputation challenges. Despite this, we consider them to be among the best in the world. We see them as corporate visionaries full of talented people trying to perform with integrity and to succeed in a competitive and complex world. They offer valuable lessons worth learning from. A few examples:

We look at large industrial companies such as DuPont, Toyota, Ford, Dow Chemical, and Alcoa, because they have cut operating costs, improved quality, and gained market share through innovative redesign of products, services, and manufacturing systems. In many cases, these measures have improved safety and environmental performance as well as economic performance. DuPont, for example, has embarked on its third century by making "sustainable growth" a central element of its corporate strategy—a concept the company defines as "the creation of shareholder value and societal value while decreasing our environmental footprint."

We profile financial institutions such as FleetBoston, Citigroup, JP-Morgan Chase, Deutsche Bank, and Goldman Sachs, because they have started to reach out to underserved markets and "bank the previously unbankable." They are providing financial services and training to low-income communities in the United States and internationally by developing innovative new products and services and combining strategic philanthropy with long-term business opportunities. In doing so they are starting to build new markets, loyal new customer bases, brand equity, and new sources of profit.

We focus on consumer goods companies such as Unilever, Home Depot, Nestlé, Procter & Gamble, Coca-Cola, Starbucks, Nike, and McDonald's, which operate in fiercely competitive, low-margin, brand-sensitive, consumer-driven markets. In different ways and for different reasons, these companies have recognized that their ability to meet changing consumer demands and protect brand equity will require them to improve their social and environmental performance along their entire global supply chains and product life cycles. They are engaging in a variety of alliances and consultation processes, often with traditional adversaries, in order to manage and measure this performance and tap into new growth markets and sources of innovation.

We highlight information technology companies such as Cisco Systems, Nokia, Dell, Vodafone, Hewlett Packard, IBM, and Microsoft, because they are developing new alliances and creating economically viable business models and social venture solutions for bridging the "digital divide." They are harnessing the power of technology not only to improve the performance and productivity of their business clients, but also to help build better-educated, healthier, and more connected communities, both in the United States and internationally.

We illustrate the role that large global operators such as Shell, BP, Chevron Texaco, General Electric, and General Motors are playing in addressing calls for better corporate governance and for what is being termed "sustainability governance"—providing increased transparency and accountability for their ethical, social, and environmental, as well as financial performance. These companies are also engaging in collective efforts with governments and with other companies to tackle tough problems such as global climate change and more equitable international development. They are helping to build market frameworks and standards that are crucial underpinnings for effective and successful global capitalism.

We analyze pharmaceutical companies such as Merck, Johnson & Johnson, GlaxoSmithKline, Novartis, and Pfizer, which are facing increased competition and challenges to their intellectual property rights while endeavoring to develop new business models and alliances to improve access to essential medicines and invest in their local communities. We look at some of the steps they are taking to live their values, some of the management dilemmas they face, and some of the business benefits that they are reaping.

We review professional services firms such as McKinsey & Company, KPMG, Monitor, Bain, PricewaterhouseCoopers, Accenture, and the Boston Consulting Group, because they are harnessing the intellectual capital and problem-solving skills of their staffs to undertake projects beyond the corporate world in some of America's most problematic inner cities and the world's poorest countries. These projects are helping to address local development challenges, as well as building the creativity, emotional intelligence, and team-working and systems-thinking skills of professional auditors and consultants.

We acknowledge the foresight and creativity of the early pioneers in the corporate responsibility and social enterprise movement, some of which have built their entire business models around an ethos of combined social and economic value. They include companies such as Ben & Jerry's, the Body Shop, Patagonia, Herman Miller, Whole Foods Market, Timberland, Fetzer Vineyards, Medtronic, Novo Nordisk, Malden Mills, the Cooperative Bank, Levi Strauss & Company, Stonyfield Farm, and Stride Rite. Although we refer to some of them in the pages that follow, their stories have been documented in detail elsewhere, and we have chosen not to focus on them for the examples in this book. We concentrate instead on companies that have more recently started to integrate social and environmental performance metrics into their corporate strategies, risk management systems, and business models.

The companies we profile are dealing with a wide variety of real-world dilemmas and business opportunities, in a climate of changing competitive pressures and rising societal expectations. We are still in largely uncharted waters. The type of experimentation, innovation, and transformation being undertaken by these companies will be crucial to developing the most effective business models and corporate practices for the twenty-first century. Our hope is that this book will contribute to the dialogue and debate on what these models and practices should look like and how they will change the boundaries and responsibilities of business. We also trust that the combination of practical examples and key lessons that illustrate each operating principle will serve as a tool kit to help people in business to implement the new leadership disciplines required to build competitiveness and trust in today's turbulent world.

Part One

Doing Business
in a
Turbulent World

Chapter One

Capitalism Rules . . . But Needs New Rules

Never before in the 33 years of the World Economic Forum's history has the situation in the world been so fragile, as complex and as dangerous as this year. We feel that we are living in a new world—with new rules and new dangers— but certainly also with new opportunities. . . . Today we need a new, an enlarged concept of business leadership!

KLAUS SCHWAB, PRESIDENT, WORLD ECONOMIC FORUM, 2003

Over the past twelve years the context for doing business has changed almost beyond recognition. This rapid and unprecedented period of change has challenged even the best-laid plans and most creative corporate visions. Anyone who wants to understand the risks and opportunities of doing business in today's world and what they mean for tomorrow's competitive advantage, and in some cases survival, must understand our recent history. It has been extensively chronicled and analyzed elsewhere. Here we offer a very brief review.

Capitalism Triumphant

The spread of global capitalism seemed unstoppable in the early 1990s. It had torn down barriers, both virtual and real—the Iron Curtain and the Berlin Wall. It had decreased state ownership and removed trade restrictions. It had mobilized virtually every nation around a common pursuit: economic progress and wealth creation. It inspired entrepreneurs, pensioners, and small-town savings clubs. It shaped the hopes of young people from inner cities in America to rural communities in Zimbabwe.

In the United States, the engine of capitalism created more than twenty-two million jobs in less than ten years. By 2000, there were nearly five million millionaires and some three hundred billionaires. The financial wealth of Americans increased by an astonishing $3 trillion a year for the years 1998 to 2000. The Dow Jones Industrial Average appeared to have overcome the laws of gravity; it increased almost fourfold in less than ten years, moving from three thousand in April 1991 to eleven thousand in May 1999, having taken fifteen years to shift from two to three thousand between 1972 and 1987.

Elsewhere around the world, in the space of less than a decade, over three billion people moved from living in centrally planned economies to economies shaped, to a lesser or greater extent, by the efficiencies and vagaries of market forces.

The twin processes of privatization and liberalization facilitated a massive transfer of assets to the private sector and a dramatic increase in international capital flows. Between 1983 and 2000, for example, world market capitalization soared from about $3 trillion to over $35 trillion. Foreign exchange flows grew from $13 billion in 1973, to more than $1.5 trillion a day in 2000. Foreign direct investment increased from about $100 billion a year in the late 1980s to well over $800 billion by 1999. According to the United Nations, the number of transnational corporations almost doubled from 37,000 in 1990 to over 60,000 in 2001, with their foreign affiliates growing almost fivefold from 170,000 to 800,000. The size and reach of individual companies ballooned, and by the turn of the century the world's five largest corporations each had sales larger than the gross domestic products of over 180 of the world's nation-states. American companies accounted for about half of the world's largest 500 companies.

Global capitalism, and the private enterprises and entrepreneurs who were driving it, gained soaring profits and an unprecedented level of prominence, affluence, and influence.

As the end of the twentieth century approached, there seemed to be little doubt, at least in most corporate boardrooms and national capitals, that capitalism was triumphant. The message appeared to be clear:

Capitalism works. It is magnificently efficient. It performs at breakneck speed. It creates jobs, expands opportunities, and introduces new technologies. It gives people access to greater benefits, conveniences, and riches today than at any time in the history of civilization. Governments should get out of the way of the market and give capitalism a free rein. Shareholder value and self-interest reign. CEO pay may be high and growing higher relative to that of average workers, but as long as the stock market keeps soaring and company earnings keep growing at a dizzying rate, who are we to complain? Surely a rising tide will lift all boats!

The CEOs who were able to deliver ever-increasing quarterly earnings were lauded as the modern-day celebrities atop the pedestal of power and prestige in a new golden age of capitalism.

Yet, as the century came to an end, there were increasingly clear signs that all was not right. Media-grabbing antiglobalization protests dominated the World Trade Organization meeting in Seattle in 1999, and financial crises rocked Mexico, Asia, and Russia. Despite the benefits that globalization had created for numerous countries and companies, the social and environmental downsides were becoming more apparent. People started to question the excesses and the costs, and they turned their attention to the role of big business.

Capitalism Under Siege

In September 2000, *Business Week* asked an uncomfortable question on its cover: "Too Much Corporate Power?" It shared the following findings of a joint *Business Week*/Harris poll[1]:

■ Over 70 percent of Americans surveyed said that business had too much power over too many aspects of their lives and too much political influence.

■ Only 4 percent agreed that companies should have only one purpose—to make the most profit for their shareholders—and that their pursuit of that goal would be best for America in the long run. Of those polled, 95 percent agreed that American corporations should have more than one purpose and that they also owe something to their workers and the communities in which they operate.

■ Only 14 percent felt that what was good for business was good for most Americans—less than half the proportion supporting the same view in 1996.

Business Week's journalists offered hard-hitting analysis of the growing disillusionment and distrust among ordinary Americans relating to excessive CEO pay; public revulsion over corporate bankrolling of politicians; concerns over the impacts of globalization; sweatshops; "in-your-face" marketing campaigns; commercialism in schools; low wages for high productivity; and high prices for poor products and services. The cover story concluded that "corporate executives would be wise to deal with the burden [of power and responsibility]—and take care to avoid the hubris that so often accompanies heady success. If they don't, a growing number of Americans stand ready to call them to account."

The time for that "accounting" has now arrived. In the span of less than three years, from 2000 to 2003, a number of political and economic events have turned the post–Cold War euphoria of global capitalism on its head.

The corporate governance crises in America and in other major capital markets have been a critical factor in undermining trust in our economic system. For over ten years companies such as Enron and WorldCom epitomized the promise of the "New Economy" and the "New World Order." They captured the spirit of the age: high-tech innovation, risk-taking, global horizons, new business models, sophisticated financial engineering, and declining regulation. None of these is necessarily problematic. In fact, most are essential to building corporate competitiveness and national prosperity. For these companies and others, however, the fundamental principles of running a good, decent business seemingly got lost.

The diverse set of public and private "checks and balances" that make our system of capitalism effective were undermined and overwhelmed by a combination of complacency, hype, arrogance, greed, and lack of oversight. As Alan Greenspan, Federal Reserve Board chairman, has described it: "Lawyers, internal and external auditors, corporate boards, Wall Street security analysts, rating agencies, and large institutional holders of stock all failed for one reason or another to detect and blow the whistle on those who breached the level of trust essential to well-functioning markets. . . . An infectious greed seemed to grip much of our business community."[2]

Although corporate governance failures were a crucial catalyst, they were not the only series of events to challenge the triumph of global capitalism. Other crucial factors included the bursting of the dot-com bubble; the financial crisis in Argentina; slowing economic growth worldwide; the events of 9/11; the increased threat of international terrorism; the waging of war; increased international trade tension; growing scientific evidence of the dangers of global climate change and environmental decline; and rising antiglobalization sentiment and growing anticapitalism campaigns. These factors have put most business leaders and their companies on the defensive. And they have placed many companies, especially those with prominent brands and global reach, under a critical and unforgiving spotlight.

In a few short years the antiglobalization and anticapitalism message has gathered strength. It can be summarized in this way:

If left to its own the capitalist system is efficient but ruthless. It creates enormous wealth but can leave poverty and inequality in its wake. It increases productivity but discards employees. Capitalism powers the stock market but closes factories and abandons whole communities. It reduces consumer prices but lowers the wages of workers. It balances budgets but deprives governments of resources needed for investment. It offers access to the wonders of the World Wide Web but leaves millions behind in a new digital divide. It generates marvelous inventions but leaves environmental pollution in its wake. It democratizes information but marginalizes people. It speeds up the flow of goods, services, and money but creates increased volatility, vulnerability, and insecurity. Globalization creates unprecedented riches but widens the gap between those who have and get ahead and those who don't and are left farther and farther behind.

There are sound and empirically rigorous counterarguments to many of these negative perceptions about global capitalism. Despite its challenges, the system of global capitalism offers greater hope for the world than alternative models that have been tested and found seriously wanting. Open markets, liberalized trade, and integration into the global economy still offer poorer countries and communities their best hope of improved living standards. In many cases it is the lack of economic growth and investment, rather than growth and investment, that is a cause of poverty and exclusion. As Joseph Nye, dean of Harvard's Kennedy School of Government, has commented, "No poor country has ever become rich by isolating itself from global markets, although North Korea and Myanmar have impoverished themselves by doing so."[3]

At the same time, there are some uncomfortable truths and long-term threats raised by the diverse and increasingly international group of people and organizations who distrust big business and who question the merits of globalization. As with the corporate governance challenge, the onus is on the private sector to demonstrate that it can be part of the solution, rather than part of the problem. Far and away the vast majority of business leaders have operated with high standards of integrity, but this is not how much of the public sees it. The private sector must demonstrate that it is worthy of public trust and confidence. Companies need to show that they can work in partnership with governments and others to help make the process of globalization not only profitable, but also more equitable and more beneficial for more people, without destroying the world's environmental capacity to nurture future generations.

For many businesspeople these leadership challenges represent un-

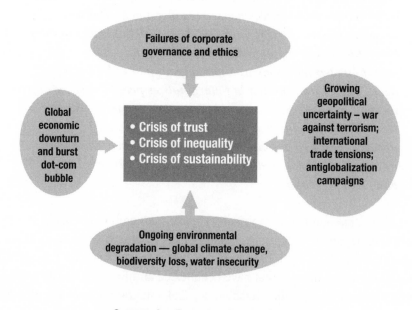

Companies Face the "Perfect Storm"

charted and choppy waters, but they cannot be ignored. Together, they represent a powerful and unprecedented collision of forces—what many corporate leaders are describing as the economic and political equivalent of a "perfect storm."

Business leaders need to face this "perfect storm" and navigate with a new compass. Despite the ongoing pressures of relentless competition, and the need to deliver short-term financial performance, no major company can ignore and fail to respond to the following threats to long-term corporate success and viability:

- The crisis of trust
- The crisis of inequality
- The crisis of sustainability

The following trends and statistics provide sobering but important reading for today's and tomorrow's leaders in business.

The Crisis of Trust

Two-thirds of Americans think that corporations make good products and compete well in the global economy, but *only one-third* feel that large corporations have ethical business practices. Just 26 percent believe that companies are straightforward and honest in their dealings with consumers and employees. These findings from a *Business Week/Harris* poll illustrate that Americans' trust in business is worryingly low.[4] In an editorial on restoring trust in corporate America, *Business Week* commented, "To many critics, Corporate America's leaders seem shockingly out of touch, blind to the deterioration in public confidence. A seemingly endless stream of bad news alleging widespread management negligence and malfeasance is chipping away at the trust vital to a free-market system."[5]

The problem isn't confined to American business. The *Financial Times,* in June 2003, released another in a long line of opinion polls showing low levels of trust in British companies and the people who lead them. In an accompanying editorial it observed that "capitalism is a system that functions on trust. It can take many years to build a culture where there is confidence in the free operation of the market. . . . Yet that confidence can quickly be eroded by unchecked greed or a cavalier attitude to commitments."[6]

This decline in trust extends to many other countries. The World Economic Forum, in January 2003, released a major global public opinion survey that asked 34,000 people across forty-six countries to assess the trustworthiness of different institutions, including global companies and large domestic companies, "to operate in the best interests of our society."[7] The survey found that not only are companies among the least trusted of any of the seventeen institutions tested, but there has been a significant and widespread decline in trust over the last two years in almost all the countries where tracking is available. More and more stakeholders are accusing big business of being untruthful, unfair, and unethical.

Some 85 million Americans invest in the stock market. After losing an estimated $7 trillion in accumulated wealth and witnessing their investment nest eggs squandered while corporate chieftains got away with millions, investors from Wall Street to Main Street are alienated and angry. They are fed up with unethical accounting practices, dishonest disclosure procedures, weak corporate governance structures, excessive executive compensation, threats to their pension funds, and analysts who offer conflicted advice and treat small investors with contempt. They are demanding that the Wizard of Oz come out from behind the curtain—transparent, accountable, ethical, and believable.

Among consumers, brand loyalty is low and cynicism about corporate claims and advertising is high, especially among the younger generation. They are demanding better product information and accountability from business, especially large companies.

Workers are tired of being told "you are the company's most valuable asset" when millions face the constant threat of unemployment, increasingly long hours, stressful working conditions, pressure to meet unrealistic goals, deceptive practices, and corporate cultures still rife with discrimination, despite a nod at legal compliance. They want to see more evidence that their management says what it does and does what it says. And ordinary citizens, too, are beginning to ask which companies they can trust. They are questioning the relationships between powerful corporations and political power brokers and focusing increased attention on corporate campaign contributions, corporate tax avoidance, and corporate lobbying.

The costs and risks of this prevailing lack of trust and confidence are high, at both the level of individual companies and in our economic system more widely. The Conference Board's Commission on Public Trust and Private Enterprise reports, "Federal Reserve Board Chairman Alan Greenspan has testified that diminished confidence in corporate earnings reports has been linked to depressed valuations of equity securities, higher debt costs, and slowing of new capital investment."[8]

Fortune magazine's editorial director, Geoffrey Colvin, observes, "In the new digital, trust-based economy, the stakes are extraordinarily high. A company's trustworthiness, embodied in brand and reputation, is increasingly all that customers, employees, and investors have to rely on. . . . Experience shows that this asset is built slowly and painfully but can be lost in an eye blink, and in losing it, you may lose everything."[9]

Trust is increasingly recognized as one of the most important assets that any company can have and one of the most precious commodities that makes our system of capitalism work. Restoring trust and confidence in the capital markets and the private sector is one of the single greatest challenges facing business. To overcome the prevailing suspicion and cynicism, companies need to demonstrate to investors and other stakeholders that they can deliver good performance with good governance and that the information they provide about the company is honest, accurate, and comprehensive.

The Crisis of Inequality

Another factor underlying mistrust and lack of confidence in our big companies and economic system is the growing public awareness of inequalities in the corporate workplace and at national and global levels. A few key trends and statistics in each of these areas illustrate the cause for concern.

Inequality in the Workplace The large gap between senior executive compensation and average workers' pay has become a prominent issue during the spate of corporate governance scandals since 2001.

In the United States, CEO compensation as a multiple of the average worker's was 42 in 1980, about 100 in 1990, and over 500 in 1999.[10] Put another way, CEOs received $500 for every $1 the average worker earned. Most stock options were also limited to top executives.[11] *Business Week* commented in one of its editorials:

What has really undermined the reputation of the managerial class is the perception that it is breaking a fundamental cultural rule central to American values: fairness. . . . This is a winner-take-all philosophy that is unacceptable in American society, especially at a time when teamwork is being extolled as the key to higher productivity and company success and all employees are putting in long hours. The size of CEO compensation is simply out of hand.[12]

This point is illustrated by the diagrams below:

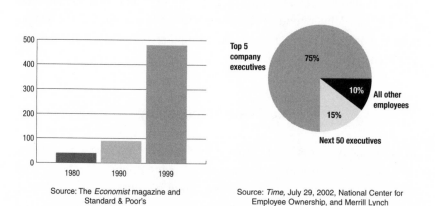

Rich Bosses
CEO pay as a multiple of average worker's
United States

The Options Debate
Estimated distribution of options outstanding as of 2000
in the United States

Top 5 company executives 75%

10% All other employees

15%

Next 50 executives

Source: The *Economist* magazine and Standard & Poor's

Source: *Time,* July 29, 2002, National Center for Employee Ownership, and Merrill Lynch

Mistrust also arises because of the gap in some cases between executive pay and performance. In their ninth annual CEO compensation survey, *Executive Excess 2002,* the Institute for Policy Studies and United for a Fair Economy pointed to the following inequalities:

■ The CEOs of twenty-three large companies under investigation for accounting irregularities earned an average of $62 million from 1999 to 2001, which was 70 percent more than the average for all CEOs in the annual *Business Week* executive pay survey. At the same time, employees of these twenty-three companies have suffered a total of 162,000 layoffs since January 2001, and between January 2000 and July 2002, the value of shares at these firms plunged by $530 billion, about 73 percent of their total value.

■ The graph below comparing CEO pay, stock prices, corporate profits, inflation, and worker pay over the eleven-year period 1990 to 2001 shows how the growth in CEO pay has far outstripped not only average worker pay, but also the other indicators of corporate performance.[13]

Inequality in America Since the 1960s the United States has experienced a period of unprecedented wealth creation, but during this time inequality between the rich and poor has risen. From the late 1980s to the late 1990s, average income of the lowest-income families grew by

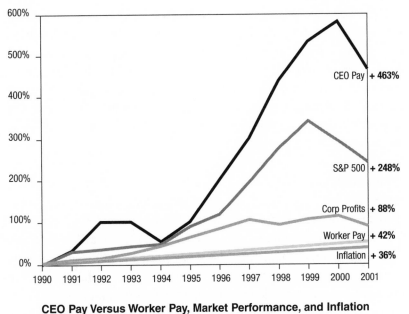

CEO Pay Versus Worker Pay, Market Performance, and Inflation

Source: Institute for Policy Studies and United for a Fair Economy, 2003

less than 1 percent, while income for the highest-income families grew by 15 percent, according to the Economic Policy Institute and Center on Budget and Policy Priorities.[14] While the number of billionaires in the country increased, so, too, did the number of people living below the official poverty line. Analysis of data from the Congressional Budget Office covering the years 1979 to 2000 shows 2000 as the time of greatest economic disparity of any year during this period, and probably the greatest since the 1930s.[15] The annual Vital Signs 2003 report states that "of all high-income nations, the United States has the most unequal distribution of income, with over 30% of income in the hands of the richest 10% and only 1.8% going to the poorest 10%."[16]

The Pew Global Attitudes Project found that in 2003, 15 percent of Americans said there had been times in the past year when they had been unable to afford food—the highest proportion in any advanced economy.[17] In its report *Hardships in America,* the Economic Policy Institute concludes that 29 percent of working families do not earn a living wage as defined by local and national budget studies. Over 70 percent of these families have to "skip meals or rent payments and forgo needed medical attention."[18] Over 40 million Americans don't have access to health insurance.

These are sobering figures in the world's wealthiest country. Many would argue that they are likely to be exacerbated by recent federal tax cuts. John Sweeney, president of the AFL-CIO, which represents thirteen million American workers, has commented, "For globalization to work for America, it must work for working people. We should measure the success of our economy by the breadth of our middle class and the scope of opportunity offered to the poorest child to climb into that middle class."[19]

Global Inequality On a global basis, there have been improvements in life expectancy, living standards, and literacy for millions of people during the past decade. The World Bank calculates that the total number of people living in absolute poverty has declined since the 1980s. Despite these hopeful signs, the levels of inequality remain high. Opinion varies on whether inequality is growing, but there is no doubt that it represents a serious leadership challenge, mainly to governments but also to companies with global interests. A few examples of what this inequality means in practice:

▪ It is estimated that about 80 percent of world income goes to the top 20 percent of people, while 60 percent of the world's population get only 6 percent of world income. The combined wealth of the world's two hundred richest people hit $1 trillion in 1999, which equals the annual income of the poorest 47 percent of the world's population. Three U.S. billionaires alone were worth more than the gross national product of the world's forty-eight poorest countries combined, home to 600 million people.[20]

▪ Americans and Europeans spend $37 billion a year on pet food—$4 billion more than the estimated annual additional total needed to provide basic health and nutrition for everyone in the world.[21]

▪ Farm subsidies of more than $300 billion a year in industrial countries allow farmers to export food crops at prices 20 to 50 percent below the cost of production, undermining farmers in developing nations. The typical European cow lives on subsidies equivalent to about $2.50 a day, while over three billion human beings in the world have to get by on $2 or less a day.[22]

It is not the role of business to solve these crises of inequality on its own, except within its own workplace. Governments in both developed and developing countries are largely responsible for the inequality that exists at national and global levels and for finding solutions. Yet the private sector cannot ignore the facts and trends; nor can it afford to sit on the sidelines as an indifferent bystander. In situations where high levels of inequality and poverty generate anti-American sentiments and a backlash against globalization and capitalism, it is in the interests of the private sector to help play a creative, problem-solving role to increase access to opportunity and hope.

The Crisis of Sustainability

The inequalities in our global income patterns also have implications for the use of the world's threatened natural resources. Just 15 percent of the world's population, who live in high-income countries in Europe and North America, account for over 50 percent of all the world's consump-

Ecological Footprint:
Amount of Land Used to Meet Human Needs
by region and income group, 1999

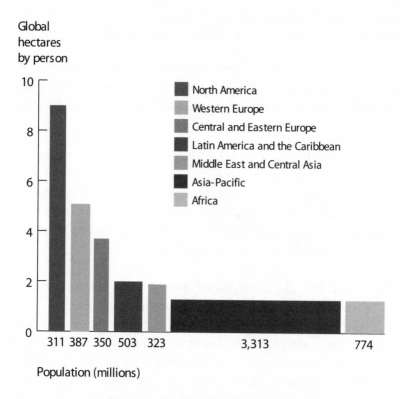

Global
hectares
by person

- North America
- Western Europe
- Central and Eastern Europe
- Latin America and the Caribbean
- Middle East and Central Asia
- Asia-Pacific
- Africa

311 387 350 503 323   3,313   774

Population (millions)

Source: *Living Planet Report,* 2002, World Wildlife Fund

tion, while the poorest 40 percent in developing countries account for only 11 percent. With less than 5 percent of world population, the United States uses 26 percent of global oil, 25 percent of the world's coal, and 27 percent of the world's natural gas. It also contributes 24 percent of the world's total emissions of carbon from fossil fuels.[23] An alarming graph from the *Living Planet 2002* report produced by the World Wildlife Fund (WWF) shows the ecological footprint—a measure of humanity's use of renewable natural resources—for seven regions of the world.

WWF reports, "The footprint per person of high income countries was on average over six times that of low income countries, and over three times greater than the Earth's biological capacity."[24]

The only way that it will be possible for millions of people to have better access to even basic needs, such as energy, water, food, and decent housing, without accelerating environmental decline even further is through new approaches to business and policy making. These include the application of new technologies, more resource-efficient production systems, more sustainable consumption patterns, better management and protection of renewable resources, and the development of new market frameworks and pricing mechanisms that reflect the true cost and value of our natural resources. Governments must play a lead role in ensuring that this happens. As we illustrate in the following chapters, however, business can play a role through leadership and creating new market opportunities.

What Does All This Mean for Your Business?

In this increasingly complex and uncertain global environment there are two certainties for corporate leaders and their companies: rising expectations and new leadership challenges.

Rising Expectations More is being expected of business and its leaders, by more people, in more places than ever before in corporate history. Pressure to deliver shareholder value remains relentless. Pressure to deliver wider societal value and good governance is also growing. These expectations are placing corporate governance and corporate citizenship firmly alongside corporate competitiveness at the heart of the business agenda.

Investors, from multibillion-dollar institutions to small-town investment clubs, are demanding greater corporate transparency and accountability. They still expect good financial performance, but are now also looking for honesty and values in executive suites and corporate boardrooms. Shareholder activism is on the rise, and the socially responsible investment movement is one of the fastest-growing fund-management sectors in the United States, Europe, and Asia.

Consumers are questioning what they read and hear and buy. They still demand quality, reliability, and good value in their products and services, but they now also want to know how these are produced and how workers and the environment are treated along the supply chain.

Employees, especially recent graduates, are searching for better work–life balance and professional growth. They still care about decent pay and a good benefits package but are now also looking for a work-place where they will feel motivated, respected, and listened to. In the absence of these their loyalty is eroding.

Governments are looking to the private sector to help them solve seemingly intractable public policy problems, from addressing social and environmental challenges to tackling national security and international terrorism, drugs, and money laundering. They still regulate business and demand corporate tax dollars but are now also looking at new ways to engage private enterprise in delivering public goods and services.

The *media* is shining a spotlight on business practices. It still follows the financial results but is now looking behind the official numbers, asking more searching questions and exposing more examples of ethical, social, and environmental failure. As a result of unprecedented communications capacity via the Internet and global media, news about corporate behavior can be highly effective in either enhancing or damaging a company's reputation and brand equity. It can turn a local problem into a global public relations crisis for a company almost overnight.

The *general public* is fed up with what they see as the growing political power and influence of big business and with high levels of inequality within the workplace. They are asking tough questions, such as: What are the values of corporations? If almost half of the world's largest "economic entities" are multinational companies, what is big business doing about global problems? Who controls the power of big business? Who is big business accountable to?

New Leadership Challenges These rising expectations are creating leadership challenges for business on a scale and level of complexity that is unprecedented. In order to sustain the trust and reputation that are crucial to successful enterprise, companies are having to demonstrate that they can produce goods and services that consumers want to buy in a manner that is competitive and profitable while responding to the rising, and sometimes conflicting, expectations of other stakeholders.

Rarely, if ever, has the private sector faced such a complex and contradictory mix of economic and political uncertainty, competitive pressures, new risks and opportunities, growing public mistrust, and high expectations, both from the market and society. Never before has a company's legitimacy and acceptance by society been so influenced by such a wide range of stakeholders, laws, and operating norms. Nor have corporate risk and reputation been so dependent on such a broad spectrum of drivers. The leadership challenge goes beyond complying with laws, protecting reputation, and controlling risks. The challenge is also about building future competitive edge. It is about anticipating the markets of tomorrow and understanding the changing societal expectations and major demographic shifts that are shaping these markets.

A few of the relentless and sometimes contradictory demands that leaders of companies of all sizes and industry sectors are facing include pressures to:

■ Satisfy financial analysts and investors, *as well as* consumers, employees, politicians, regulators, local communities, and vocal citizen groups.

■ Demonstrate both short-term profitability *and* long-term growth.

■ Produce more in terms of products and services, *but* use less in terms of the depletion of natural resources.

■ Simultaneously provide low-cost products *with* high-quality customer service, while seeking brand differentiation in a world of increasingly commoditized products and services.

■ Cut costs, restructure, and lay people off *and* continue to attract, retain, and motivate the most talented and skilled employees.

■ Balance confidentiality in an increasingly competitive business environment *with* greater transparency and accountability to more stakeholders on more issues—both financial and nonfinancial— than ever before.

The central challenge that business leaders face in this complex environment is continuing to deliver shareholder value while also delivering societal value. Doing this requires them to focus on all the normal levers of value creation, from cost competitiveness to customer focus. At the same time, it requires them to address a new and constantly emerging set of responsibilities and opportunities related to the company's ethical, social, and environmental performance.

These emerging responsibilities and opportunities are moving to the mainstream of the business agenda. They are not about good intentions or the chairman's favorite charity. They are not about "political correctness" or about business becoming the world's moral arbiter. And they are not about a utopian vision of some far-distant future. They are about "leading-edge" business practice in a world that already exists. They are about corporate profitability, strategy, and long-term competitive advantage, and about managing risk and reputation in an increasingly complex operating environment. They demand that we move beyond "business as usual," and they call for new business practices to equip companies for the twenty-first century. Some of the key shifts in thinking and approach that are required are outlined in the table on page 31.

These shifts require corporations to act according to clearly stated principles and values, to be more accountable and transparent, and to engage more actively with their stakeholders while continuing to innovate and produce products and services that consumers want and that deliver sound returns to investors. This is the core business leadership challenge of our time. Meeting this challenge offers our best hope for a system that stimulates and sustains economic growth while also building trust and promoting greater opportunity and environmental sustainability. As Peter Sutherland, chairman of Goldman Sachs and BP, has commented, "I believe it is part of building good sustainable businesses to help establish safe, secure, and peaceful societies. Business thrives where society thrives."[25]

But isn't there a danger that what we're calling for might result in distracting business from its principal function of providing goods and services and maximizing profitability and return to shareholders?

In the face of economic uncertainty, increased security risks, and unrelenting competition, isn't this a time more than ever for companies to turn inward and focus on their core business issues?

Why shouldn't business be left to do what it does best while government tends to the rest?

Toward New Business Practices for the Twenty-first Century

	Business as Usual	Business Leadership for the Twenty-first Century
Competitive Advantage	Quality, speed, and value of products and services	Quality, speed, and value of products and services PLUS quality of stakeholder relationships, reputation, ability to leverage synergies globally and locally, and development of new business models and innovations to reach underserved markets
Structure	Monolithic and top-down	Lattices of networks, alliances, and partnerships
View of Time	Short-term view of business decisions and their impacts	Long-term view, with short-term deliverables
Focus	The company (internal and independent)	The company PLUS stakeholders (external and interdependent)
Measures of Value	Tangibles—financial capital and physical capital	Tangibles AND intangibles—intellectual capital, social capital, relationship capital, reputation, quality, brand value, alliances, innovation, technology
Relationships with Stakeholders	Paternalistic, tight-lipped, and transactional	Transparent, accountable, and partnership oriented
Employee Proposition	Loyalty in exchange for security	Commitment in exchange for motivation, personal growth, and employability
Customer Proposition	Loyalty in exchange for a low-cost product	Selection in exchange for a low-cost, high-quality product AND corporate reputation
CEO's Role	Arbiter and power broker on a pedestal	Integrator and bridge builder within a network
World-class Performance	Price, quality, and financials	Price, quality, financials AND good governance, ethics, social and environmental performance
Purpose	Focus on shareholder value	Focus on shareholder value AND societal value
Core Mission	Value creation	Value creation AND values

Isn't business already perceived as too powerful and intrusive? Doesn't more corporate do-gooding create a kind of global neocorporatism?

These are fair and legitimate questions, and here are some answers.

Might greater social responsiveness distract business from the business of making money and dilute profitability and return to shareholders? We maintain that profits and principles are not mutually exclusive. Rather than being seen as contrasting or competing interests, profits and principles need to be linked. Far from destroying shareholder value, we believe that values can help create and sustain it. At the very least, the principled company can protect its corporate bottom line. But more often than not, it can actually contribute to it. We explore this "business case" argument in more detail throughout the book.

Doesn't protecting people's rights and responding to other societal demands and expectations belong to the government and the public sector? Public responsibilities do belong in the hands of the public sector, and some functions of society need greater governmental commitment and involvement, to be sure. But many global challenges—such as climate change, international trade, international terrorism, the provision of basic health care, and tackling the digital divide—are too large, intractable, and costly for any one sector to be expected to address or resolve. So too are many local challenges—such as urban regeneration, school reform, and homeland security. Indeed, for a new approach to capitalism to take hold, governments will need to do more, not less. But it's hard to imagine governments solving many of these and other lingering, unresolved issues on their own. Not only has government demonstrated inadequate capacity and lack of competence on many issues, but public resources are declining and new approaches are required. And business leaders can't have it both ways, demanding better schools, safer communities, lower taxes, and more market-driven approaches to social and environmental problems such as pollution or worker training, and then stepping away from involvement or any degree of responsibility for the public interest.

Isn't business already too powerful? It is undeniable that corporations exercise unprecedented influence in the new global economy. More corporate engagement beyond core business activities could lead to even greater public suspicion and backlash. These are concerns that business leaders of major companies cannot ignore, but they are no excuse to sit on the sidelines. The skills, resources, and networks of business can be a vital force for good. They need to be mobilized effectively, efficiently, and transparently and focused on where they can offer a comparative advantage and make a measurable difference. This may not overcome all the criticism leveled at business for being too powerful and unaccountable, but it could help a great deal to demonstrate the willingness of the corporate world to exercise rights with responsibility. As the *Financial Times* has argued, "If businesses want to make good profits, and to protect their good names, they must stand up and argue their case—for globalization, for free trade, and for responsible corporate behavior."[26]

Chapter Two

Building Tomorrow's Competitive Advantage Today

We define our direction as sustainable growth—the creation of shareholder and societal value while decreasing our environmental footprint along the value chains in which we operate.

CHAD HOLLIDAY, CHAIRMAN AND CEO, DUPONT

The success of big business and the well-being of the world have never been more closely linked. Global issues of the environment, health, diversity and human rights once at the periphery of management decision-making are fast becoming central to the way we work.

JORMA OLLILA, CHAIRMAN AND CEO, NOKIA

Creating Shareholder and Societal Value

If you pick up the annual report or CEO statements of almost any leading company around the world, the word "value" is likely to appear prominently. Value creation has become the business mantra for the twenty-first century. From factory floors to the corporate boardroom, there is recognition that the leadership companies of the future will be those that base their missions and their corporate strategies around creating, measuring, and managing value. The critical questions, for both business and society, are what types of value will be created and for whom?

Shareholder Value For the vast majority of business leaders, the challenge is first and foremost about creating shareholder value. Pressure to meet this challenge continues unabated, despite a more cautious and circumspect investment climate in the post–dot-com bubble and post-Enron world. Failure to deliver long-term profitability and financial value undermines the potential for any other type of value creation.

Employee and Customer Value Most business leaders recognize that long-term shareholder value cannot be delivered without having clear strategies and management systems in place to create measurable value for customers and employees. As customer choice expands dramatically in many countries and industries, and the intellectual capital of skilled employees becomes an increasingly important factor in achieving competitive advantage, no business can afford to ignore their needs and aspirations.

Is this enough to ensure competitive advantage and sustainable success in the twenty-first century? A small but growing number of companies and business leaders don't think so. They are going further.

Societal Value[1] These pioneering companies are certainly running their businesses with a clear commitment to delivering shareholder value and focusing on the needs and aspirations of customers and employees. They have incorporated initiatives to drive production and process excellence, adopted new methods for calculating economic value added, and embraced cutting-edge disciplines of employee engagement and customer satisfaction. At the same time, they are explicitly aiming to produce measurable benefits not only for their investors, employees, customers, and business partners, but also for host communities, countries, and society in general. They are measuring these benefits in terms of economic, social, and environmental contributions and in terms of stakeholder relationships that are based on mutual respect and trust. They are systematically managing for value with values. And they are publicly stating and accounting for these values, both inside the company and externally.

We believe the companies that are focused strategically on creating and delivering all these different types of value—shareholder value, employee value, customer value, and societal value—are the ones that will provide the answers to the following questions:

Who will be the corporate leaders of tomorrow, and what will be the growth industries?

Who will retain and sustain investor confidence in an increasingly competitive and risk-averse global marketplace? How will the analysts on Wall Street and in London, Frankfurt, and Tokyo be judging the "buys," the "holds," and the "sells" in 2010? Where will venture capitalists be placing their bets?

What will individual consumers, investors, and talented employees be looking for in the companies that they buy from, invest in, and work for?

Where will governments be focusing their regulatory muscle, and what companies will the social and environmental activists be targeting?

Where will your own company stand? Competitive, profitable, trusted, and admired? Muddling along? Vilified by key stakeholder groups? Somewhere in between? Or relegated to the pages of history? The trends described in the following pages and the way you respond to them are likely to be crucial in determining the answers to these questions.

Don't just take our word for it. The 108-year-old Dow Jones Indexes have also identified the emergence of a new class of value creators with their launch in 1999 of the Dow Jones Sustainability Index (DJSI) series.

Sustainability for Competitive Advantage

The Dow Jones Indexes are used the world over as barometers of corporate health and national wealth. For over a century, they have been tracking the companies and industries that have shaped America's and the world's development. Throughout this period they have often been "one step ahead of the game." They have accurately anticipated and reflected emerging global trends and the changing competitive landscape of business, from the railroads to the virtual highway and from America's own economic history to the emergence of the global economy. In August 1999, Dow Jones & Company joined forces with Zurich-based SAM Sustainable Asset Management to launch another new family of indexes, called the *Dow Jones Sustainability Indexes* (DJSI). These were the world's first major benchmarks for reflecting the financial performance of sustainability leaders, defined by the DJSI as companies that follow "a business approach to create long-term shareholder value by embracing opportunities and managing risks deriving from economic, environmental and social developments."[2]

The DJSI World index is made up of companies in the top 10 percent in terms of their sustainability record, out of a starting universe of the largest 2,500 firms in the Dow Jones Global Index by market capitalization. It includes over three hundred leading companies from some sixty industries and over twenty countries. As of June 2003 it had a combined market capitalization of US$4.6 trillion. It includes some of the world's great companies and most respected brands, many of which are profiled in this book: Johnson & Johnson; DuPont; BP; Shell; Nike; Procter & Gamble; Unilever; Nestlé; Dow; Citigroup; Alcoa; GlaxoSmithKline; 3M; Home Depot; Vodafone; and Nokia. DJSI uses rigorous quantitative and qualitative analysis to evaluate companies on their economic, social, and environmental value added, including their governance structure and traditional financial performance measures. The leaders selected are those companies that perform the best across all of these dimensions.

Although it is still in its early days, to date the performance of DJSI World has been encouraging. Against the MSCI World (Morgan Stanley Capital International), DJSI World underperformed in its first year of existence, when it suffered overproportionately from the steep fall of technology stocks as well as an overweighting in large caps. Since September 2000, however, it has shown better performance against the MSCI each subsequent anniversary of its existence. Performance against the Dow Jones Global Index has also been promising.

The big question is whether the Dow Jones Sustainability Indexes and similar initiatives that are emerging in other capital markets are blips on the screen of history or part of a historical paradigm shift.

They were launched at the height of the longest economic boom in history. Were they the "last hurrah" of a buoyant market? Will they continue to be seen as a specialist approach that is fine for "tree lovers and bunny huggers" but not a serious focus for the trillions of dollars in investment capital and credit that shifts around the globe in a restless search for greater returns? Or have Dow Jones and its partners seen a critical new trend and future market transformation emerging before most companies and investors have seen the same potential? Have they already started to pick the value creators of the future?

We are convinced that they have. We believe that the most successful companies of the future will be those that focus on creating shareholder value *and* societal value, by combining outstanding economic performance with outstanding ethical, social, and environmental performance and by building accountable, transparent, and trusted relationships with all key stakeholders.

We base our prediction on:

■ *The changing "rules of the game":* Economic, demographic, social, political, and technological trends are changing societal expectations, regulations, and market conditions, in essence the "rules of the game" under which business operates. In doing so, they are also changing the overall context for competitive advantage.

■ *The emergence of new business risks and opportunities:* The changing rules of the game are creating a new set of business risks and opportunities, especially for companies operating on an international basis. Initial empirical evidence establishes a positive correlation between companies that deliver good ethical, governance, social, and environmental performance and good financial performance—a link between shareholder value added and what we have termed societal value added.

■ *Who the leaders are:* What is more, the type of leadership companies that are adopting a more integrated approach to managing for both shareholder and societal value are some of the world's most successful enterprises and most consistently respected brands. They have long-standing track records for being performance-driven and for adapting to new market risks and opportunities. The fact that so many of them are investing considerable management time and money in embracing this new approach is surely no coincidence or short-term fad.

Let's look at these arguments in a bit more detail.

The Changing Rules of the Game

The role of business is, and must continue to be, the efficient use of capital to produce goods and services that meet customer needs and aspirations in a manner that is legal and profitable. Competitive advantage will continue to go to those companies that meet customer needs and aspirations in a manner that is more cost effective, more targeted, more differentiated, or more attractive to more customers than that of their competitors.

There is mounting evidence, however, that some of the rules of the game that determine cost-effectiveness and attractiveness to customers are fundamentally changing, creating new risks and opportunities for companies. Concepts such as "efficient use of capital" and "customer needs and aspirations" are changing as new types of intangible capital become more important to business success and as consumers become more aware of the wider economic, ethical, social, political, and environmental impacts of business. Milton Friedman famously stated, "There is one and only one social responsibility of business—to use its resources and engage in activities designed to increase its profits so long as it stays within the rules of the game."[3] Over the past ten years we have witnessed some fundamental changes in the "rules of the game." These changes are redefining what we mean by the "social responsibility of business" and its relationship to corporate competitiveness and success.

Over the past decade evolving societal expectations, together with the forces of political transformation, economic globalization, and technological innovation, have changed forever the context in which business operates. They have created a combination of new competitive pressures on companies and new expectations of the private sector. We briefly review some of these trends below.

1. New Horizons: From Peoria to Pretoria
The new horizons offered to multinational companies by the process of globalization offer great business potential tempered by unprecedented organizational and management challenges. They also create new social and environmental challenges, as well as the growing need to understand and respect different cultures and local histories. Companies are under growing pressure to implement the same level of ethical, labor,

and environmental standards in distant foreign countries as they have at home.

2. Demographics: From Homogeneity to Diversity

After America's 2000 census, Kenneth Prewitt, former director of the U.S. Census Bureau, commented, "We are in the early stages of diversifying our population in a manner historically unprecedented."[4] The trend is similar in many other countries that are important markets for business. Diversity is no longer a nice-to-have "add-on" for business, or an issue simply of affirmative action or regulatory compliance. Nor is it only a case of social justice. The direct bottom-line argument for diversity is growing—the employees, customers, investors, and communities of the future *will* be diverse. Corporations ignore this trend at their peril. Whatever measures you choose to take, the trends are compelling. The growth in the economic power of minorities, women, gays and lesbians, disabled people, multiethnic youth, and the aging population presents substantial business opportunities and challenges. And this is not just a challenge at the national level. Mastering multicultural competency is also an issue for companies operating globally, especially in a world of increased political and cultural sensitivity.

3. Capital: From Tangibles to Intangibles

There is now clear evidence of the crucial importance of nonfinancial, intangible assets in determining corporate value. A growing number of studies have shown that 50 to 90 percent of a company's value is based on such assets, depending on the industry sector. These nonfinancial or intangible assets include innovation; reputation; brand equity; business alliances; management capabilities; technology; employee relations; customer relations; and environmental and community issues. They are often spoken about in terms of different types of capital: intellectual capital or human capital; social capital or relationship capital; and environmental capital.[5] All of these are increasingly thought to be as important as financial and physical capital in determining corporate value drivers and value creation. Despite growing recognition of their importance, these crucial corporate assets are not adequately captured by our current systems of global auditing, assurance, and public reporting. Furthermore, almost all of these intangible assets are influenced in some way by a company's ethical, social, and environmental practices and its reputation for trustworthiness and reliability.

4. Technology: From Infotech to Nanotech

Information technology has ushered in an age of just-in-time, just-what's-required goods and services and 24/7 working hours. It has increased the knowledge intensity of most products and placed e-commerce, e-learning, e-privacy, and e-inclusion firmly on the corporate agenda. It has led to hypercompetition and hyperconnectivity. And it has empowered both customers and anticapitalist activists. Together with the growing potential of biotechnology and nanotechnology, information technology offers immense commercial opportunities and new ethical, social, and environmental challenges. In the unrelenting drive toward ever-greater technological innovation, productivity gains, and process efficiencies, companies are increasingly required to understand and manage the wider societal impacts of new technologies.

5. Connections: From Independence to Interdependence

Many issues that used to be treated as local or national are now global in scope, and many issues that used to be seen as separate are now closely linked in terms of their causes and impacts. The events of September 11, for example, redefined our concepts of national and international security. They brought home the complex interdependence between the political and economic spheres, public policy and private interest, global capitalism and local cultures. They emphasized the growing risks that companies face in an interdependent world. These risks require more comprehensive security strategies in terms of employees, technologies, and networks. They also require new efforts to help tackle some of the interdependent challenges associated with globalization: challenges that were once the sole responsibility of governments, such as spreading economic empowerment, addressing climate change, tackling corruption and money laundering, and ensuring good governance.

6. Actors: From Government to Nongovernment

During the past decade we have witnessed a dramatic growth in the number, reach, and influence of companies and other nongovernmental organizations. The number of multinationals, for example, has grown from 37,000 to over 60,000 in ten years, and the number of transnational nongovernmental organizations (NGOs) from about 20,000 to over 44,000. As September 11 demonstrated, an open global economy where nongovernmental organizations have unprecedented access to technology can be harnessed for evil as well as good. The challenge for political, business, and civic leaders is to control the negative threats and mobilize the positive potential of nongovernmental players. The business community must also develop new ways of cooperating and engaging with a wider range of stakeholders than ever before, all of whom have some type of interest in the impact of business on society.

7. Activism: From City Streets to Virtual Highways

Anticorporate activism is not new, but in the past decade it has grown dramatically in scale, scope, and sophistication. In a networked world, activists with access to the global media and Internet can ensure that there is no place for companies to hide in terms of any unethical or suspicious corporate behavior. Campaigners have a growing array of tactics at their disposal. These range from traditional methods of confronting companies, such as demonstrations, consumer boycotts, and media campaigns, to increased shareholder activism, civil lawsuits, cyberactivism, and critical engagement, where they may work with a company on a particular issue but maintain the right to withdraw. Public trust in many of these groups is high, and what they put on the Internet about companies, accurate or not, is difficult to refute. A small crisis for a company in one part of the world can wreck havoc on its reputation globally. Wherever possible, companies need to build strategies for engaging with their critics—whether in the local community or globally—in as open, accurate, and transparent a manner as possible. This creates risks, as well as opportunities, and calls for new management skills and competencies.

8. Governance: From Assertion to Accountability

Growing activism isn't limited to so-called anticapitalist campaigners and idealistic students. Hard-nosed shareholder activism is also on the rise. The days when shareholders, and other key stakeholders, unquestioningly believed what they were told by companies have gone. There is now suspicion and cynicism among many investors, customers, employees, and community leaders regarding anything that is seen as one-way corporate public relations. This tendency has been greatly intensified by the recent crises in corporate governance. Institutional investors, which own over 60 percent of the top one thousand U.S. companies and 50 percent of total equities in the United States, are starting to use their clout and act as real owners of the companies they invest in. They are not only putting pressure on boards to deliver in terms of their company's financial performance, but also are starting to demand better disclosure of information and better results in terms of nonfinancial performance. In the face of such demands, companies need to find new ways of communicating with their shareholders and other stakeholders. This includes more regular dialogue and the provision of externally verified, clear, and accessible information on the company's social and environmental performance, in addition to its financial results.

Every single one of these trends places new competitive pressures *and* new societal expectations on business. Some of the trends are resulting in the emergence of "soft" laws, such as self-regulatory structures and industrywide voluntary guidelines. Others are being hard-wired into national legislation and regulation, and even international conventions and frameworks. In some cases they are influencing the market frameworks and fiscal incentives under which the private sector operates, as is the case with new stock exchange listing requirements and environmental taxes. They are also having an impact on consumer choices and on the choices made by employees and investors. These trends offer growing opportunities for companies that embrace strategies to deliver shareholder value *and* societal value. They create growing risks and costs for those companies that do not. They create a new competitive context for business, and they underpin a growing business case for companies to get serious about combining private profitability with a sense of public purpose.

The diagram on page 44, from PricewaterhouseCoopers, illustrates the growing importance of intangible, nonfinancial capital and diverse stakeholders in the creation of long-term corporate value. As Alois Flatz, head of research at SAM Sustainable Asset Management, argues, "By recognizing that long-term success means living off income rather than capital reserves, and that human capital, customer capital and natural capital are as important as financial capital, companies embracing sustainability will generate an enduring capability to create value in the longer run, thereby outperforming their peers who may focus on a more narrow set of capital and shorter-term success factors."[6]

A key impact of the changing rules of the game has been to create new risks and opportunities for companies related to their ethical, social, and environmental performance, which can have a material impact on the company's success and even survival.

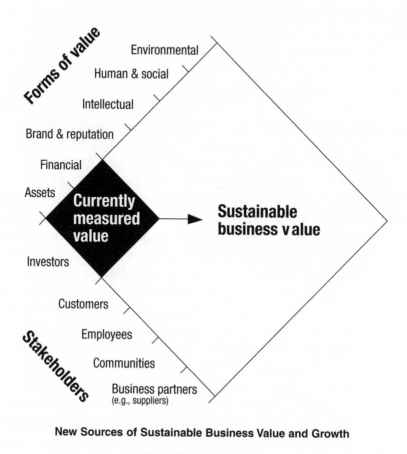

New Sources of Sustainable Business Value and Growth

Source: PricewaterhouseCoopers

The Emergence of New Business Risks and Opportunities

Studies undertaken on the "business case" for good ethical, social, and environmental performance usually look at the costs and risks of "getting it wrong" and/or the benefits and opportunities of "getting it right." We summarize some of the key factors in both of these categories in the chart on page 46.

At a very minimum we can say that efforts by companies to deliver outstanding ethical, social, and environmental performance are unlikely to seriously undermine their financial performance. In most cases they have a good chance of enhancing it, especially over the longer run, and especially in open and transparent market conditions.[7]

Four key points are worth making in analyzing the business case for responsible corporate practices:

1. Responsible business does not always "pay" but it usually makes long-term sense. In many cases it is simply the right thing to do, especially when companies aspire to operate according to a set of core values or business principles.

2. The costs of "getting it wrong" are growing in terms of damage to reputation, costly litigation, increased regulation, and even liquidation.

3. Chief executive officers are playing a growing role in publicly articulating the case for responsible business.

4. There is growing empirical evidence and research to support this business case.

We look at each of these in turn in the following pages.

1. Responsible business does not always "pay" in terms of direct or immediate impact on the bottom line. But it usually makes long-term sense, and in many cases it is the right thing to do, especially in a world where business plays a powerful and influential leadership role and where trust is so crucial.

There are obviously cases where responsible companies will incur greater costs on a certain project, miss an opportunity, or be underpriced by a company accepting bribes, working with corrupt officials, paying unfair low wages, or using cheaper but environmentally damaging technologies.

Equally, there are cases where a company using unethical practices will do better than companies that do not—at least in the short term. Given the growing emphasis on transparency and accountability, however, this will be increasingly difficult to achieve, especially for publicly quoted companies. As the *Financial Times* has observed, "Managing big companies unethically can produce gain but usually it is short-lived.

Costs, Risks, Benefits, and Opportunities

Potential costs of "getting it wrong"—i.e., unacceptable ethical, social, and/or environmental performance—can lead to crises, undermine or destroy a company's financial value.

- Corporate failure

- Criminal charges and imprisonment of corporate officers

- Litigation costs

- Government fines, increased regulatory supervision, and greater compliance burdens

- Higher costs of capital and insurance premiums

- Problems with stock exchange listings, unsuccessful public offers, and inability to attract investment capital

- Lost customers, especially key customers

- Higher operating costs and/or inefficiencies

- Reputation damage through media exposés, consumer boycotts, lawsuits, activist campaigns

- High employee turnover and low employee morale and engagement

- Poor quality control

- Opportunity costs due to distraction, time spent on litigation, crisis management, and compliance burdens

- Inward, compliance-oriented focus, poor executive–board relations, and risk-averse, hostile, and suspicious corporate culture

- Accelerated depletion of intangible assets such as innovation and good relationships and lost competitive edge

Potential benefits of "getting it right"—i.e., good ethical, social, and environmental performance, leadership role on important issues—can protect or enhance a company's financial value.

- Improved risk management, better risk profile and credit ratings

- Avoidance of costly regulation

- Better access to capital through greater investor confidence, lower insurance premiums, and more favorable credit terms

- Reduced operating and resource costs

- Improved process efficiency and effectiveness

- Enhanced intangible assets, such as good reputation, brand equity, product and service quality, successful innovation, increased employee motivation and productivity, positive stakeholder relationships

- Better organizational functioning through creation of a more integrated performance-driven culture and employee learning and motivation

- Easier to attract and retain talented employees and loyal customers

- More attractive as a reliable strategic partner and credible M&A candidate

- Recognition as a neighbor of choice by local community leaders and public authorities

- Increased differentiation of existing product and service offerings

- Greater opportunities for innovation and for new product, service, and market development

- Competitive advantage through lower costs, differentiated products, or new products, services, and customer solutions

Sources: Adapted from J. Nelson, *Business as Partners in Development* (1996); J. Nelson, *Building Competitiveness and Communities* (1998); and J. Nelson and S. Zadek, *Partnership Alchemy* (2001)

Long-term success demands ethical behavior that encourages the trust on which all social endeavors ultimately depend."[8]

Over the longer term, the benefits of "getting it right" on ethical, social, and environmental issues are likely to translate directly or indirectly into better overall operational performance and profitability. These benefits include:

- Better risk management

- Better relationship management in terms of employee, customer, community, and government relations and, increasingly, shareholder relations

- Better responsiveness in anticipating and meeting changing consumer needs, emerging societal expectations, and new regulations

- Better resource and cost management

- Better reputation management

- Greater readiness to innovate and experiment with new products, services, processes, markets, alliances, and business models

2. The costs of "getting it wrong" and facing major problems in terms of damage to reputation, costly litigation, increased regulation, and, in severe cases, liquidation are increasingly high and likely to grow.

Given the trends we have identified in this chapter, delivering or being perceived to deliver bad ethical, social, or environmental performance is increasingly likely to have a negative impact on reputation and financial performance. This is especially the case when well-known companies are deemed to be responsible for a major fraud or for a health, environmental, corruption, or human rights crisis.

Some of the most serious costs of getting it wrong include:

- Reputation damage resulting from consumer boycotts, shareholder activism, negative media coverage, or Internet campaigns against a company

- Costly and high-profile litigation, sometimes resulting in expensive compensation or remediation

■ Increased regulatory overview, fines, and imposition of new regulation

■ In severe cases, jail sentences for company executives and the demise or liquidation of the company

Depending on the severity and extent of the problem and the company or industry sector's existing reservoir of goodwill, all of these can have a negative impact on corporate performance and financial results, and sometimes can lead to a death spiral.

The most obvious recent examples of the cost of "getting it wrong" can be seen in the unfolding outcomes of the corporate governance and integrity scandals that engulfed Enron, Andersen, Adelphia, Global Crossing, WorldCom, Martha Stewart Living, Omnimedia, ImClone, Ahold, Parmalat, and others. The case of Andersen is in many ways the most sobering one of all. In January 2002, Andersen was describing itself as follows: "Andersen is a global leader in professional services. . . . [it] employs 85,000 people in 84 countries. Andersen is frequently rated among the best places to work by leading publications around the world. It is also consistently ranked first in client satisfaction in independent surveys. Andersen has enjoyed uninterrupted growth since its founding in 1913."[9] Less than a year later, this venerable eighty-nine-year-old company was gone. In an industry sector highly dependent on public trust, customer loyalty, and professional integrity, the company could not survive the negative fallout caused by the unethical behavior of a tiny handful of its 85,000 mostly hardworking, dedicated, and honest employees. Many of these employees have found jobs with other professional services firms, but the economic costs and loss of trust associated with the demise of Andersen have been large. While such occurrences are extremely rare, no company can afford to ignore the growing complexity and variety of risks associated with its nonfinancial performance. Probably fewer than 50 percent of large companies, however, have established integrated, comprehensive, enterprisewide risk management strategies and systems.

Corporate collapse is clearly the greatest cost of getting it wrong, at least for the companies and stakeholders directly involved. There are a growing number of other examples, perhaps not as dramatic, of how getting it wrong can negatively impact the bottom line.

The growth in litigation related to ethical, social, and environmental performance is an obvious case in point. Class action and other lawsuits being filed against companies cover a growing variety of labor, occupational health and safety, product safety, human rights, and environmental issues—both contemporary and historical. These include ongoing asbestos-related claims. According to *Fortune* magazine, in 2002 these claims involved more than 200,000 cases pending in the United States against more than a thousand companies, many of which had never even made products containing asbestos.[10] Some major companies that have been generally impressive performers have faced or been threatened with bankruptcy as a result.

Litigation also includes suits filed against companies in reparation for historical "wrongdoings," ranging from links with the former Nazi regime in Germany to relationships with apartheid South Africa and association with the slave trade. There are also emerging themes such as obesity lawsuits against fast-food companies and lawsuits against pharmaceutical companies to increase access to essential drugs in poor countries and communities. There are implications for many major corporations in the *Nike v. Kasky* case, which reached the U.S. Supreme Court in 2003 and related to a corporation's freedom of speech around issues of public policy and social and environmental performance, and the question of whether discussions on such issues should be seen as "commercial speech" or not. There has also been an increase in the use of the Alien Tort Statute of 1789. In a nutshell, this enables citizens from other countries to sue companies in the United States for their behavior in overseas markets. Some of the world's major companies, including a few of those whose good practices we describe in this book, have faced or are facing legal action under this statute as a result of real or perceived problems with their social or environmental performance in other countries.

Dealing with such litigation, some of which is accompanied or inspired by media exposés, activist campaigns, and consumer boycotts, has become part of the cost of doing business. This is especially the case for American companies and those operating in the litigious American system. Few major global companies, however, can avoid it in today's operating environment any more than they can escape the reach of sexual harassment and discrimination suits. But just as the best protection in these cases is proactive policies and procedures, those companies that have clear ethical, social, and environmental policies in place will have the best defense. If they can demonstrate rigorous due diligence and effective accountability processes, they are less likely to incur massive costs, reputation damage, and financial settlements.

Even without litigation there are new financial costs and risks for companies related to social and environmental issues that were simply not there five years ago. These include the growing momentum, driven in large part by institutional investors, behind requests for increased public disclosure on companies' social and environmental performance, especially when this may have a material impact on the company's risk profile, its product pipeline, or its market opportunities. The risks and opportunities of climate change is one area that has received increased investor attention during the past couple of years. Even when public disclosure on these issues is not legally mandated, a company's failure to be transparent can result in negative media coverage, costly remediation efforts, and reputation damage.

3. Chief executive officers are playing a growing role in articulating the emerging "business case" for responsible business.

A number of leading CEOs are playing a growing public role in making the "risk and opportunity" case for responsible business. As should be apparent from the chart on page 46 and the examples given above, corporate responsibility and the creation of wider societal value are no longer simply a question of philanthropy or what a company does with its profits once it has made them. It is a question of *how* the company makes these profits in the first place—how it manages its nonfinancial risks, as well as its financial risks, and how it develops opportunities to make increased profits through addressing ethical, social, and environmental needs. This goes to the heart of corporate strategy, corporate profitability, corporate risk management, and corporate leadership.

There is growing evidence from CEO surveys, speeches, and leadership initiatives that business leaders are placing increased emphasis on improving their wider societal performance and linking it directly to their financial performance.

In its sixth annual Global CEO Survey, carried out in 2003, PricewaterhouseCoopers surveyed over thirteen hundred CEOs from around the world. Reflecting a growing trend from previous years, 69 percent agreed that corporate social responsibility is vital to profitability, and 60 percent stated that these issues would not assume a lower priority in the current difficult economic climate.[11]

In 2003, the U.S. Chamber of Commerce, Boston College, and the Hitachi Foundation jointly released the largest-ever corporate survey of the state of corporate citizenship in the United States, and the first of its kind to include small- and medium-sized businesses. According to 82 percent of the respondents, good corporate citizenship helps their bottom line, and 86 percent of them claimed to have invested more or the same in corporate citizenship over the past year.[12]

In December 2002, UK-based Business in the Community surveyed over two hundred chief executives, chairmen, and directors from ten European countries on the top issues that will influence their performance in the next five years. They identified attracting and retaining talented staff, ability to innovate, and corporate reputation, all of which could be influenced by their wider societal performance. Nearly 80 percent of them agreed that companies that integrate responsible practices into their mainstream business will be more competitive, and 73 percent agreed that "sustained social and environmental engagement can significantly improve profitability."[13] Yet less than one-third of these European business leaders had systematically assessed the risks and opportunities presented to their company by ethical, social, and environmental issues. And only half had set targets for their company's performance in these areas.

Also in 2002, the World Economic Forum, which brings together over a thousand of the world's business leaders and leading companies, launched a global corporate citizenship initiative. In a CEO statement, developed in partnership with the International Business Leaders Forum, a group of leading CEOs stated:

First and foremost, our companies' commitment to being global corporate citizens is about the way we run our own businesses. The greatest contribution we can make is to do business in a manner that obeys the law, produces safe and cost effective products and services, creates jobs and wealth, supports training and technology cooperation, and reflects international business standards and values in areas such as the environment, ethics, governance, labor and human rights. This involves making every effort to enhance the positive multipliers of our activities and to minimize any negative impacts on people and the environment, everywhere we invest and operate. A key element of this is recognizing that responsible business must move beyond philanthropy and be integrated into core business strategy and practice.[14]

4. There is growing empirical evidence to suggest a sound business case for responsible corporate practices.

Over the past few years a growing number of academic research projects and attitude surveys have been undertaken to identify and examine the "business case" for responsible business—the case for "doing well by doing good."

A number of longitudinal and cross-border attitudinal surveys and public opinion polls are testing people's views on the changing role of business in society. One of the most influential to date has been *The Millennium Poll,* conducted by Environics International, in collaboration with the U.S. Conference Board and the International Business Leaders Forum. This was one of the largest-ever public opinion polls to test people's attitudes on the role of business. It surveyed over 25,000 people across twenty-three countries on five continents.[15] Two of its key findings:

   Two-thirds of citizens said that they want companies to go beyond their historical role of making a profit, paying taxes, employing people, and obeying laws. They want companies to contribute to broader societal goals as well.

   Actively contributing to charities and community projects doesn't nearly satisfy people's expectations of corporate social responsibility—there are ten areas of social accountability rated higher by citizens in countries on all continents.

At the same time, a growing number of academic studies, backed by empirical research, are also starting to examine the link between the financial, social, and environmental performances of companies. A sizable number of these studies point to a positive relationship between a company's financial performance and its social and environmental performance. Although some are inconclusive, very few point to a negative link. This is still an emerging field of study. It is early days in terms of being able to track long-term trends, and there is still much debate around methodologies. Nevertheless, many of the research findings to date debunk the all too commonly held view that suggests an inevitable trade-off: profits against principles, and shareholders against other stakeholders.

In the Appendixes we provide lists of what we consider to be some of the most useful contacts, academic studies, and references for readers wanting more detailed information on, and arguments in favor of, the business case for action. In this book we focus our own arguments on the actual stories and experiences of the over sixty companies we have profiled throughout the following chapters.

Who Are the Leaders?

Many of the companies profiled in this book have been long-standing pioneers and innovators in new technologies, products, services, processes, and ways of doing business. They have led the business "take-up" on other major management trends such as Total Quality Management, Six Sigma, and managing intellectual capital. The fact that all of them are now looking more strategically at how to manage both the risks and the opportunities of their wider ethical, social, and environmental performance is surely no coincidence. It is unlikely that such an influential and progressive group of companies, all leaders in their respective industry sectors, would be investing so much leadership effort and such substantial amounts of time and money on a short-term fad or a mere public relations exercise.

As illustrated on page 54, when managing their wider impacts on society, these companies are moving beyond a mind-set that is bounded by *compliance* with laws and regulations; the *control* of risks, costs, and liabilities; and *community investment* or philanthropy. They see compliance, control, and community investment as necessary but insufficient building blocks to becoming outstanding corporate citizens. They are also aiming to *create new value* for stakeholders, including but not only shareholders. They are implementing strategies to create new products and services, change operational processes, build new alliances, enter new markets, support new institutional structures, and in some cases even transform business models so that they meet social and environmental needs as well as customer demands and aspirations. They are looking to create societal value as well as shareholder value. They are

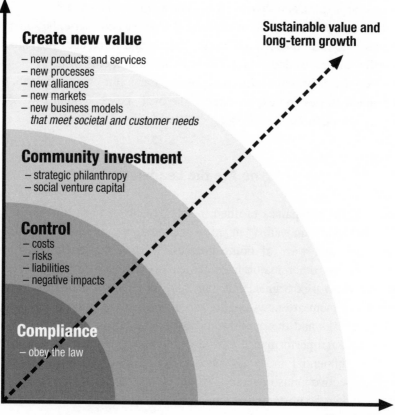

Societal value added

Create new value
- new products and services
- new processes
- new alliances
- new markets
- new business models
  that meet societal and customer needs

Community investment
- strategic philanthropy
- social venture capital

Control
- costs
- risks
- liabilities
- negative impacts

Compliance
- obey the law

Sustainable value and long-term growth

Shareholder value added

Strategies for Building Shareholder and Societal Value Added

Source: Adapted from J. Nelson, *The Business of Peace* (2001)

thinking of their impact on society in terms of not only corporate social responsibility, but also corporate social opportunity. In short, they are aiming not only to "do no harm," but also to "do positive good."

As these companies aim to deliver both shareholder and wider societal value, their performance is not always consistent. Some have demonstrated outstanding performance in one area while simultaneously facing public or investor censure for their performance in another. Citigroup, for example, has played a leadership role in issues such as diversity, reaching underserved markets, and tackling environmental challenges, but has made some mistakes in terms of conflicts of interest between its research and investment banking activities. BP has become one of the world's most competitive energy companies and raised the bar for its industry sector on tackling climate change, but at the same time it has faced negative media coverage and regulatory censure for problems in its Alaskan safety practices. GlaxoSmithKline has led the way on improving access to life-saving medicines in poor countries and communities but has also been the target of a backlash from some of its investors over executive compensation. Almost every major company struggles with similar inconsistencies and dilemmas in delivering superior financial, social, and environmental performance. It is these dilemmas that create a leadership challenge, making it imperative that senior management play a role.

At the same time, "best practice" companies sometimes get singled out and punished for being first movers, suggesting that there may be a price to pay for being a corporate pioneer as opposed to just a freeloader or one of the pack. And the bar for what is considered "best practice" keeps rising. In a post-Enron environment, explicitly linking profits with principles is a prerequisite for helping to restore trust and confidence while delivering long-term value to shareholders. Yet that still does not make it simple. So we cannot offer an "easy fix" or a panacea. Instead we offer a broad framework for leadership action, supported by examples from some of the world's most respected companies. Putting the seven principles into practice, although not always easy, *is* achievable. There are direct and indirect business benefits for getting it right, and there can be substantial costs for getting it wrong. Practicing these principles can lead to genuine competitive advantage for the firm—as well as meaningful improvement for society.

In *Part Two* we show the seven principles in action and identify companies that demonstrate that by putting these principles to work, business can succeed, society can make progress, and capitalism itself can be strengthened.

Part Two

Putting Principles into Practice

How Companies Are Mastering the New Rules of the Game

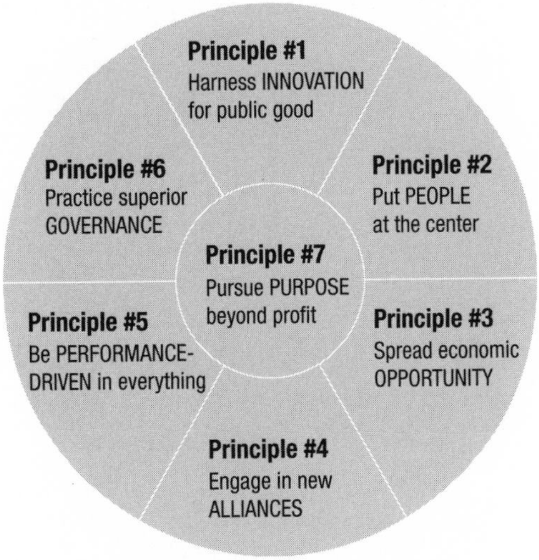

Principle #1
Harness INNOVATION
for public good

Principle #6
Practice superior
GOVERNANCE

Principle #2
Put PEOPLE
at the center

Principle #7
Pursue PURPOSE
beyond profit

Principle #5
Be PERFORMANCE-
DRIVEN in everything

Principle #3
Spread economic
OPPORTUNITY

Principle #4
Engage in new
ALLIANCES

Harness Innovation
for Public Good

The ability to turn good ideas into deliverable solutions has never been more important to the success of business and society. Innovation is the lifeblood of corporate competitiveness, value creation, and sustainable growth. It is also vital to solving many of the major challenges that our world faces. Great companies understand the immense opportunities and responsibilities of innovation. As a result, they go further than others by integrating ethical, social, and environmental considerations into their innovation and R&D efforts. They carry out due diligence to minimize any negative impacts and they create new value by developing profitable customer solutions that meet environmental, safety, and social needs, in addition to providing customers with good quality, reliability, and value.

They also look to their philanthropic programs as a source of innovation and they support institutional innovation to improve the effectiveness and efficiency of public policy and market frameworks.

Why Innovation Matters

*Ultimately, innovation holds the potential to address our
most pressing social and human challenges. Many policy
discussions assume the existence of a sharp trade-off between
goals such as health, environment, safety, and short-term
economic growth. However, a healthy rate of innovation
increases the likelihood that new technologies will emerge
that substantially temper or even eliminate such trade-offs.*

MICHAEL PORTER, PROFESSOR, HARVARD BUSINESS SCHOOL

If there is one thing that everyone agrees on as a fundamental requirement for business success, it is the importance of innovation. In today's
rapidly changing and globally connected economy, innovation is crucial
for both national and corporate competitiveness. Here are findings from
three of the many studies that support this point:

■ The World Economic Forum's annual global competitiveness
report is the most comprehensive and systematic analysis of the
competitive positioning and potential of over seventy nations
around the world. In the 2002 report, Professor Michael Porter
comments, "Innovation has become perhaps the most important
source of competitive advantage in advanced economies, and
building innovative capacity has a strong relationship to a country's overall competitiveness and level of prosperity."[1]

■ The U.S. Council on Competitiveness concluded in its survey
Going Global: The New Shape of American Innovation, "Every
company ranks the capacity to innovate—the transformation of
knowledge and ideas into new products, processes, and services—
as a top priority. Innovative capacity plays a dominant, and probably decisive, role in determining who will prosper in the global
arena. For companies, innovation creates a strategic market advantage in a fiercely competitive economic environment. For countries, the ability to leverage innovation not only to achieve national

goals (improved security, health, and environment) but to increase productivity and attract investment from an array of global sources is the key to continuous improvements in the standard of living and quality of life."[2]

■ In October 2001, the McKinsey Global Institute released a major study that aimed to determine future economic growth potential in the United States by examining the drivers of the country's unprecedented labor productivity boom from 1995 to 1999.[3] Contrary to popular opinion at the time, the study found that investment in information technology was not the most important factor in productivity growth, although it had a key impact in some industries. Rather, the study concluded that the major drivers of productivity were competition, and product, service, and process innovations—in short, new ways of doing business with or without new technologies.

At a time of great political uncertainty and economic downturn, it is easier for most companies and their leaders to focus on cutting costs, avoiding risks, and keeping heads down, rather than increasing the time, money, and effort allocated to product, process, and organizational innovation. Yet it is at times like this that innovation is more important than ever, for both corporate and national competitiveness. There is enormous potential for the business sector to harness its skills, technologies, competencies, and networks to support innovation in both the social and the environmental areas. This is a potential that is largely untapped by most major companies. It offers companies an opportunity to develop new ideas, new alliances, new products, new services, new processes, and new markets that can enhance their own value proposition—both directly and indirectly—and at the same time make a meaningful contribution to the world.

Any company, in any country or industry sector, can aim to harness innovation for public good. In essence, this can be defined as *innovation undertaken with an explicit added goal of protecting or creating wider societal value* in addition to *customer and shareholder value, through systematically taking ethical, social, and environmental factors into consideration.*

What Can Companies Do to Harness Innovation for Public Good?

First, they can embed a broader vision of innovation into their core business strategy. They can:

■ Analyze the environmental and social impacts of *existing products, services, and processes,* and work on innovative solutions to enhance the positive impacts and minimize any negative impacts that these may have.

■ Integrate environmental and social considerations and due diligence into all *new product development and process changes.* Aim to produce better-quality products and services and to implement better processes that meet customer needs with fewer negative impacts on the environment and society.

■ Look for opportunities to develop *new products and services that very specifically address an environmental problem or meet a social need.*

Second, they can look for ways to innovate in the company's philanthropy and social investment programs. In particular, they can develop innovative approaches to *support and empower social entrepreneurs.*

Third, they can work with government authorities and other partners to develop *institutional innovations,* such as *innovative public policy frameworks* and *voluntary market mechanisms* that enhance the effectiveness and efficiency of regulation and enable leading companies to raise the bar beyond compliance.

None of these approaches is entirely new. Product, process, and institutional innovations have been at the forefront of human progress since humans first made fire. They have determined our scientific and economic advances, as well as our political and social progress. Since innovations and ideas were first commercialized, they have been the source of some of the world's great personal fortunes and great companies. Outstanding companies, their leaders, and their innovators have long thought of innovation in terms of wider purpose and contribution. As Thomas Edison, the founder of General Electric, once said, "I never perfected an invention that I did not think about in terms of the service it might give others."[4]

What *is* new is the sense of urgency and the importance of innovation for both private enterprise and public purpose. Product, process, and institutional innovation are more crucial than ever to corporate success and survival in today's highly competitive global economy. They are also among our best hopes for tackling the urgent socioeconomic and environmental challenges that the world faces. Indeed, absent corporate involvement and innovation, efforts by governments to resolve daunting challenges—from global warming to widespread poverty—are destined to fall far short of their potential, or even to fail altogether.

The private sector, probably more than ever before in history, has the wherewithal to make a substantial difference, but it cannot do this alone. Public-sector policy frameworks, incentives, and funding are necessary. Academic rigor and research are essential. Citizen acceptance and support are vital. But one thing is certain: the quantity and quality of innovation that the world needs to prosper will simply not happen without a sense of entrepreneurship and without the investment of private-sector skills, technologies, funds, competencies, and networks.

Many of the companies that we have profiled in this book are at the leading edge of such innovation and transformation. In some cases this has been driven by major reputation crises and activist campaigns resulting from social, ethical, or environmental failures in their business. In others they have been faced with the challenge of turning around an ailing company or responding to new competitors. A few have been ahead of the game. They have been able to meet changing expectations or avoid the risks now so apparent to others because they properly anticipated future trends and incipient market demands. This has enabled some of them to lay the foundations for competitive advantage and in certain cases to raise the bar for their entire industry sector. What are some of the lessons we can draw from the companies that harness innovation for public good?

Making It Happen

One: Embed into Core Business Strategy

Great companies embed their efforts to harness innovation for public good into their core business strategy. They aim to *create new value* for shareholders and society by developing new products, services, processes, and business models, or by enhancing the design or redefining the use of existing ones—and doing so in a way that either decreases negative social and environmental impacts or positively contributes to solving social and environmental problems.

There are two broad areas of innovation in a company's core business activities that can be particularly valuable in terms of contribution to society or the environment, in addition to creating financial value and reputation benefits for the company:

■ *Eco-innovation or eco-efficiency*—aimed at developing products, services, and processes that meet consumer needs with less of an environmental footprint

■ *Innovating to serve low-income communities*—aimed at developing new technologies, new supply and distribution systems, or new business models that can extend the affordability, access, and availability of products and services that help to improve the quality of people's lives

The World Business Council for Sustainable Development (WBCSD) first coined the term *eco-efficiency*. The WBCSD is a coalition of over 150 companies from different countries and industry sectors that has played a pioneering role in mobilizing business leadership for social and environmental progress. It defines eco-efficiency as "the delivery of competitively priced goods and services that satisfy human needs and bring quality of life, while progressively reducing ecological impact and resource intensity throughout the life cycle, to a level at least in line with the Earth's estimated carrying capacity."[5]

A task force of WBCSD member companies has developed a framework to help businesses implement eco-efficiency in their own operations, which we describe in the box below. They point out, "Many companies have made eco-efficiency part of their overall business strategy. . . . Eco-efficiency for them has become a major driver of innovation and progress, a vehicle that helps them meet the economic *and* environmental targets they have set."[6]

In the following pages we consider Toyota and its eco-friendly Prius car; describe P&G's efforts to provide low-income communities with affordable products that meet environmental and health needs; and profile William McDonough & Partners, a firm of architects and designers world renowned in the area of eco-effective building and design. These three different examples of product and process innovation offer generic lessons for most companies and industry sectors.

A Framework for Operationalizing Eco-efficiency

There are four key areas in which business can implement eco-efficiency:

▨ **Reengineer processes:** Improve monitoring and management practices, change existing technology, amend operating procedures, and make changes to raw material inputs in order to reduce resource use; reduce pollution; improve quality, efficiency, and productivity; and save operational costs.

▨ **Redesign products and services:** Facilitate product disassembly, reduce material intensity, and promote product recycling and reuse in order to meet consumer needs with less environmental impact.

▨ **Revalue by-products:** Turn waste into a resource for other processes or for other companies. At its optimum this may form part of a closed-loop process of "industrial ecology" where businesses work together toward a target of zero waste from their combined industrial activities.

▨ **Rethink markets:** Develop new markets and meet customer needs in a less material- and energy-intensive manner. For example, increase the knowledge intensity of products or provide an equivalent service to replace the product.

Source: World Business Council for Sustainable Development

Toyota: Product Innovation to Preserve the Environment

First established in the United States in 1957, and listed on the New York Stock Exchange in 1999, Toyota is now one of America's top four automakers, with impressive growth statistics and profitability. In 2003, its U.S. operations and dealerships employed over 130,000 Americans, it purchased more than $15 billion worth of parts and materials from North American suppliers, and the company sold more vehicles in the United States than in Japan.

Over the past decade the Toyota Production System has possibly been the focus of more benchmarking and study visits than any other company's production process. Toyota has become a byword for cutting-edge management practices such as continuous improvement (*kaizen*), team empowerment, innovation, supplier relationship management, and flexible production. What has been less well known in the past, but is becoming more recognized every day, is the fact that Toyota has applied these practices not only to producing high-quality, good-value cars, but also to enhancing safety and preserving the environment. The concept of *"muri, mura, muda"* permeates the corporate philosophy. It translates as "eliminate waste," and Toyota is proving that it is possible to do just that in an innovative, cost-effective, and competitive manner.

In 1997, for example, it became the first auto company in the world to mass-produce a hybrid vehicle. By combining gasoline and electric power, the Prius, which is Latin for "to go before," produces up to 90 percent fewer harmful emissions than the average car on the road today and cuts gas consumption in half. It offers drivers better fuel efficiency, decent acceleration performance, and practicality, while cutting negative environmental impacts. The Prius sedan is currently the bestselling gas/electric hybrid vehicle in America and an increasingly popular purchase by city governments. It has earned Toyota environmental and design awards, as well as extensive free media coverage, the majority of it positive.

Although the car still represents a tiny slice of the U.S. vehicle market, the development and marketing of the Prius offers a good example of a company anticipating future market trends and developing affordable, cutting-edge technology and new products that have offered it first-mover advantage. As other car companies play catch-up on the R&D, marketing, public awareness, and reputation fronts, Toyota is introducing the second-generation Prius, rolling out the trendy youth-oriented Scion, road-testing a hydrogen-powered fuel cell hybrid sport-utility vehicle, and continuing to grow market share with key brands. When the second-generation Prius reached U.S. showrooms in October 2003, dealers received over 10,000 orders before the car was even available.

At the same time, the company recognizes that alliances with its competitors are a key factor for creating the necessary public policy incentives and consumer awareness to grow the size of the market for environmentally innovative products. Eco-innovation is not simply about gaining more market share, but also about growing the overall market for products that serve people in a way that does less damage to the environment. As managing director Hiroyuki Watanabe, the man responsible for the Prius, comments, "We have a basic notion that unless we find a solution for environmental problems, we will not be able to achieve sustainable growth in coming years. The only way to achieve this—it's not just smart R&D—is by interacting with the government and public."[7]

The company, drawing in part on its Japanese heritage, has a long-standing business philosophy centered on the explicit goal of "achieving stable, long-term growth, through the development of business activities that contribute to society." Over the past two decades, environmental leadership has become a core component of this management philosophy.

Today eco-innovation stands shoulder to shoulder with cost competitiveness and globalization as central strands of the company's corporate strategy and future growth plans. It is not an add-on and it is not incidental. Like everything else that Toyota has become famous for excelling at, eco-innovation is seen as systematic, strategic, and serious business. The thousands of businesspeople around the world who study the Toyota Production System could usefully look at this component of the company's performance.

P&G: Product Innovation to Serve the Poor

Procter & Gamble is one of America's largest makers of household goods. Established nearly 170 years ago, it was a pioneer in popularizing the concept of consumer branding and brand marketing. Today, with a portfolio of nearly three hundred brands available in 160 countries around the world, P&G's products touch the lives of millions of people on a daily basis. Few companies know more about the importance of brand loyalty and consumer trust, or about the emotional as well as the functional connections that people make with brands. Linked to this is growing awareness of the need to integrate health, safety, and environmental considerations into product development, over and above what is required by law.

In the past few years P&G has focused relentlessly on controlling costs, improving competitiveness, and starting to grow again, after a period of poor performance. Innovation sits at the heart of its recovery strategy and is the company's primary driver for future growth. At the same time, the company has made a strategic, board-level commitment to integrate the principles of sustainable development into its core business activities, including its innovation processes. According to P&G director George Carpenter, "P&G continues to embrace sustainable development as a business strategy, as well as a corporate responsibility. We believe we can grow our business and deliver ever-greater shareholder and stakeholder value by bringing innovations to the marketplace that address the frustrations and aspirations of consumers at all economic levels."[8]

Despite massive competitive pressures and a strong focus on managing costs, P&G has moved beyond a compliance-based, risk-management mind-set aimed at ensuring that its products are safe and environmentally sound. Although this remains an important foundation of its R&D efforts, today P&G is proactively creating new social and environmental value by combining what it views as corporate social responsibility with what it calls corporate social opportunity: the production of new products that improve consumers' lives, while also making important contributions to environmental quality and society.

Innovation at P&G is approached as a deliberate process. Executives speak of the "Innovation Equation," which has been characterized as follows: "Good ideas flowing friction free across the enterprise . . . times the multiplier of external connections with best-of-breed partners . . . plus seed funding so good ideas get oxygen fast . . . equals big, predictable, profitable innovation."[9] The company is particularly focused on increasing the percentage of innovation coming from alliances with external partners from less than 10 percent today to over 50 percent in the future. It estimates that it could increase innovation fivefold with such alliances.

New types of R&D partnerships, often with nontraditional allies, are especially important in helping the company develop products that have the potential to be economically viable and at the same time serve the poor. Reaching low-income communities with products that are of reliable quality and good value is not only an important part of P&G's publicly stated values. It also represents an area of long-term growth potential for the company, given that four-fifths of the world's population is economically, socially, and politically marginalized.

After four years of partnership-building and R&D in this area, P&G is starting to launch a variety of new products and services. These include the PuR Water Purifier developed in collaboration with the International Council of Nurses and the U.S. Centers for Disease Control and Prevention (CDC) to increase access to clean water. It is estimated that some five thousand children die every day in developing countries from diarrheal diseases due in large part to lack of clean water. This simple-to-use, low-cost water purifier therefore has the potential to save thousands of lives. The company is also in discussion with relief agencies to supply this product in emergency situations caused by war or natural disaster.

Working once again in partnership with CDC and public health officials, P&G is testing the ability of another product to improve hygiene and cut the incidence or severity of childhood disease in Pakistan and China. This is Safeguard antibacterial soap, another simple, low-cost solution that has the potential to reach millions of people by leveraging the company's R&D and marketing capabilities with public funds and community outreach.

Low levels of nutrition are another impediment to the quality of life in many countries. P&G has worked with the United Nations Children Fund (UNICEF), among others, to establish the Global Alliance for Improved Nutrition, aimed at increasing access to nutrient-fortified foods. One of the initial products P&G has developed is called Nutristar, a fruit-flavored drink powder that directly addresses nutritional deficiencies.

A deliberate process of innovation, backed by rigorous environmental and social due diligence and proactive engagement with external partners, is helping to put P&G back in the top ranks of market performers. At the same time, this approach is enabling the company to actively contribute to both the debate about and the practice of sustainable development, with the potential to improve the quality of life for millions of people in developing countries.

William McDonough: Process Innovation to Build the "Next Industrial Revolution"

William McDonough and his partners illustrate how a small group of people with a clear vision, the right skills and technology, and an ability to work in partnership with nontraditional allies can convert innovative ideas into profitable business models that have an impact far beyond their own operations. Working with a European partner, Dr. Michael Braungart, McDonough has developed an approach called the Cradle to Cradle Design process. It aims to help companies design "closed loop" systems for their products and processes that eliminate waste and have a restorative impact on the environment and on people. McDonough works with leading companies such as Ford, Nike, Herman Miller, BP, Wal-Mart, the Gap, IBM, SC Johnson, and Visteon to help them move beyond eco-efficiency toward what he describes as "eco-effectiveness": process and product designs that are "life-sustaining" rather than simply sustainable and "regenerative and restoring" rather than just efficient.[10]

In 2000, for example, Ford Motor Company announced a $2 billion plan to transform its historic Rouge complex in Michigan into a futuristic model of sustainable manufacturing, one that will combine flexible assembly lines and lean manufacturing processes with innovative advances in energy and water efficiency, worker safety, and nature conservation. Bill McDonough and his colleagues have played a central role in helping Ford to shape this vision, and they are now working together to put it into action.

To many people, the Rouge complex is an icon of the ups and downs of twentieth-century industrialization. It is linked to the birth of "vertically integrated" manufacturing processes and America's love affair with the car in the early 1900s, to the beginnings of unionization in the 1930s and a violent response from management, through to economic decline in the face of more efficient "virtual manufacturing" processes, and to growing safety concerns and increased awareness of environmental costs in the 1980s and '90s. Almost one hundred years after it was first built, the Rouge is undergoing a rebirth, with the potential of becoming a standard-bearer of the "Next Industrial Revolution."

Among other innovations, the revitalization of the Rouge plant includes the world's largest ecologically inspired "living roof" and interior design features that will utilize renewable energy, save water, improve working conditions, and potentially increase productivity, cut costs, and cut pollution. These are difficult times for Ford and others in the U.S. auto industry, but as Bill Ford Jr., Ford's CEO and chairman, has commented, "Difficult business conditions make it harder to achieve the goals we set for ourselves, including corporate citizenship. But it doesn't mean we will abandon our goals or change our direction."[11]

Other major companies are working with McDonough and Michael Braungart to move in similar directions. These collaborations range from Herman Miller's new manufacturing processes to Shaw's recyclable carpets. They include processes and products that are productive and profitable, and at the same time high quality, safe, and environmentally restorative, eliminating the concept of waste.

Two: Be Rigorous About Due Diligence

Successful innovation and the harnessing of new technologies—especially information technology, biotechnology, and nanotechnology—offer immense commercial opportunities and potential solutions to wider societal challenges and human needs. At the same time, they raise new ethical, social, and environmental risks and dilemmas.

As Rick Belluzzo, former president of Microsoft, has commented:

> *For all its benefits, technology that drives such tremendous economic and social change is not without its pitfalls. With each innovation comes a new set of challenges—how do we shape our society around this new technology? How will it be used by those with good intentions—or misused by those who wish to do harm? Who will benefit most from new technology, and who will get left behind?*[12]

All new products, services, and technologies have wider ethical, social, and environmental implications. These are especially critical, however, with respect to information technology, the emerging fields of biotechnology, and nanotechnology, and the mapping of the human genome.

Failure to carry out due diligence and publicly address the unintended consequences of new technologies can slow market testing and commercialization, destroy a good product launch, and seriously undermine a corporate reputation. Due diligence is essential for sound risk management and long-term market and societal acceptance.

Monsanto's unsuccessful attempt to introduce genetically modified foods into Europe in the late 1990s has become a classic example of how important it is to carry out due diligence and consult widely with a broad cross-section of society. In a nutshell, the company's efforts to enter the potentially lucrative European market with genetically modified products was fatally undermined by effective activist campaigns that led to negative media coverage, growing consumer opposition, and declining supermarket support. Monsanto's scientists were among the best in the world. But they and their business colleagues failed to anticipate or respond to changing societal expectations.

As Kate Fish, Monsanto's vice president for public policy, has commented in retrospect:

Monsanto's assumption was that our technology was more efficient, safer, caused less erosion, used less fuel and was ecologically better. The farmers and Wall Street loved it and we equated "new" with "better." But European consumers saw it as "scary science." Trust in government and American multinational companies was low. They couldn't see the benefits. They felt there were unexplored risks to the food chain, the technology was moving too fast, and they were not sufficiently consulted. From their perspective, "new" didn't necessarily mean "better."[13]

Since then Monsanto has implemented comprehensive policies, made public pledges, and undertaken concerted efforts to address these concerns. But the company continues to face an uphill battle in regaining public trust and market acceptance. Once damaged, a corporate reputation is immensely difficult and costly to rebuild. In today's networked "CNN world," prevention usually makes far better business sense than cure.

In short, carrying out extensive due diligence and consultation is crucial. No matter how great the commercial potential of a new product or technology, no matter how high its acceptance in one part of the world, no matter how strong the endorsement of regulators and scientists—if the general public and potential consumers have legitimate and unanswered concerns about its safety, or its ethical and environmental risks, the product or technology won't fly.

While most companies already integrate market and financial risk analysis into their innovation processes, far fewer systematically integrate wider ethical, social, and environmental risk analysis—despite the fact that these types of risks may themselves lead to market and financial risk, over and above their potential negative impact on people and the environment. Leadership companies are starting to address this anomaly. Those that are able to anticipate and stay ahead of changing societal expectations, consumer concerns, and new regulations will be well positioned to avoid costly mistakes and ensure wider acceptance and faster commercialization of their products.

What are these leadership companies doing to carry out more comprehensive due diligence?

Life Cycle Analysis and Management First, they are looking at innovations as an ongoing process, as outlined in the diagram below: a process that covers the full life cycle of products and services, not only the process of initial research, development, and commercialization. They are focusing on the generation of new products, services, and processes, but also on the use and disposal of existing products, and in some cases their redesign, reapplication, recycling, or renovation.

Policies and Guidelines for R&D Second, they are implementing internal policies and guidelines to integrate wider due diligence procedures into each stage of the innovation cycle.

The Innovation Life Cycle

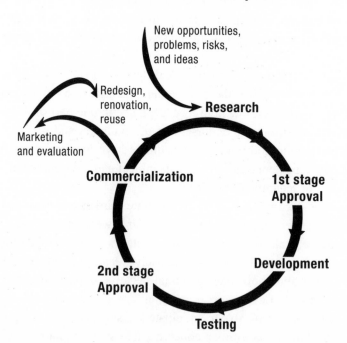

The example provided by Novartis illustrates how one research- and innovation-driven company is implementing the above approach to address the challenge of due diligence.

Novartis: Linking Innovation with Accountability

Swiss-based Novartis is a global leader in pharmaceuticals and consumer and animal health products. It is among the five largest European companies listed on the New York Stock Exchange, and some 45 percent of its sales are in the North American market. In 2001, the company publicly made a strategic commitment to become one of the world's leading corporate citizens. It cited the following business drivers behind this action: First, "it reflects our personal values and beliefs." Second, "it helps us to manage risks." This includes shaping the agenda rather than observing from the outside, being part of the solution rather than part of the problem, and acting rather than only reacting to outside pressure. Third, "it supports our long-term goals. In particular, attracting the best talent, adding to our reputation, and addressing concerns of an increasing segment of stakeholders."[14]

How does this commitment translate into practice? The development of innovative and sometimes ethically risky new technologies and medical treatments lies at the core of the Novartis business model. Encouraging innovation and ensuring that it is responsible and responsive to stakeholder needs and concerns is therefore a core element of both the company's value proposition and its new corporate citizenship strategy.

In its Policy on Corporate Citizenship Novartis commits to "assess health, safety and environmental implications to ensure that the benefits of new products, processes and technologies outweigh remaining risks." It also publicly commits to periodically review its assessments in the light of new concerns or evidence, and to take a precautionary approach to innovation by engaging in scientific peer review and considering benefits and risks in a transparent manner.

Dialogue with external stakeholders is central to this process of due diligence. Novartis has carried out a comprehensive process to identify its key stakeholders. It is now establishing different strategies to consult with them on the key risks, dilemmas, and opportunities that the company faces at the different stages of the innovation life cycle:

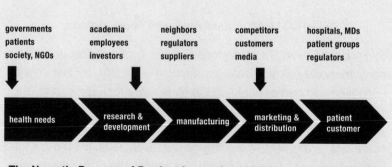

The Novartis Process of Product Innovation: Dialogue with Stakeholders

Source: Corporate Citizenship at Novartis, 2001/2002

An important step in Novartis's due diligence process has been the establishment of an external Ethics Advisory Board made up of world-renowned experts in various disciplines from genetics and biology to law, ethics, and theology. Its role is to carefully analyze research projects in order to make sure these are compliant with the company's internal ethical guidelines. The board will also play a role in monitoring implementation of the company's policies on specific bioethical issues, many of which have immense potential to improve the quality of human life but pose obvious ethical dilemmas and risks. At the same time, the company is working to integrate health, safety, and environmental issues into its business performance reviews and developing a more extensive "Balanced Scorecard" approach to accommodate these alongside financial, operational, and quality performance metrics.

The issues that Novartis is dealing with may be different from those of other companies and industries, but the strategy is relevant for almost any company that undertakes research and development efforts. All R&D has some ethical, social, and environmental implications for society. A clear statement on R&D responsibilities, supported by a life cycle approach to new product development and systematic dialogue between company research teams and independent, external advisors, makes sound business sense, *and* sound ethical sense. It can help the company manage risks and at the same time improve its accountability and transparency.

Stakeholder Dialogue Third, in researching, testing, and gaining approval for new products and services, they are going beyond traditional scientific research, market analysis, and legal compliance to listen and learn from other external stakeholders—often people from groups that the company does not normally interact with, but who could be key to influencing the broader public acceptance of a new technology or product.

Three: Invest in Social Entrepreneurs

In addition to embedding innovation for public good into core product development, due diligence, and life cycle management processes, companies can also create new value for themselves and for society by investing in social entrepreneurs. These are people who apply the skills and mind-sets of entrepreneurship in working for the public interest.

Although social entrepreneurs usually operate in the nonprofit or voluntary sector, their mind-set and set of skills can be found in any organization—public, private, or voluntary. Their critical defining feature is the application of innovative, entrepreneurial, and performance-driven approaches to solving societal problems and the ability to act as bridge-builders between different sectors and organizational cultures.

Companies can invest in social entrepreneurship in a number of ways: first, through creating a climate for social entrepreneurship within the company itself; second, through helping to promote public policy that enables social entrepreneurs to flourish; and third, through investing directly in such people and their social enterprises in the communities and countries where the company operates.

The growing practice of venture philanthropy provides a good example of such direct investment. It is a process whereby companies and individual business leaders apply some of the principles of venture capital to support social enterprises. They share their management skills with these enterprises as well as providing seed financing, and they engage in active, performance-driven partnerships. We compare some of the differences between venture philanthropy and traditional philanthropy in Principle #4 (alliances).

So what does a social entrepreneur look like? What types of people should companies look to invest in? Our Harvard colleague Iqbal

Quadir offers one inspiring example. From Wall Street to rural Bangladesh and more recently the classrooms at Harvard, Iqbal is a wonderful example of the emerging potential of social entrepreneurship. Another inspiring example is Bill Drayton, former McKinsey consultant and founder of Ashoka, a network that empowers other social entrepreneurs around the world.

Iqbal Quadir and Bill Drayton are just two of a growing number of people who are applying business skills and an entrepreneurial mindset to solving local and even global challenges. There are other examples throughout this book: Alan Khazei and Michael Brown, the founders of City Year who convinced BankBoston, Timberland, and others to support their vision of developing young leaders; Michael Porter, a Harvard Business School professor who founded the Initiative for the Competitive Inner City; Rick Little, founder of the International Youth Foundation; and Robert Davies, founder of the Digital Partnership. In each case these people have worked with business in innovative and challenging new ways to tackle social, economic, or environmental challenges.

Defining a Social Entrepreneur

The Schwab Foundation for Social Entrepreneurship, established by Dr. Klaus Schwab, the founder of the World Economic Forum, defines a social entrepreneur as someone who:

- Identifies and applies practical solutions to social problems by combining innovation, resourcefulness, and opportunity.

- Works in any area such as health, education, environment, enterprise development, microfinance, rural development.

- Innovates by finding a new product, a new service, or a new approach to a societal problem.

- Embraces business principles and efficiency.

- Focuses on social value creation.

- Is entrepreneurial and continuously adapts, refines, and innovates the idea.

Source: Schwab Foundation for Social Entrepreneurship

From Wall Street to Bangladesh: Bringing Connectivity and a Healthy Return to Rural Villages and Investors

Iqbal Quadir was a budding venture capitalist in New York in the early 1990s. But he remained haunted by memories of being isolated and cut off as a child in rural Bangladesh where he spent a year during a civil war. So he vowed that one day he would put his business acumen and technological sophistication to work back home. But how?

Would it be possible to bring mobile phone service to millions of rural villagers in Bangladesh, especially women? Who would back his business plan and invest in his unlikely new venture? Where would he find partners on the ground to help him navigate the thicket of local bureaucracies to obtain the necessary permissions? How could he be certain that potential customers, all of whom are poor and have virtually no credit history, would be decent credit risks? What if his business could spark a revolution in connectivity and, by applying state-of-the-art technology to a backward environment, he could help spark yet another revolution—one involving democracy, participation, and political accountability?

Talk about an unlikely, untested business proposition! Eight years later, the numbers tell the tale:

■ GrameenPhone today has nearly 1,200,000 subscribers throughout Bangladesh, has experienced in excess of 100 percent annual growth since its inception, and has turned a profit for investors ahead of schedule. Cell phone users now outnumber fixed-line telephone subscribers in Bangladesh.

■ In 2001, GrameenPhone was identified by London-based mobile phone market research firm EMC as the fastest-growing and single largest mobile phone company in South Asia.

■ Village Phone operators, who subscribe to GrameenPhone's services and allow their neighbors to make phone calls upon payment, are making profits of about $700 a year, twice the per capita income in Bangladesh. This Village Phone program is now available in thirty-five thousand villages, giving telephone access for the first time to more than fifty million people, who are now enjoying market information for their products and able to easily contact friends and loved ones living elsewhere in the country or abroad.

■ Investors are pleased with performance. Telenor, the largest phone company in Norway, is seeing its 51 percent stake in GrameenPhone help propel it into previously untapped markets.

What began as an impossible dream has turned out to be a home run for its founder, his native Bangladesh, and his customers and investors. A key to its success was Quadir's designing the project to use Grameen Bank's borrowers as a distribution network for telephone services. Grameen Bank is a financial intermediary that extends microloans to poor villagers through a process that basically applies "tough love" through strong technical assistance and insistence on mutual accountability. GrameenPhone's Village Phone program lets a bank borrower use her loan proceeds to set up a small retailing shop at her home, selling phone services.

A hundred years earlier, an equally unlikely capitalist had an equally revolutionary idea. At a time when competitors were driving prices upward and cutting wages for their employees, Henry Ford had a radically different idea—cutting prices and raising wages dramatically. If his workers couldn't afford the product they were producing, why would they feel connected and committed to his enterprise? If a mass market didn't develop for his automobile, how would he ever sustain business growth and profitability? Vilified by many and accused of being a communist by some, Ford built a great company—by challenging conventional assumptions and by harnessing his technological prowess in a revolutionary way. Henry Ford—meet Iqbal Quadir. This unlikely pair of capitalists shows us a path to rethinking private enterprise, the role of innovation, and its relationship to society at large.

From McKinsey to Microenterprise: How Ashoka's Founder Has Mobilized Capital for Social Entrepreneurs

Bill Drayton, the founder of Ashoka, has been a pioneer in the application of a venture capital model for investing in exceptional individuals with new ideas for public service, using a combination of financial stipends and professional support services. Before establishing Ashoka in 1980, Bill Drayton spent about ten years working with the management consulting firm McKinsey and then serving as an assistant administrator at the Environmental Protection Agency, designing innovative tradable "pollution rights" as a market-based alternative to environmental regulation. Since then, he has applied his business skills, networks, and passion to investing in social entrepreneurs and promoting awareness of their critical role in society. Ashoka invests in people with ideas for tackling societal problems and who meet the following criteria: creativity in goal-setting and problem-solving; entrepreneurial spirit and temperament; an idea with potential for nationwide impact; and strong ethical fiber.

Since 1981, Ashoka's investments have enabled over a thousand people in forty-two countries to achieve larger-scale social impact in areas such as education, the environment, health, human rights, and economic development. These individuals, who have had an impact on entire communities and nations, include Gloria de Souza, a teacher in India who has developed a methodology for teaching environmental issues that has spread through schools across this vast country. Mary Allegretti, whose work has helped to save over twelve million acres of Amazonian rain forest. And Rodrigo Baggio in Brazil, who has worked with companies, foundations, and government bodies to tackle the digital divide with projects that are reaching over 160,000 students and mobilizing hundreds of volunteers.

Ashoka maintains close links with Drayton's old employer McKinsey, which is one of a growing number of companies that are helping to build the capacity of social entrepreneurs and raise awareness of the potential of social venture capital. In different countries around the world, McKinsey consultants apply their problem-solving skills to helping Ashoka Fellows develop business plans, implement strategy, and strengthen organizational capacity. In Brazil, for example, McKinsey and Ashoka have worked in partnership to create the Center for Social Entrepreneurship, aimed at building the field of social enterprise. It helps to mobilize resources and build support structures through a wide range of training and management advisory services. It also organizes an annual business plan competition and helps to broker partnerships between social and business entrepreneurs.

Other professional services firms are also forming strategic alliances with social entrepreneurs. The Boston-based Monitor Group, for example, has provided resources, consulting services, and coaching to New Profit Inc., a nonprofit venture philanthropy firm founded by Vanessa Kirsch and Kelly Fitzsimmons that aims to effect large-scale social change by applying venture capital approaches to philanthropy. It utilizes the Balanced Scorecard approach and other leading-edge management tools to help fund and build the management skills of social enterprises. Bain Consulting has set up a dedicated business unit—Bridgespan Group—to provide consulting services to social entrepreneurs and their organizations. Accenture, PricewaterhouseCoopers, the Boston Consulting Group, KPMG, and other firms are looking at ways to combine support for social entrepreneurs with their own leadership development programs—using this as an opportunity to get their employees to "think outside the box" and develop new skills to apply in their consultancy work with commercial clients.

Business Leaders as Social Entrepreneurs Successful business entrepreneurs can themselves be highly effective social entrepreneurs. Arguably the greatest contribution that Bill Gates has made through the establishment of the multibillion-dollar Bill and Melinda Gates Foundation has been not only the money, although this is clearly crucial, but the manner in which the money is being invested and the application of new thinking to old problems. The foundation has enormous financial muscle, but it also reflects the mind-set of one of history's most successful and paradigm-changing business entrepreneurs. Gates and his colleagues want to change the way governments, companies, health experts, and community leaders think about tackling disease among the world's poor people. They are working not only to fund new research and health projects in some of the poorest places on earth, but also to reform or build institutional structures, local management capacity, and public policy frameworks. They are combining intellectual capital with financial capital to tackle some of the world's most intractable obstacles to meeting health needs.

Other great contemporary philanthropists have taken similar approaches. These include: hedge-fund pioneer George Soros and his active intellectual and financial engagement in building open, democratic societies and tackling bribery and corruption; CNN founder Ted Turner and his commitment to create new partnerships for international development, including greater use of the media to raise public awareness; Home Depot cofounder Arthur Blank, who has applied innovative approaches to youth development; eBay pioneers Pierre Omidyar and Jeffrey Skoll, who have fostered networks of social entrepreneurs; Paul Newman, who has inspired the CEO-level Committee to Encourage Corporate Philanthropy; and Lynn Fritz from UPS, who is applying his family fortune and his knowledge of world-class logistics to help improve the effectiveness and efficiency of disaster relief in developing countries. These and many other millionaires are building on the traditions of great American philanthropists such as Rockefeller, Ford, and Carnegie, who made their money through business and returned large amounts of it to the society and communities that helped to build this wealth.

There are two key differences today. First, many of today's business philanthropists are applying their business minds and entrepreneurial problem-solving skills, as well as their money, to tackle social problems. Second, it is not only high-profile millionaires, but also thousands of businesspeople who did well in the boom years of the 1990s who are putting something back, both financially and professionally, into their community—people like Kelli Givens, a former New York businesswoman who set up community centers in her McDonald's franchises in Harlem and is now an international volunteer running Habitat for Humanity in southern Africa. Or David McKay, a successful businessman from Colorado, who made his money in the healthcare sector and has now founded Pii—the Peace Initiatives Institute—aimed at developing innovative and creative approaches to build understanding and tolerance among young children in zones of conflict such as Northern Ireland. These two examples, and many others like them, illustrate the enormous potential for companies and individual businesspeople to apply social innovation to their philanthropic and community investment efforts.

Four: Support Institutional Innovation

New types of innovation are crucial not only at the level of the company and the community, but also at the level of public policy and national and international institutions. In our chapters on good governance and new alliances, we describe a number of innovative new types of engagement between the public and private sectors. Some of these are aimed at improving corporate performance. Others are focused on creating market mechanisms as an alternative to command-and-control regulation in areas such as health, safety, and the environment. In all cases the emphasis is on finding innovative ways to leverage limited public resources by mobilizing the problem-solving skills, networks, and market orientation of business.

Examples of institutional innovation profiled later in the book include the Environmental Protection Agency's Partners for the Environment Program; the Forest and Marine Stewardship Councils; the Global Alliance for Workers and Communities; and the Global Compact.

Five: Implement Support Systems and Incentives

If investing in eco-innovation, social innovation, and institutional innovation offers so much potential for managing corporate risks, enhancing stakeholder relationships, and harnessing competitive opportunities, what makes it happen? How do companies embed it into their business operations and decision-making? How do they take great ideas to fruition, either by changing existing processes, structures, or business models, or by profitably bringing new or redesigned products and services to market? How do companies translate a new idea into societal value *as well as* customer value and shareholder value?

First, they need to create the right corporate culture—a culture that is passionate, purposeful, and experimental and one that is supported unreservedly by senior management, including during periods of cost-cutting and risk aversion. Second, companies need to encourage "cross-boundary" learning experiences and "out-of-the-box" thinking—taking people out of their normal environments and exposing them to new types of ideas and organizations. Third, they need to make seed capital available.

Create a Culture for Change Committed champions can be found at all levels of a company that harnesses innovation for public good, not only the executive office and the R&D department. In an article for the *Harvard Business Review* in 2002, for example, Daniel Vasella, chairman and CEO of Novartis, was asked to describe the key factor that encourages innovation in his company.[15] He commented:

> *One way we try to foster innovation—both the technological innovation that leads to new drugs and the organization innovation that improves the way we do business—is to align our business objectives with our ideals. Doing so reaches people's intrinsic motivation. Certainly, extrinsic motivation is important; we offer stock options to our scientists and sponsor company research awards that enhance a researcher's visibility both within and outside Novartis. But I believe that people also do a better job when they believe in what they do and in how the company behaves, when they see that their work does more than enrich the shareholders.*

Companies that harness innovation for public good encourage experimentation and risk-taking and tolerate failure, as long as the company's core values and principles are observed. The people in the R&D department get out and about, not only inside the company but also externally. Few companies do this better than 3M.

3M and Eco-Innovation

A legendary experimenter, 3M has a platform of some one hundred core technologies that support over fifty thousand products and on average the development and commercialization of about four hundred new products a year. The company is also a pioneer in the field of eco-efficiency and eco-innovation. Today, one out of every eight scientists at 3M is experimenting with compounds or processes aimed at minimizing the company's impact on the environment.

Inspired by the vision and imagination of Dr. Joseph T. Ling, 3M launched its renowned Pollution Prevention Pays (3P) program back in 1975. Its pioneering work on eliminating pollution at the source and thereby making financial savings, environmental gains, and innovation advances provided input for the U.S. Pollution Prevention Act of 1990. It has also had a far-reaching impact on other corporate best practices and government legislation all over the world. For 3M, the program has led to new products and processes, financial gains, closer customer interaction, and increased employee motivation. Since 1975, more than 5,200 employee-driven 3P projects have prevented 2.2 billion pounds of pollution worldwide and saved 3M more than $950 million in manufacturing and pollution control costs.

Company programs that have encouraged eco-innovation include 3M's well-documented 15 percent rule, which enables employees to spend part of their work time exploring new ideas and experiments. In addition, employees can apply for 3M Genesis Grants, which provide seed funding to develop prototypes and market tests for products that may not get funded through standard channels.

Support Cross-Boundary Learning Companies that innovate for public good are often excellent at listening and learning across traditional boundaries. They listen and learn from customers *and* critics, from peers *and* competitors, from academics *and* activists. They also integrate cross-boundary experiences into their leadership development and learning programs by creating cross-function, cross-culture, cross-division, cross-sector, and cross-border learning opportunities. These include community assignments, project visits, job exchanges, company-wide communities of practice, cross-company and cross-sector learning laboratories, and active engagement with young people.

Much cross-boundary learning happens within a company among its own employees. Even here there is enormous scope for improvement in most global corporations, even within the same physical location, let alone internationally. In terms of cross-boundary learning between employees and people external to the company, there are two basic strategies that a company can adopt. It can adopt an *outside-in approach,* appointing external advisors or inviting external stakeholders to come into the company for a short-term visit, a series of dialogues, or a longer-term secondment or consultancy. Many of our company profiles throughout the book illustrate examples of such approaches for engaging with external stakeholders and new ideas.

Alternatively, the company can adopt an *inside-out approach,* whereby people in the company go out and get exposed to new perspectives, experiences, and ways of thinking and operating. This can range from fairly standard corporate procedures, such as customer visits, to community engagement programs in neighboring communities, to highly innovative international development assignments. Once again, even in the seemingly obvious area of active customer engagement, many companies fall short, especially when it comes to developing an understanding of nontraditional or emerging markets. Our profile of Unilever, in Principle #4 (alliances), illustrates the innovative way in which this company is reaching out to low-income consumers in countries such as India, Brazil, and Ghana—building new markets, customer loyalty, and product offerings in the process.

There is also untapped potential for companies to use their employee volunteering and community engagement programs as an important source of ideas and inspiration for the workplace. On pages 88 and 89 we profile a few different examples of mechanisms that leading companies are using to engage their best managers in learning beyond the business environment.

Cross-Boundary Learning
Through Community Engagement

IBM's Reinventing Education Initiative Established in 1994, this program is run by IBM in partnership with schools across America and in other countries. The company provides a combination of money, technology, researchers, systems engineers, and consultants to help its school partners develop and implement innovative technology-based solutions to specific education challenges. The program has reached over ten million children and resulted in measurable improvements in performance, teaching quality, and school management. At the same time, it has had clear benefits for the company that go beyond reputation enhancement and good community relations. According to Harvard Business School professor Rosabeth Moss Kanter, "These projects have also helped IBM teams develop new solutions with commercial applications, such as voice recognition technology based on children's voices or data warehousing for large groups of users."[16] She describes the social sector as a Beta Site for business innovation and argues, "Traditionally, business viewed the social sector as a dumping ground for spare cash, obsolete equipment, and tired executives. But today smart companies are approaching it as a learning laboratory."[17]

UPS's Community Internship Program UPS, one of the world's largest package-delivery companies, is an innovator that takes the idea of "community as learning laboratory" seriously. Through its Community Internship Program, founded back in 1968, more than one thousand managers have spent four weeks living and working in poor communities. In the process they have developed new skills, gained new insights and inspiration, and improved their understanding of the needs of current and potential customers.

PWC's Ulysses Program As a professional services firm of over 120,000 people operating on a truly global basis, Pricewaterhouse-Coopers recognizes that its employees need to develop not only the best professional skills, but also the ability to work in diverse cultures and challenging situations, using emotional intelligence in addition to their intellect and technical expertise. The firm has launched an innovative "learning journey" for some of its high-potential junior partners to help them develop the global vision, realism, ethics, and courage that are needed for future leadership of the firm. Multicultural and cross-functional teams are selected to spend eight weeks working with local partners on community development projects in remote and challenging locations before returning to share their lessons with other colleagues.

Business in the Community's "Seeing Is Believing" Visits In this UK-based initiative, top business leaders, at the CEO or board level, are led by one of their own peers on carefully structured visits to innovative community projects. The aim is to open their eyes to leadership initiatives being undertaken by people in disadvantaged communities and to generate ideas for their own involvement and that of their company, beyond writing checks. Tailored community visits are also managed for senior managers and boards of directors from the same company. In a related initiative, supported by KPMG among others, senior managers are paired in joint mentoring arrangements with head teachers at schools. Both initiatives provide an opportunity for two-way learning and new ways of looking at the world and at problem-solving.

Provide Seed Capital and Incentives Companies committed to innovation for public good back up the "soft" incentives and opportunities for experimentation and cross-boundary learning with hard cash, stretch targets, and rigorous performance indicators. They create internal markets for ideas and awards for risk-takers and paradigm-breakers, ranging from venture capital funds to global award programs. Nestlé's Life Venture's Fund offers one example.

Nestlé's Life Venture's Fund

In the exciting and excitable stock markets of the 1990s, many analysts and business journalists viewed Swiss-based Nestlé as distinctly unexciting. It was seen as evolutionary rather than revolutionary, long term rather than quick return, boring rather than booming. These labels didn't concern CEO Peter Brabeck-Letmathe. As he sees it, "The Nestlé Corporate Business Principles state openly that we favor long-term business development over short-term profit. While we are committed to making a healthy profit, we instruct managers not to do so at the expense of long-term, sustainable development."[18] In fact, the company's performance was more than respectable during this period; from 1970 to 2000, its shares outperformed the Morgan Stanley World Index in U.S. dollar terms by 25 percent.

"Innovation-renovation" is one of four central pillars that underpin Nestlé's long-term strategy. Its research facilities in different countries make up the world's largest food and nutrition research network, with roots in many local cultures. The network also provides a framework for embedding health, safety, environmental, and nutrition considerations into the company's R&D processes. A recent innovation has been the launch of Life Ventures SA, a venture capital fund that offers an interesting model for other companies. Established in 2002, this fund aims to provide Nestlé with a better pipeline of science, technology, and know-how opportunities through investing in minority stakes in startups with innovative R&D projects. Run by an independent management team, the fund specializes in areas related to food and life sciences, as well as packaging and commercial applications with a strong emphasis on sustainable development.

Despite the potential shareholder and societal benefits of harnessing innovation for public good, in most companies there are numerous internal obstacles to achieving this goal. Indeed, there are obstacles to any type of innovation. These obstacles are both cultural and structural. They include "turf battles," bureaucracy, extreme short-term focus and earnings pressures, cost cutting, low employee morale, unreasonably high levels of risk aversion, technical or scientific arrogance, poor information systems, organizational inertia, and fear. They are likely to undermine all but the lowest-risk, lowest-cost opportunities for eco-innovation and social innovation. This is especially the case in periods of economic downturn and uncertainty, and yet arguably this is the very time when companies should be exploring more creative ways to be competitive than simply cutting costs, jobs, and research.

If corporate bureaucracies and cultures are stifling the type of innovation that is *clearly* crucial to the bottom line, they are even more likely to obstruct innovation that has a less proven, or a less direct, impact on corporate performance and profitability. One of the most vital leadership roles of senior management is to make sure that these obstacles are removed. They need to champion a systematic and structured approach to innovation that aligns policies and incentives in a manner that integrates ethical, environmental, and social considerations into innovation processes.

Our final profile in this chapter looks at how DuPont is harnessing innovation for public good. The company has survived for over two hundred years because of its ability to anticipate societal and market trends and to innovate and periodically transform its business model in response to these. Today, the company is integrating a vision for sustainable growth into its core business strategy and innovation processes. Although at an early stage, this integration offers useful ideas for others.

DUPONT
Innovating for Sustainable Growth

As DuPont starts our third century of business, we view sustainable growth as our key defining strategy. By integrating sustainable strategies and practices into our business plans, we will be best positioned to capitalize on emerging trends in a way that builds tremendous value for

*our shareholders while also improving the environment
and society as a whole. . . . During the decade of the
1990s we improved our environmental footprint by about
60% and shareholder value increased by nearly 340%. I
will not try to convince you of the mathematical causality
of those two facts. I would suggest that they are more than
coincidental.*

GARY PFEIFFER, CHIEF FINANCIAL OFFICER, DUPONT

On July 19, 2002, Joshua Zhang from China and Margarita de Ceballos from Colombia joined ten of their DuPont colleagues from around the world, together with their chairman and CEO Chad Holliday, on the floor of the New York Stock Exchange. They were there to ring the closing bell in celebration of a major milestone in DuPont's history. In a month when stock-market values were plummeting and the media pundits were lamenting the greed and short-term focus of American capitalism, DuPont celebrated its two hundredth anniversary—the oldest industrial company listed on the Fortune 500.

On the same day, its senior management team met with key financial analysts and investors to discuss the future. Their central mission, they stated, was to become a sustainable growth company—defined as increasing shareholder and societal value while decreasing the company's environmental footprint. Speaking the previous year at the Chicago Executives Club, Chad Holliday had stated, "The challenge of sustainable growth is not a philosophical issue. It is a nuts-and-bolts business reality. . . . We made it the primary objective of our company because we believe sustainable growth will be the common denominator of successful global companies in the twenty-first century."[19]

The company aims to fundamentally transform itself to build tomorrow's competitive advantage and to better serve both today's and tomorrow's markets. Harnessing innovation for public good by incorporating ethical, social, and environmental considerations into all types of corporate innovation is a central element of this transformation plan.

Two Centuries of Innovation

Over the past two hundred years DuPont's scientific innovation has reflected, and in many cases supported, America's own economic progress and national security. When Neil Armstrong stepped onto the surface of the moon, twenty-three layers of his twenty-five-layer spacesuit were made from DuPont materials. The company has invented nearly 75 percent of the forty-plus major polymers commercially produced today, forming the basis for numerous other businesses and products with household names. DuPont plastics have made cars more fuel-efficient, and its nylon airbags have helped to make them safer, while its products are used in protective clothing for police officers, firefighters, and rescue workers around the world. The company's pioneering work in new aerosols and refrigerants has helped to ease negative environmental impacts on the ozone layer, and its scientists are exploring fascinating new possibilities for biotechnology, from plants that clean up pollution to foods that help prevent brittle bones and cancer.

As with all the companies profiled in this book, the social and environmental impacts of DuPont's products and processes have not always been positive. It has been targeted by environmental campaigns as one of America's largest polluters, and looking to the future, it faces the challenge of dealing with the uncertain consequences of biotechnology. Yet for over two hundred years the company has produced thousands of products and services that have improved the quality and longevity of people's lives. At the same time, it has successfully adapted and learned from past experiences, undergoing several transformations of its business model in the process. The company cites two critical factors in its longevity and success, both of which reflect our seven operating principles:

▨ *The first success factor is DuPont's grounding in a long-standing set of corporate values that cover safety, health, and environmental stewardship, integrity, and high ethical standards, as well as treating people with fairness and respect.* These are not a recent development. DuPont's founding fathers recognized the human and economic importance of safety back in the 1800s, and safety was declared a line management responsibility in 1811. One of the company's earliest safety rules was that "no employee may enter a new mill or rebuilt mill until a member of top management has personally operated it." DuPont was one of the first companies in the world to institute an employee medical plan, a pension plan, and a formal, companywide safety policy. It was also one of the first companies to recognize the risks and opportunities of environmental issues in the 1970s, albeit with some prodding from environmental campaigners. When Chad Holliday briefed security analysts and institutional investors in July 2002 on the company's goals for higher earnings growth and improved return on invested capital, he noted, "These values provide the foundation for the company and its employees to manage change during difficult and challenging times."[20]

▓ *The second success factor is DuPont's commitment to scientific discovery and market-driven innovation as a means to gain competitive advantage and create value, and its ability to transform and reinvent itself in order to grow.* The company has undergone three fundamental transformations over the past two hundred years—into high explosives in the latter nineteenth century, into chemicals and polymers in the twentieth century, and into biotechnology, information technology, and other integrated sciences today. As D. S. Kim, president of DuPont Asia Pacific, describes it, "What has not stayed the same over time is the products we make and the markets we serve; these have changed dramatically. . . . our sustainability has been more related to 'who' we are than to 'what' we make."[21]

How are these past lessons and experiences being leveraged to support the company's vision of tomorrow? What are the cornerstones of its transformation process aimed at sustaining and gaining competitive edge in the next century?

Sustainable Growth for the Future

As DuPont looks to the next one hundred years, the company has placed its bets on a strategy it terms *sustainable growth*—increasing shareholder and societal value while decreasing the company's environmental footprint.

In the words of Paul Tebo, the company's vice president for safety, health and environment, and a thirty-three-year DuPont veteran who has worked in research, strategic planning, engineering, and line management positions, "We recognize that, even though we have been sustainable in terms of longevity for the past 200 years, we will probably not survive and prosper in this century unless we transform ourselves into a 'sustainable growth' company—all along the value chains in which we operate, and wherever we operate around the world."[22]

The company is already a number of years along this path, and the results to date look encouraging. Over the past ten years DuPont reports that it has increased production by 35 percent and delivered the highest earnings growth in some thirty years. At the same time, it has kept total energy use flat, conservatively saving the company over $1.5 billion. It has cut global air carcinogens by 87 percent, global air toxins by 76 percent, and global hazardous waste by 37 percent, and delivered a 68 percent reduction of global greenhouse gases, based on the Kyoto basket of gases. In addition, the company's safety and health performance continues to be about five times better than the chemical and petrochemical industry average and twenty times better than the average for all industries. And diversity statistics are impressive for a science-based company, with women running two of the company's five growth platforms and over one hundred support networks or affinity groups aimed at creating a more inclusive and welcoming environment for all people.

What does sustainable growth look like in practice?

Since 1998, DuPont has built its strategic vision of sustainable growth on a foundation of *three core strategies:* vigorously pursue *knowledge intensity* in all businesses; significantly *increase productivity* by using Six Sigma methodology; and deliver new products through the power of *integrated science.* Implementing all three of these core strategies to deliver both shareholder *and* societal value is an explicit goal. Building on the three core strategies, in early 2002 the company created *five market growth platforms* for organizing its businesses. They are illustrated on page 96. In all five of these growth platforms the market opportunities are large, there are unmet needs, and there is a pre-

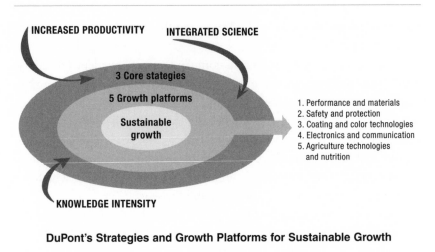

INCREASED PRODUCTIVITY   INTEGRATED SCIENCE

3 Core stategies

5 Growth platforms

Sustainable
growth

1. Performance and materials
2. Safety and protection
3. Coating and color technologies
4. Electronics and communication
5. Agriculture technologies
   and nutrition

KNOWLEDGE INTENSITY

DuPont's Strategies and Growth Platforms for Sustainable Growth

Source: DuPont

mium on innovation and a clear opportunity to deliver societal as well as shareholder value.

DuPont's three core business strategies are applicable for many companies. What are some of the ways they are harnessing these strategies to deliver a combination of financial, social, and environmental benefits?

Core Strategy #1: Knowledge Intensity The company defines knowledge intensity as a strategy to get paid for what the company knows rather than simply for what it makes. It involves harnessing and creating value from DuPont's many years of experience, its technical know-how, and its brand equity. Although physical products and materials remain central to DuPont's value proposition, major new opportunities are possible by delivering value to customers based on the company's knowledge, either in combination with or separate from its products and materials. These opportunities have the potential to create environmental and social value, as well as profits.

The company's creation of a safety and protection business as one of its five growth platforms is one example. This business draws on the fact that industrial safety has been a core value and operational speciality of the company for two centuries, and this knowledge can now be leveraged, together with the company's extensive range of safety products, to deliver profitable services to other companies. In 2001 DuPont's highly knowledge-intensive safety consulting business tripled, achieving 20 percent top-line revenue growth while helping customers to reduce both injuries and costs.

Knowledge intensity also has the potential to reduce the use of depletable forms of raw materials and energy while lowering environmental impact. In Canada, for example, DuPont signed a commercial agreement with Ford Motor Company, stating that it would get paid on the basis of "cars painted" rather than gallons of paint sold to Ford. By leveraging its extensive know-how on paint application technology, over four years DuPont has used less paint and seen a 50 percent reduction in volatile organic emissions. Ford's costs are down by almost 35 percent, and application efficiency is greatly increased, resulting in added value for DuPont that more than offsets the reduction in paint sold.

Core Strategy #2: Increased Productivity Increased productivity can deliver shareholder value while decreasing a company's environmental footprint by driving down costs, cutting waste, and reducing the use of energy. DuPont has made a major commitment to the Six Sigma process, which focuses on eliminating defects from work processes, with the aim of cutting costs and cycle time and increasing customer satisfaction. Within its first year of implementation in 2000, Six Sigma was in place in every DuPont business and region, with some five thousand ongoing or completed projects. These delivered an annualized financial benefit of nearly $1 billion in pretax earnings, along with substantial reductions in the company's environmental footprint. The environmental benefits cited by one DuPont business have included reduced energy and water consumption, cuts in greenhouse gas emissions and land-fill waste, less shipment of hazardous materials, and adoption of inherently safer manufacturing process technology.

Core Strategy #3: Integrated Science This strategy has the potential to combine chemistry, engineering, physics, biology, information technology, and other technology platforms to address a wide variety of social and environmental needs on a commercially viable basis. In 2001, for example, DuPont created a fuel cell business that draws on its experience in polymer chemistry, coatings, and electrochemical technologies. Fuel cells have the potential to supply clean power for transportation, homes, and commercial buildings in a way that substantially reduces environmental impact and could someday power cellular phones and laptop computers. Another example is a DuPont business called Qualicon. It combines chemistry and biotechnology to create commercial tests that can cut the time needed to detect and identify pathogenic bacteria from days to hours—helping to reduce disease and death rates. In the United States alone, foodborne illnesses affect as many as 76 million people a year with more than nine thousand deaths.

Innovation underpins these three strategies and lies at the core of the company's vision for the future. DuPont has targeted one-third of its total revenues each year to come from new innovations—defined as products and services commercialized in the last five years.

How DuPont Is Harnessing Innovation for Public Good

Undertaking Due Diligence The company is analyzing the environmental and social impacts of existing and new products, services, and processes, with the aim of "doing no harm." All of DuPont's businesses conduct product stewardship reviews on a regular basis to assess the environmental impact of new and existing products. In 2001, the company introduced formal guidelines to its R&D organizations that require them to integrate potential societal and environmental impact assessments into the development process for all new products and services.

Creating New Value DuPont looks for opportunities to create new value by developing products, services, and technologies that specifically address an environmental problem or meet a social need. There is potential for this in all of the company's five growth platforms—with particular opportunities and risks in the area of biotechnology. One example is the company's Integrated Agricultural Plan in Colombia, launched in 1999 with a group of local partners from the public and private sectors, that provides small-scale farmers with a package of technical, financial, and commercial assistance. This partnership enables the farmers to obtain financial credit, training, technology, and agreed pricing contracts to help them improve their productivity, and to do so in a manner that also decreases price uncertainty and commercial risk, while minimizing negative environmental impact and health and safety risks. It also helps to grow future markets for the companies and is a commercially viable business proposition.

As chief financial officer Gary Pfeiffer has observed, "Today we in DuPont serve about one billion of the six billion people in the world—primarily in the developed economies. If we are to be a sustainable growth company, we must serve the entire population in a way that is good for society, our shareholders and the environment. That is our challenge for the next 100 years."[23]

Supporting Institutional Innovation DuPont is working with other companies, government authorities, academics, and nongovernmental organizations to support institutional innovation. The company has been a key leader, for example, in the chemical industry's Responsible Care program, which we describe under Principle #6 (governance), and is active in a number of the innovative EPA programs described under Principle #4 (alliances). It is also working with other companies, academics, and environmental groups such as Environmental Defense, the Pew Center on Climate Change, and the World Resources Institute to speed policy action and to develop innovative market mechanisms aimed at tackling global climate change.

Mobilizing Philanthropic Innovation A key element in the company's philanthropic innovations is leveraging its core competencies and products, as well as its charitable contributions, for wider social benefit. One example is the cloth developed and donated by DuPont and manufactured by Precision Fabrics of Greensboro, North Carolina, which has provided a simple, inexpensive, but highly cost-effective technology for preventing the tropical disease guinea worm. There were more than 3.2 million cases of the disease reported in Asia and Africa in 1986; today, a decade after the launch of the program, the known cases have fallen below 150,000.

Core Leadership Disciplines

DuPont exemplifies many of the core leadership disciplines we have identified in other corporate visionaries. These include the following:

Enlist Committed Champions at All Levels of the Company

Ultimate responsibility for the company's sustainable growth strategy rests with the board of directors. DuPont's thirteen-member board is diverse in terms of nationality, gender, ethnicity, professional background, and areas of expertise. It has also established a dedicated Environmental Policy Committee consisting of independent directors with a valuable mix of business, environmental, and social credentials.

Another sign of commitment from the top is the fact that business unit heads are measured against their sustainable growth performance, not only the financials. They are also encouraged to assess the specific risks and opportunities for societal value creation in their own business units. Champions are encouraged at different levels and locations in the company through a variety of award programs.

Consult with External Thought Leaders

Community-level Consultation Community advisory panels and other formal structures for community interaction have been established at all of DuPont's manufacturing sites around the world. These have been key in building better communications and trust, as well as providing useful market information, business advice, and linkages.

Integrating External Input into Business Planning Stakeholder involvement in business planning processes is still at an early stage but is being experimented with both at the level of business units and on a national basis. DuPont in Canada, for example, has a national-level external advisory panel consisting of environmental, government, and business leaders.

Consultation on Sensitive Issues Biotechnology is central to DuPont's growth plans, and DuPont believes strongly that this technology has the potential to address many global problems, including malnutrition, obesity, aging diseases, certain types of cancer, soil erosion, water quality, climate change, and agricultural productivity. Despite this potential, DuPont recognizes the high levels of public concern around the world associated with the uncertain scientific data and potential unintended consequences of biotechnology. This public concern creates risks and potential costs for the company in terms of its reputation, and of potential activist campaigns, consumer boycotts, sabotage, lawsuits, and regulations.

As a result, DuPont has embarked on a process of stakeholder engagement as a core element of its strategic plan to harness biotechnology. In 1999, it established an initial set of principles and made a series of public commitments on how it would develop biotech as a business opportunity. At the same time, it established an external biotechnology advisory panel consisting of six international experts. The panel's role is to guide and challenge the company in its development, testing, and commercialization of biotech, to audit its progress, and to provide independent reports available to the public on a regular basis.

In June 2003, the company adopted a new set of principles on biodiversity, based on guidance from the advisory panel and other stakeholder feedback. This exemplifies the dynamic learning process that needs to underpin meaningful stakeholder consultation. It is not simply a matter of hosting stakeholder dialogues. Far more important is how these feed back into the company and influence its policies, strategies, and business decisions.

Ensure Consistency and Credibility

Speaking at the World Summit for Sustainable Development in 2002, Chad Holliday outlined what he saw as the four key things that are necessary for a company to be credible in implementing change toward sustainable development:

> *First, a public commitment, codified in a way that says something meaningful to your company. Second, you must have ways to measure that with very specific goals and indicators. Third, you must report on progress in a transparent way that is meaningful to your stakeholders. And fourth, get external stakeholders engaged at the outset before you are locked in. This includes other companies outside your company, others around your company, such as employees and customers, and young people in your company and in universities. You can expect criticism, that the goals are either not ambitious enough or time is too short, but you can sleep better at night because you know you are doing the right thing.[24]*

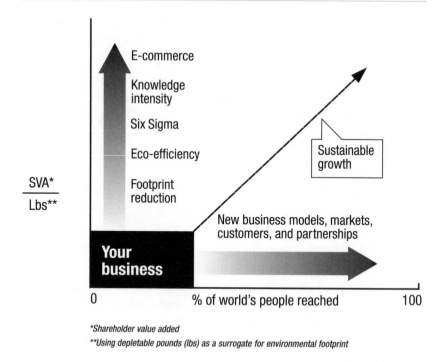

Shareholder value added

**Using depletable pounds (lbs) as a surrogate for environmental footprint

DuPont's Strategy for Achieving Sustainable Growth

Source: DuPont

The following two actions that DuPont has taken over the past ten years to implement goals and metrics for social innovation and eco-innovation are especially worth mentioning.

Setting Clear Targets In 1994, DuPont's former CEO set a new corporate-wide goal: zero injuries, illnesses, and incidents. This challenged conventional thinking at the time, but the mantra *the goal is zero* became central to the company's mission and its corporate culture. The "goal is zero" target has now been extended to waste and emissions along the company's value chain. As the World Business Council for Sustainable Development has observed, "While the sustainable growth transformation and the attainment of zero goals throughout the whole value chain will take time, already the zero challenge is driving new innovations through the business globally. . . . The challenging targets are forcing DuPont businesses to rethink products and approaches and come up with new innovative solutions."[25] Four new companywide targets have now been set for 2010 and committed to publicly: reducing greenhouse emissions from global operations by 65 percent using 1990 as a base year; keeping energy use flat; sourcing 10 percent of global energy use in 2010 from renewable sources; and achieving 25 percent of revenues from nondepletable resources. The company believes that if expectations are clear and managers are held accountable, then results will follow.

Establishing Rigorous Metrics A particularly innovative metric that DuPont has developed is based on shareholder value added per pound of product. This metric helps the company to measure and monitor its progress in creating more shareholder value without using or creating more pounds of product and the associated depletion of natural resources and production of waste. DuPont uses pounds of product to serve as a surrogate for its overall environmental footprint. It recognizes that to become a sustainable growth company, it needs to demonstrate that it is profitable to produce more with less in terms of environmental impact, while at the same time developing new business models and partnerships to serve the growing populations in emerging economies, many of whom live on very low incomes. As Chad Holliday describes it, "We want our employees and everyone associated with the company to understand that our mission of sustainable growth involves the pursuit of a noble purpose while growing profitably."[26] The figure on page 102 illustrates the company's strategy for sustainable growth.

Like all leadership companies, DuPont has moved beyond a compliance mind-set to also embrace a value creation mind-set. It is the first to admit that it has a long way to go. Changing a two-hundred-year-old, engineering-based culture and influencing organizational behavior and management structures throughout a large global company takes time and persistence. There is also the ongoing challenge of engaging effectively with external stakeholders. The company's commitment to biotechnology poses future risks, and it faces strong competition in many areas. Despite these challenges, DuPont's sustainable growth strategy offers an ambitious mainstream business vision for the future and some useful ideas on the types of strategy, systems, and metrics that other companies can adopt. Taken to scale and replicated by others, this approach illustrates the potential of harnessing innovation for competitive advantage and for social and environmental progress.

Harnessing Innovation for Public Good

One: Embed into core business strategy.

Two: Be rigorous about due diligence.

Three: Invest in social entrepreneurs.

Four: Support institutional innovation.

Five: Implement support systems and incentives.

Put People at the Center

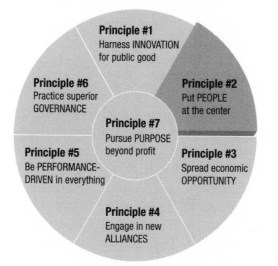

Putting people at the center is about the quality of relationships that a company has with its employees, its customers, its investors, its business partners, its local neighbors, workers along its supply chain, and other people who contribute to its success or who are affected by its operations.

It involves identifying these key stakeholders and then building relationships with them that are based on mutual respect, mutual benefit, transparency, and accountability, all of which are crucial to building trust.

It involves listening to stakeholder interests and concerns. It requires measures to ensure that the company's operations do not have a negative impact, and wherever possible have a positive impact, on people's basic health, safety, and quality of life, their participation in the company's success, and their personal growth and potential.

Why a Focus on People Matters

We as a management team are spending a lot of time reminding ourselves what are the core values of this company, the ones that we believe deeply in. . . . we changed our mission statement as a company and we did it because we believe that in the end it's all about people. That's what it is. It is people. Absolutely technology matters, but it is all about people.

ORLANDO AYALA, GROUP VICE PRESIDENT,

WORLDWIDE SALES, MICROSOFT, 2002

The quality of a company's relationships with its employees and other key stakeholders along its value chain—customers, shareholders, suppliers, public officials, and host communities—is crucial to its success and its ability to anticipate or respond to changing competitive conditions and societal expectations. In today's knowledge-intensive, global economy, it is the ideas, interests, diversity, and energy of the people who work in and interact with a business, more than anything else, that underpin innovation and drive the creation of value and wealth.

Failure to treat people with respect and fairness undermines motivation and loyalty in the case of employees and chases away business in the case of customers. In extreme cases, for example, in the case of labor, civil rights, or human rights problems, a company may incur reputation damage and costly litigation if it is deemed to be responsible for, or even complicit in, these problems. Cynicism and skepticism about business, its motives, and its actions create mistrust and threaten to tear the social fabric that is necessary for business to thrive.

The link between sustaining long-term productivity, performance, and profit and having good relationships with people should be obvious. As the diagram on page 107 illustrates, a company's relationship with any group of people is almost always a two-way process. There is usually an element of reciprocity—an element of "give and take," both tangible and intangible—in terms of products, services, and different types of capital. This includes financial, intellectual, human, and social capital.

Financial capital means money, and that's important. But intellectual capital means ideas and innovation; human capital means skills, health, energy, and enthusiasm; and social capital means trust. They *all* matter for corporate success. The most effective and efficient way for a business to attract and retain these different types of capital is through transparent, accountable, and ongoing relationships with people. This calls for good relationships not only with the company's major institutional investors, key customers, and a few "high flyers" at the top of the corporate hierarchy, but with all the people who work in the company and along its supply chain and with all customers, regulators, suppliers, and community partners.

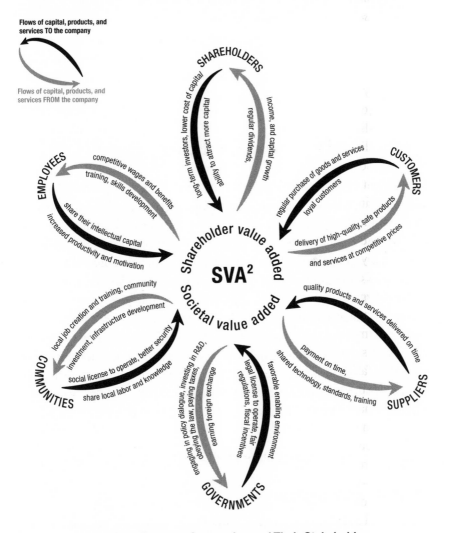

Interactions Between Companies and Their Stakeholders

Source: J. Nelson, *Building Competitiveness and Communities*, 1998

Despite the logic of building strong relationships with the different groups of people who have an impact on the company or are affected by its activities, most companies fail the test. They face unnecessary risks and they miss incredible opportunities as a result. Most companies have never undertaken a companywide stakeholder analysis or relationship mapping exercise, let alone developed systematic approaches for managing and measuring different types of relationships.

By genuinely putting people at the center, leading companies are doing a better job of managing their risks, reaping performance benefits, and improving the quality of people's lives. They are changing the corporate view of stakeholder relationships from burdensome, time-consuming, and superficial management activities to energizing, proactive, and strategic business opportunities.

Making It Happen

So how does a company genuinely *put people at the center*? What strategies can you use as a manager to develop a people-centered approach to managing risk and reputation; increasing efficiency, productivity, and quality; encouraging new ideas, creativity, and innovation; and enhancing performance and profit? What can you do to genuinely enhance the quality of people's lives while also improving your company's performance?

In the following pages we suggest five broad strategies for putting people at the center. They are especially relevant for employees, whether you manage 10 people, 100 people, or 100,000 people. They are also relevant, to a greater or lesser extent, in building and managing relationships with people working along the company's supply chain, with customers, and with people in local communities. In certain cases they are relevant to relationships with individual investors and business partners.

One: Identify Key Stakeholders and What Matters to Them

People in the Workplace

Every day millions of people go to work in companies that range from small, owner-operated businesses to some of the world's largest enterprises. How many of these people get up each morning with the aim of maximizing profits for the shareholders? Some, certainly, but most people aspire to something much greater. Their motivations include a desire to improve their own standard of living and quality of life; to do "good work" of which they feel proud; to feel challenged, respected, listened to, and valued; and to be part of a team, a community, a sense of purpose, or something bigger than themselves.

Yet we continue to emphasize the employee as economic agent, as economic entity. We speak of employees as "our greatest asset." The *Concise Oxford Dictionary* defines *asset* as "property available to meet debts; any possession; person or thing having any useful quality"—a utilitarian and economic term that does not exactly imply personal motivation, meaning, and purpose. As Adrian Levy, founder and former chairman of Canadian consulting firm RLG, comments, "People are not the most important asset of a company. They *are* the company. Everything else is an asset."[1]

The most important and direct links between people and corporate performance involve employees and customers. A company with a positive, motivated, and inclusive culture, where people feel that they matter for who they are, not just as "cogs in a money-making wheel," is a great place to work. It is also likely to be more diverse and to deliver higher productivity, good ideas, good quality, good customer service, and ultimately good performance and profits. In *The Service Profit Chain,* Harvard Business School professors James Heskett, Earl Sasser, and Len Schlesinger concluded, "Simply stated, service profit chain thinking maintains that there are direct and strong relationships between profit; growth; customer loyalty; customer satisfaction; the value of goods and services delivered to customers; and employee capability, satisfaction, loyalty, and productivity."[2] Between 1986 and 1995, the common stock prices of the companies they studied increased 147 percent, nearly twice as much as the price of their closest competitors' stocks.

The importance of nonfinancial motivations was one of the key findings in a research project conducted by consultants McKinsey & Company, entitled *The War for Talent.*[3] They studied seventy-seven large U.S. companies in a variety of industries, surveying nearly four hundred corporate officers and six thousand executives from the "top 200" ranks in these companies. Only 23 percent of the executives surveyed cited high total compensation as absolutely essential to motivating the best talent, compared to 58 percent who cited values and culture as being essential, 56 percent who emphasized freedom and autonomy, 51 percent who cited exciting job challenges, and 50 percent who stressed good management. McKinsey identified nineteen "employee value proposition" dimensions. Some of these related to compensation, but most were intangibles linked to values, culture, and good management. The top-quintile companies in terms of shareholder value outperformed the mid-quintile companies in thirteen out of nineteen of these "soft" people-centered dimensions.

Yet, despite all the lip service paid to the importance of employees and clear evidence of a sound business case for respecting their motivations and aspirations, corporations often fail to achieve this in practice. Stress; overwork; badly and insensitively handled layoffs; lack of genuine fairness, care, concern, trust, and diversity; and an emphasis on profits over people remain the reality in far too many workplaces.

WalkerInformation's survey *Integrity in the Workplace* found that fairness at work, including fair pay and fair implementation of policies, was listed by respondents from forty-eight U.S. states as the most important factor in ensuring employee loyalty and motivation, followed by care and concern for employees. Yet only 50 percent of employees felt there was fairness in pay and only 45 percent felt there was fairness in the way policies are carried out. Only 44 percent felt there was an atmosphere of genuine care and concern for employees, and only 41 percent saw real trust in their companies. Ironically, 66 percent of senior managers believe their company shows care and concern, even though fewer than half their middle managers and rank-and-file employees think this is the case.[4]

There is a growing need to "raise the game" and look more creatively at how best to relate to the people whose work contributes directly to a company's success. Peter Drucker comments in a 2002 *Harvard Business Review* article, "They're Not Employees, They're People," "Every organization must take management responsibility for *all* the people whose productivity and performance it relies on—whether they're temps, part-timers, employees of the organization itself, or employees of its outsourcers, suppliers, and distributors."[5] This raises the question: How far along a company's value chain can it realistically be expected to take responsibility for the health, safety, and welfare of workers? At the very least, in today's global economy, companies need to understand who the people are along their value chain and what some of the company's risks and opportunities may be in terms of its relationship to these people.

People in the Marketplace

Every day hundreds of millions of people around the world purchase goods and services that help them to meet their basic needs; make their lives more efficient and more convenient; provide entertainment, leisure, and luxuries; and impact on their livelihoods. Businesses, large and small, are responsible for researching, developing, sourcing, producing, marketing, selling, and delivering these goods and services. To suggest that all these activities are values free and can be carried out solely on the basis of private gain, without any sense of public interest or focus on the people who buy and use the goods and services, is to seriously misunderstand the opportunities and responsibilities of private enterprise.

The nature of these responsibilities and opportunities varies from company to company and from industry to industry. A company that is providing essential goods and services, for example, such as energy, water, basic foods, or medicines, clearly faces different opportunities and responsibilities than one producing luxury goods and services. In any great company, however, large or small, the customer relationship goes beyond the sole purpose of making a profit or making a one-time transaction. Yet not enough companies define their corporate purpose in terms of the contribution that their products and services make to people's lives. Equally, not enough companies think through the positive and negative impacts of their products and services on people's lives. Even fewer companies think about these impacts along the whole life cycle of a particular product, from sourcing to final use and disposal.

Companies that explicitly place concepts of service, or improving the quality of people's lives, or building trusted relationships with people at the core of their value proposition are still the exceptions rather than the norm. They include companies such as Marriott, with its ethos and culture of "The Spirit to Serve"; Unilever, with its corporate purpose to "anticipate the aspirations of our consumers and customers and to respond creatively and competitively with branded products and services which raise the quality of life"; and Johnson & Johnson, whose first commitment in its Credo is to "the doctors, nurses and patients, to mothers and fathers and all others who use our products and services."

Statements of public commitment are necessary, but not sufficient. If the employees who interface with customers and other stakeholders don't walk the talk, great damage can be done to a company's reputation and reservoir of public trust. Citigroup's strategic aspiration to "establish trusted relationships with consumers," for example, was undermined by a few of the company's analysts—a tiny number compared to the company's over 250,000 employees—who treated small-scale investors and customers with disdain and contempt when they publicly promoted purchases of stock that in reality they considered to be bad performers or worse.

People in the Community

Millions of people around the world who have never worked for companies, and many who have never purchased their products and services, are affected—for good and ill—because those companies are operating in their community. As in the workplace and marketplace, business has an opportunity to make a positive impact on such people's lives even if they are not direct employees, customers, or investors.

At a minimum, every company needs to think seriously and systematically about how to protect its neighbors from any adverse economic, health, safety, and environmental impacts resulting from its activities. In certain industries and locations—for example, high-impact industries like infrastructure, oil, gas, and mining, or locations where governments are weak or corrupt—companies face serious risks of causing a negative impact on people's lives.

Over and above managing risks and avoiding a negative impact on local communities, companies can think creatively about ways to increase the participation of local people in their affairs, especially when these affairs directly affect those people. They can also think about possibilities for spreading social and economic opportunities to people living in the surrounding community.

Two: Understand the Emerging Human Rights Agenda

Most analysis of the relationship between companies and people focuses on customers and employees. In the case of customers, the emphasis has been on customer service and meeting customer needs with good quality, good value, and safe products and services. In the case of employees, the emphasis is largely on improving human resource practices: compensation, benefits, stock ownership, diversity, equal opportunity, work–life balance, training, job security, labor or industrial relations, and health and safety. These are all crucially important to corporate performance and to the goal of putting people at the center.

For companies operating globally, however, these issues are no longer enough. They capture only part of the picture. In today's global economy, it is increasingly necessary for companies to think about their relationships with people along their entire supply chain and in all the local communities where they operate. And it is increasingly important to think about these relationships not only in terms of managing human resources, but also managing human rights.

Although the concepts of consumer rights, civil rights, and labor rights have been an ongoing issue for many American companies since the 1960s, human rights have barely been on the corporate radar screen. Few corporate executives are familiar with the United Nations Universal Declaration of Human Rights. This is starting to change, however, driven by a combination of activist campaigns, negative media coverage, and, for some companies, litigation and reputation damage.

We summarize below a few of the human rights campaigns and lawsuits that have started to impact major corporations over the past five years. Until recently, few if any of these issues were considered a strategic concern for the companies and industries in question. Today, they take up a growing percentage of management time and raise serious risks for some companies in terms of reputation, litigation, and agitation.

- Companies in the *apparel industry* have faced proxy resolutions, investigative journalism, consumer boycotts, and lawsuits related to sweatshop conditions in their supply chain, often in contractors' factories that the companies neither own nor directly manage. Nike, Gap, Disney, and Wal-Mart are among the companies that have been targeted.

▪ Companies in the *energy and mining sector* have faced similar types of activism targeted at their operations in politically volatile or conflict-prone countries such as Azerbaijan, Burma, Colombia, Ecuador, Angola, Sudan, and Indonesia. Accusations have focused on issues such as indigenous people's rights, corporate relationships with public and private security forces that have been guilty of abusing people's rights, the use of forced labor, corruption, and unfair revenue distribution. Shell, Rio Tinto, Unocal, ExxonMobil, ChevronTexaco, Talisman, and BP have all faced criticism, and in some cases costly lawsuits, over these issues.

▪ The *diamond industry* has been charged with selling "conflict diamonds" to Western consumers—diamonds that are illegally mined in Africa and responsible for fueling gruesome civil wars, which have had a particularly tragic impact on women and children.

▪ Some of the world's leading *food and beverage manufacturers* have been challenged for using child labor on plantations, for failing to pay a living wage, for being complicit with draconian government actions against trade unions in some of the facilities and countries where they operate, or for negative health impacts associated with consumption of their products. Cadbury Schweppes, Nestlé, Chiquita, Starbucks, McDonald's, and Coca-Cola are among the companies that have been targeted.

▪ Companies in the *banking industry* have faced media exposés, activist campaigns, and lawsuits related to their past roles in supporting slavery in the United States, storing gold stolen from Jewish families by the Nazi regime during the Holocaust, supporting the former apartheid regime in South Africa, and more recently laundering, even if unintentionally, money belonging to drug barons, warlords, dictators, and international terrorist groups. Deutsche Bank, Citigroup, JPMorgan Chase, FleetBoston, and others have been targeted for some of these issues.

▪ *Information technology, hardware, and telecommunications companies* are being questioned on the sale of products to governments that may use them to repress their citizens, undermine privacy, or prevent freedom of expression. The sourcing of coltan, a mineral found mostly in the Congo and used in mobile phones, circuit boards, and computer equipment, is also becoming an issue for some companies in the high-tech sector. There is evidence that access to coltan mines has been a cause of conflict in this war-torn region, funding rebel armies and killing or displacing innocent civilians. Companies such as Motorola, Intel, BT, and Vodafone have needed to address some of these questions.

Pharmaceutical companies have come under growing media and public pressure and faced several legal battles over human rights issues. In their case, the central issue has been access by poor people to life-saving medicines. Most notable has been the issue of access to HIV/AIDS drugs in developing countries in Africa and elsewhere. The question of providing lower-priced drugs for poor communities in the United States, especially for the elderly, is also becoming an issue. Merck, GlaxoSmithKline, Pfizer, and Novartis are some of the leading brand names that have come under pressure on these issues.

No global company can afford to ignore the growing debate on business and human rights. At the very minimum, there is the need for corporate executives to become better informed about the issues and more aware of the risks that they pose for their companies.

Once a company has done a comprehensive analysis or relationship mapping exercise involving its key stakeholders and considered some of the key human rights risks that may affect its industry sector, what are some of the other actions that it can take? Three broad goals for putting people at the center can be summarized under the headings *protection, participation,* and *personal potential,* as illustrated in the figure on page 116.[6]

Each of these three Ps can be used as the basis for developing policies, setting targets and performance indicators, measuring and reporting on progress, and benchmarking against other companies. As with every other principle outlined in this book, policies are necessary but not sufficient. The goals of protection, participation, and personal development must become embedded in the company's culture and daily operations, backed by clear leadership and performance systems.

Increasingly, "people measures"—both quantitative and qualitative—

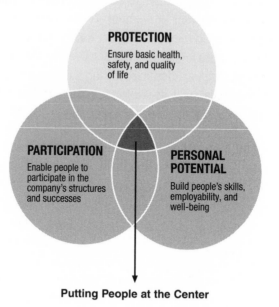

Putting People at the Center

need to be on an equal footing with financial measures when assessing a company's performance and its long-term potential. In leading companies, creative approaches are being developed to measure relationships with employees, customers, investors, and local communities. These measures can become a crucial tool for improving the accountability, as well as the overall performance, of the company.

What are some of the key issues for companies to consider under the three areas of protection, participation, and personal growth?

Three: Protect Basic Health, Safety, and Quality of Life

In most developed countries, many of the areas outlined below are already well regulated. World-class companies, however, aim beyond legal compliance. They also aim to apply similar standards everywhere they operate, including developing countries, where local regulations are often not as rigorous as they are in North America, Europe, and Japan.

In the Workplace Protection includes, first and foremost, a safe and healthy working environment, including a range of occupational health and safety issues. In certain industries and countries, the need to address HIV/AIDS in the workplace is becoming a crucial strategic business issue, and we look at this challenge on page 118.

Protection also includes protecting basic labor rights and human rights in the workplace and along the supply chain, including freedom of association and expression, privacy, and the prevention of child labor. It also includes protecting people from unethical behavior by managers and fellow workers, such as sexual harassment or bullying.

In today's difficult and competitive business environment, protection of employees usually does *not* include guaranteed job security, especially in publicly quoted companies. It should, however, include efforts by management to protect the dignity of people whose business functions have been made redundant. This includes efforts to deal with restructuring, downsizing, and layoffs in as humane a way as possible, providing people with counseling, advice, training, severance, and other support to ease the transition. Badly and insensitively handled layoffs, especially alongside massive remuneration packages that reward executives even when performance has been poor, are key factors that raise mistrust and cynicism in a company. Stories of employees who learn of their firing by text-message, e-mail, or reading about it in the newspaper, or who arrive at work to find that their security pass no longer works, not only create bad press, but tend to linger in the memories of remaining employees for a long time afterward, undermining morale, motivation, and loyalty.

In the past few years, there have been very few companies that have not had to cut costs, restructure, or reduce jobs. The companies that take their commitment to people seriously, however, have made efforts to ease the distress, uncertainty, and human costs that these measures often create. They have often worked through a clearly articulated set of options, such as voluntary leaves of absence, natural attrition, work sharing, early retirement, relocation and retraining, and severance pay. Cisco Systems and Accenture, for example, both developed programs that offered employees a choice of working in community organizations on reduced salaries and benefits but with continued links to the company and the possibility of going back to a job when economic conditions improved.

For Consumers Protection includes making sure that people are not directly harmed when using the company's products and services or are clearly warned about any potential harm associated with them. It may also include ensuring customer privacy and setting standards for responsible advertising, depending on the industry and products in question. In the case of products and services that are essential to life—such as life-saving medicines and water—companies that aim to put people at the center are developing innovative solutions to increase access for people who cannot afford them. In some cases these are part of philanthropic activities, but in certain industries they are becoming part of the core business proposition.

For Local Communities Protection means efforts to ensure that communities are safe from negative environmental and health impacts directly linked to the company's operations, including industrial accidents and road accidents associated with its activities. In some countries, where governments may not be democratic, it also means efforts to protect local people from human rights abuses carried out by security forces that are protecting the company's assets, or abuses associated with the use of the company's products.

Helping People Deal with HIV/AIDS

The HIV/AIDS epidemic is one of the greatest public health crises the world has ever experienced. Over 40 million people are currently infected around the globe, and the UN estimates that without strategic interventions that number could increase to 100 million by 2010. The epidemic is a human tragedy that is also creating economic calamity in some countries. It is a health issue that no company can afford to ignore if it is operating globally or with a large global workforce and supply chain. Research shows that the epidemic imposes high costs on business.[7] These include lower productivity; loss of skills; increased direct costs; and, in some countries, declining profits and investments as the epidemic adversely affects consumer and business confidence.

A few corporate leaders are starting to provide not only awareness and prevention programs in the workplace, but also comprehensive treatment and care services to employees and their dependents. Levi Strauss was an early pioneer. In mid-2002, the global mining company Anglo American became the first company to offer its infected workers free access to antiretroviral drugs. The following examples illustrate how two other companies are tackling the challenge.

GlaxoSmithKline's Strategy to Provide Affordable Access to Medicines

As a leading international pharmaceutical company we can make a real difference to healthcare in the developing world. We believe this is both an ethical imperative and key to business success. Companies that respond sensitively and with commitment by changing their business practices to address such challenges will be the leaders of the future.

GSK, *FACING THE CHALLENGE*, 2001

GlaxoSmithKline (GSK) is one of a growing number of "dual nationality" companies that span the shores of the United States and Europe, created in December 2000 from the merger of Glaxo Wellcome and SmithKline Beecham. During the past few years, it has played a leadership role in the growing trend of moving beyond philanthropy to developing new business models to increase affordable access to medicines. Increasing access to HIV/AIDS treatments in developing countries, where few people can afford the prices paid in the United States or Europe, has been a key part of the challenge.

In 2001, a case bought by thirty-nine drug companies against the South African government was due to be heard in court. It involved claims that a new law, which included provisions that would allow patents to be overridden, was unconstitutional. The companies had a sound legal case, but they were unprepared for the massive public backlash not only in South Africa, but also internationally caused by the portrayal of the case as an attempt to prevent the importation of low cost generic drugs. Spurred on by activist campaigns and negative media coverage, parts of the European and American public accused the profitable pharmaceutical industry of putting profit before people's lives. GSK received letters from some of its major institutional investors raising concerns about the reputation risks associated with the debate. This was a classic example of changing societal expectations leading to new rules of the game for business, resulting in the need for revised business models. On April 18, 2001, all thirty-nine companies settled the case in return for the South African government agreeing to implement the new law in accordance with its international obligations. The *Wall Street Journal* described the industry, usually seen as reliable, trusted, and philanthropically generous as "reeling from an unprecedented wave of public scorn."[8]

At the time of the South African case, GSK was already developing a more integrated strategy to improve access to medicines in the developing world. In May 2000, it had joined forces with Merck, Roche, Boehringer Ingelheim, Bristol-Myers Squibb, and the United Nations to offer developing countries price reductions on HIV/AIDS treatments. It was already running, as were other drug companies, philanthropically based product donation programs for tropical diseases such as malaria and elephantiasis, as well as for the prevention of mother-to-child transmission of HIV/AIDS. For almost ten years it had been running a community investment program called *Positive Action,* which assists projects in many countries focused on HIV education, care, and community support. But increasingly, this philanthropy-based approach was no longer sufficient to meet changing societal expectations as the scale of the HIV/AIDS crisis grew. Its community investment and product donation programs have benefited millions of people and continue to do so, but GSK realized that it had to go further. The company knew that it needed to respond with a strategy that was credible, doable, and economically viable for the long term.

In June 2001, GSK launched a groundbreaking strategy for improving health care in the developing world and improving affordability and access to essential medicines. It was the first of its kind in the industry. The company's commitment, outlined in *Facing the Challenge,* is based on a three-pronged strategy: first, a business strategy for sustainable not-for-profit preferential pricing on treatments for selected disease in selected countries; second, a strategy to maintain GSK's research and development targeting diseases that particularly affect the developing world (at present less than 10 percent of total global expenditure on health R&D is focused on such diseases); and third, a commitment to continue building GSK's community partnerships program around the world. This is an example of a company that is bringing traditional philanthropy more in line with core business competencies and core business competencies more in line with addressing societal expectations and needs.

GSK also committed to develop performance measures and report publicly on its progress. A year later, it was able to report twelve very concrete actions covering a range of undertakings that included preferential pricing, R&D commitments, product donations, and community investments. Seven of these initiatives were focused on HIV/AIDS treatments. At the same time, the company established a board-level corporate social responsibility committee, which consists of independent nonexecutive directors. This committee has oversight of all corporate citizenship matters and advises the board on social, ethical, and environmental issues that have the potential to either seriously impact GSK's business and reputation, or create new business opportunities.

By 2003, the company had secured over 150 arrangements to supply preferentially priced HIV/AIDS medicines in fifty-six of the world's poorest countries. Along with other pharmaceutical companies, it had further reduced the not-for-profit preferential prices of its HIV/AIDS medicines. GSK continues to face a highly competitive and uncertain market but has made its strategy for affordable medicines an integral element of its overall corporate strategic direction. In doing so, it believes that it will be better positioned in the years ahead to meet customer needs, societal expectations, and investor demands worldwide.

MTV's Commitment to Spreading the HIV/AIDS Message

*The AIDS fight needs everything the business world can
offer, from leadership to marketing, media, supply chains,
organization, infrastructure, and most importantly, people.*

BILL ROEDY, PRESIDENT, MTV NETWORKS INTERNATIONAL

Viacom subsidiary MTV Networks International reaches over 1 billion young people in 166 countries via some 43 channels in 18 languages. In particular, it reaches the globally connected and technically savvy teen generation. This is not only a massive and strategically important market in the making, but also a demographic group that will have crucial implications for future peace and prosperity. Nearly 50 percent of the world's population is below the age of twenty-five, and their education, health, awareness, and attitudes will have an important bearing on future political, economic, and social trends.

Over the past decade, MTV has become the world's leading multimedia brand for youth—a brand that young people can relate to, but also trust. Among its many diverse programs, MTV provides a forum for young people to exchange opinions with world leaders, celebrities, and other young people from around the world on issues that matter in their lives, such as drugs, racism, war, and their hopes and fears for the future. As the severity of the global HIV/AIDS epidemic started to become apparent and the risks to young people more obvious—6,000 young people are infected a day—MTV made a strategic commitment to harness its core competencies and the trust it had built with its youth audiences to reach out on this sensitive and stigmatized issue. Its goal in doing so is not only to inform, challenge, and educate its audience on how to avoid becoming HIV positive, but also to eradicate the stigma, discrimination, and rejection experienced by those who are infected with HIV/AIDS.

The company also aims to raise public awareness of the severity of this tragic epidemic through special programming such as the Emmy Award–winning series *Staying Alive* and the *Fight For Your Rights: Protect Yourself* campaign. These programs are about providing young people across the globe with awareness of HIV/AIDS, as well as enpowering them to protect themselves from infection. *Staying Alive* is produced in association with the Kaiser Family Foundation and in partnership with the United Nations AIDS program and the World Bank. The program premiered in 1998, hosted by George Michael. Artists such as Ricky Martin, Sean "P. Diddy" Combs, Mary J. Blige, and Beyoncé have hosted subsequent productions. *Staying Alive* is produced "rights free," meaning that it can be used free, with no strings attached, by any broadcaster anywhere in the world. To date it has reached over a billion people.

Beyond original programming, MTV conducts an annual Global Sexual Behavior Poll, which helps to assess risk behavior among young people. For several years Bill Roedy, president of MTV Networks International, also took a personal leadership role as chair of the Global Business Coalition on HIV/AIDS. He got engaged at a time when the Global Business Coalition was in its early stages, with few members, a low profile, and insufficient funding to meet the scale of the task it faced. Under Roedy's leadership, supported by a small team, the organization's profile has been raised. It has built closer links to the United Nations and attracted many new members. Today, the business coalition is a global force and a collective voice for business in the fight against HIV/AIDS, with over 150 corporate members from a wide diversity of countries and industry sectors.

MTV's efforts to raise awareness of HIV/AIDS are serving the needs of its audiences without letting down its shareholders. The company is doing what it does best and mobilizing its core competencies for a wider societal purpose. And by working in partnership with other companies and international agencies, it is spreading vital health messages and reaching audiences in a way that few publicly funded campaigns could hope to achieve on their own.

Four: Enable People to Participate in the Company's Structures and Success

In the Workplace Participation can mean a variety of things. It can mean a genuine commitment to equal opportunity and diversity. Anyone with the appropriate skills, competencies, and experience should be able to participate and progress within the company's management structure regardless of gender, race, religion, sexual preference, or physical disability. In assessing diversity, a company needs to consider both the breadth of diversity and the depth—that is, not only the percentage of women, minorities, nonnationals, gays and lesbians, and disabled people, but also their presence throughout the organization, including the board and senior management levels and along the company's supply chain.

Participation also includes a commitment to formal and informal consultation structures, aimed at listening to and learning from employees throughout the organization. These can range from formal dialogue with trade unions, where these exist, to survey mechanisms and dialogues facilitated by third parties, to informal brainstorming sessions, learning networks, and one-to-one conversations. The key is to listen and respond to employees' ideas, concerns, hopes, and opinions. Even if employee input is not always acted on when final decisions are made, management should explain how decisions have been made and why. Extensive employee consultation may raise the risk of "paralysis by analysis"—too many internal task forces, learning networks, and dialogues and not enough decision-making. Getting the balance right and taking responsibility for making and explaining decisions, after a genuine process of consultation, is a key role of leadership.

Participation and consultation in the workplace is not a one-time formal process but something that happens day in and day out, creating a culture where people feel genuinely engaged. It can be especially important in difficult periods of restructuring and downsizing. There is growing evidence that management teams who consult their employees during such times and, where relevant, work with rather than confront their trade unions come up with creative ideas on how to minimize the human costs of major corporate change. Such consultation has helped numerous companies develop alternatives to layoffs, such as job sharing, sabbaticals, job furloughs, and pay cuts. Yet all too often, these are the very times when management huddles behind a closed door—creating an even greater sense of uncertainty and insecurity.

Participation in the workplace is also about creating a sense of community and a caring, compassionate working environment. These words may sound laughable in an era of "lean and mean" working environments, but many people are searching for meaning and a greater sense of community. Outstanding companies try to offer this by establishing support systems to help minimize the human costs of crises and trauma—from corporate restructuring and workplace accidents to traumatic events in employees' personal lives.

Finally, participation in the workplace is about ensuring that employees are fairly included in the recognition and rewards that come with successful performance. Again this can range from formal structures, such as employee share ownership plans (ESOPs) and company award programs to small and simple rewards given on a regular basis at the discretion of line managers. ESOPs offer great potential. There are some eleven thousand employee-owned companies in the United States, employing an estimated ten million people. A growing number of publicly quoted companies have also established ESOPs, but there is room for much greater action. Employee share ownership is not without its risks, however. In recent years, there has been a growing focus on employee 401(k)s as a risk, as well as a benefit, for employees. The risk is associated with lack of diversification and overexposure of employees to the company's own stock, as the employees of Enron learned to their cost. Responsible companies are paying for independent investment advice for their employees or, at the very least, ensuring that their employees are given educational materials and plan statements that emphasize the benefits of diversification and the risks of overconcentration in the company's own stock.

For Consumers Participation includes being part of consumer focus groups and other efforts to improve feedback between customers and the company, as well as efforts by the company, where relevant, to increase the diversity of its customer base.

For People in the Local Community Participation includes regular consultation between the company and community leaders, aimed at discussing areas of common interest and/or addressing problems and crises. This can include open-door policies, factory visits, and regular information flows to keep local people informed about the company and its activities. It also includes efforts to ensure that people in local communities are able to participate in benefits associated with having the company as a neighbor. This can include philanthropic support, partnerships with local groups, and sharing core corporate competencies, such as management skills and premises, with community partners.

So what does participation look like in practice? We provide an illustration in the area of promoting diversity among employees, customers, business partners, and local communities.

Celebrating and Building Diversity

No company in America can afford to ignore the challenges and opportunities of the country's increasingly diverse population. Every way you look at it, there is a strong case for companies to address diversity in the boardroom, in the workplace, in the marketplace, along the supply chain, and in local communities. Politically, socially, ethically, and economically—the arguments are clear and compelling. We won't rehearse them here, but we leave you with the statistics on page 127 from organizations such as DiversityInc, the U.S. National Council on Disability, Catalyst, and Age Concern. The statistics tell their own story.

Diversity and multicultural competency are not strategic business issues only within the United States. They are also issues for companies operating internationally. Increasingly, diversity is not only about the number of women and minorities on a company board or in its management ranks. It is also about having more foreign nationals in these positions and having local nationals in senior management positions in different countries around the world. The business rationale should be obvious, but few multinational companies, American or otherwise, have truly diverse senior management structures. Companies such as Unilever, Nestlé, Shell, Alcoa, and Citigroup are among those that are leading the way.

American Demographic Trends that No Company Can Afford to Ignore

DiversityInc cites the following numbers from the U.S. 2000 census and other sources in their report *The Business Case for Diversity* (www.diversityinc.com):

▪ Women and people of color will represent approximately 70 percent of *new* entrants to the U.S. workforce by 2008.

▪ Companies owned by people of color and women are the fastest-growing small-business segment, increasing 150 percent between 1992 and 1997 and representing $495 billion in revenue.

▪ The collective buying power of African-Americans, Asian-Americans, Latinos, and American Indians reached $1.3 trillion in 2001, up from $647 billion in 1990.

A few other diversity statistics worth keeping in mind:

▪ Estimates for the number of gay men and lesbians vary from 3 to 10 percent of the U.S. population, and their buying power is predicted to reach about $444 billion by 2004, according to marketresearch.com.

▪ Women currently account for 46.6 percent of the workforce. In 2000, they held 49.5 percent of managerial and leadership positions at Fortune 500 companies and 12.5 percent of corporate officer positions, and represented 4.1 percent of the top earners, more than double the figure in 1996.

▪ The U.S. National Council on Disability estimates that there are 54 million Americans with disabilities.

▪ At the start of twentieth century, there were almost no centenarians in the United States. The 2000 U.S. Census recorded over 50,000 people who are one hundred or older, and it is estimated that this figure could reach over 600,000 in the next fifty years.

▪ There are about 31.6 million teenagers in the U.S. between twelve and nineteen years old—an increasingly diverse, technologically savvy, and globally aware generation. Children under eighteen are twice as likely to identify themselves as being of more than one race, and in 1997, about 33 percent of all children and youth were multiethnic. The ratio of white to nonwhite people over the age of seventy is about 5 to 1; under the age of ten it is 1.5 to 1.

Sources: DiversityInc, U.S. National Council on Disability, U.S. Age Concern, Catalyst

In addition to diversity among their employees, there is also a growing imperative for companies to respect and encourage cultural diversity in their global operations in terms of their advertising, marketing, and supply chain strategies. The growing backlash against what has been termed as *cultural imperialism* or *Americanization* in countries as diverse as France, India, and Egypt needs to be countered with increased cultural awareness and respect. Clear strategies are needed to deliver local solutions to local people and build local opportunities, even when leveraging off global brands and global networks.

Many of the companies profiled in this book rank well on measures of diversity performance and have programs in place to drive continuous improvement. In particular, J&J, IBM, American Express, UPS, Ford Motor Company, Merck, Avon, Marriott, and Cisco Systems come up again and again in surveys and academic research as leaders in diversity. So does Citigroup, which we profile here.

Citigroup's Efforts to Promote Diversity

The concept of diversity lies at the heart of Citigroup's successful value proposition—diversity of products and services, diversity of locations, and diversity of people. This includes diversity of people not only in the workplace, but also in the marketplace, along the supply chain, in distribution channels for the company's products and services, and in local communities where the company operates.

In the early 1990s, the former Citibank faced difficult times. Today, it is one of the world's most profitable companies, outperforming most of its competitors with double-digit growth across many lines of business. And it is doing so in many parts of the world, including in major growth markets such as China and India, where the bank celebrated hundred-year anniversaries in 2002. In addition to the company's geographic and business portfolio diversification, people diversity has been a central factor in Citigroup's revival and success. According to Ana Duarte McCarthy, director of global diversity, "We believe that diversity greatly enhances our business proposition for our employees, customers and shareholders."[9]

One of the key elements of the company's employee diversity strategy is its global emphasis. A look at Citigroup's list of country managers and senior executives reads like a mini–United Nations. The company states that 98 percent of its over 250,000 employees are locally hired in the hundred-plus countries where the company operates. In many developing countries the company is seen as an alternative to business school—thousands of former Citibank employees have gone on to run their own businesses and work in government ministries of finance, economics, and development. Two of the company's five business heads are women and women represent a growing percentage of employees—now over 50 percent in the United States.

With regard to its customers and communities, the company has a long-standing record of reaching out to minority and women customers in the United States, with tailored marketing and customized products and services. Its community investment program also has a focus on supporting education and economic empowerment of minority and other marginalized communities. In the United States, the company made a historic ten-year commitment of $115 billion in 1998 to increase lending and investment to low- and moderate-income communities. Again this is a philosophy that extends beyond the United States. In 1996, the bank launched an innovative micro-lending initiative, which has now supported thousands of micro-entrepreneurs, most of them women, in over forty countries.

In terms of business partners, the company's Supplier Diversity program in the United States channeled $500 million in business during 2002 to minority- and women-owned businesses. Diversity sourcing goes beyond traditional procurement areas of office products and services. It is being extended into technical and professional services such as legal, marketing, accounting, and investment advice. Citigroup is also working to bring diverse partners into its core business portfolio. The company's initial public offering of its Travelers Property Casualty business, for example, set a new precedent in diversity. Citigroup selected four minority comanagers for the IPO. In addition, over twenty minority- and women-owned broker-dealers participated in the underwriting syndicate. Between 1997 and 2001, such firms also participated in over 350 municipal underwriting syndicates in which Citigroup was a senior manager. These are two examples of how a company can harness its influence in its own industry sector to encourage greater diversity at the heart of its business, not simply in its office-cleaning services.

What are some of the lessons that stand out in Citigroup's on-going commitment to global diversity? First, *clear policies and direction from the top.* The company has developed detailed nondiscrimination and harassment policies. Equally important, senior management sends a clear message: merit matters more than ethnic or cultural background.

Integrated processes are the second key factor in embedding diversity into corporate culture and business operations. They constitute the company's plan of action and enable it to move from policy to practice. These processes range from the formal to the informal within Citigroup. The company has established a cross-business Diversity Operating Council, which consists of senior managers from its businesses. It meets twice a month. This enables managers to share ideas and best practices across different business units and engages them in the development and implementation of the overall diversity program. A number of business units have also established their own councils. There are employee "hotlines" in place and employee networks including a women's network, an African heritage network, a Hispanic/Latin network, a Pride network, a working parents network, and a multicultural network. In recent years, a series of diversity leadership events have been held on both a regional and a business unit basis, bringing together existing and potential diversity champions. Diversity targets are also being integrated into performance appraisals and executive development models.

Targeted programs are a third key factor. At Citigroup, these range from standard corporate programs, such as affirmative action and formal diversity training workshops, to more innovative initiatives. The company has established a holistic work/life program that offers options such as flexible working hours, employee assistance, domestic partner benefits, and an award-winning childcare initiative. The company's Supplier Diversity Program works with business partners to give them business but also offers mentoring and technical advice, as well as access to the company's leaders. Its community investment and microlending programs are run as comprehensive, integrated initiatives that draw on the bank's core competencies and have clear performance targets, rather than simply being ad hoc philanthropic donations.

Fourth, *active partnerships* have been key. The company works closely with minority MBA organizations in its recruitment, with disability organizations on projects to employ and serve disabled people, with minority support groups to provide financial products and education to minority communities, with microfinance intermediaries to reach thousands of women microentrepreneurs, and with other major companies to advocate for greater diversity, in the United States and beyond.

Citigroup's increasingly strategic and systematic commitment to diversity has failed to make headlines during a period when the bank, along with other Wall Street institutions, has been in the spotlight over conflicts of interest between its research and investment banking units and for its role in advising on the complicated structured financing arrangements used by discredited companies such as Enron. Behind the scenes, however, the senior-level commitment to build diverse teams and bring diverse perspectives to all aspects of the company's business continues to be embedded in daily operations. This is positioning the bank well for the future to serve an increasingly diverse population in the United States and globally.

Five: Build Personal Potential by Enhancing Skills and Employability

A focus on building people's personal potential is particularly relevant in the workplace and in local communities. In the workplace, this includes training and development, ranging from basic skills development for less skilled workers to executive and leadership development and mentoring for managers. It also involves a focus on moving from basic quality-of-life issues, such as protecting people from unsafe, unhealthy, or abusive working conditions, to enhancing quality of life through encouraging better work–home balance and physical and mental well-being. This can include flexible working hours, job sharing, part-time working, sabbaticals, family leave for births and deaths, telecommuting, health screening and education, flexible health benefits, and ergonomically designed working spaces. It can also include a wide range of on-site facilities such as child-care centers, gyms, restaurants, medical services, counseling, and so on.

From a community outreach perspective, building personal potential includes encouraging employees to engage in volunteering efforts, which can help to develop their leadership competencies and other types of skills and awareness and provide them with a broader sense of purpose and an opportunity to serve, while also supporting local communities and societal issues beyond the company. Other initiatives to consider from a community outreach perspective include assistance to families of employees. Study scholarships for employees' children, for example, can be especially valuable for lower-income workers. Also important is support for local schools, such as philanthropic support for better educational materials and equipment and corporate efforts to support education reform and youth development programs, especially for youth at risk.

We will look at a number of these approaches under the next principle, which involves spreading economic opportunity.

Our final example of putting people at the center is drawn from Alcoa, with an emphasis on the company's efforts to achieve its ambitious safety goal of "zero injuries and illnesses" and on how this and Alcoa's other core values are embedded in its management and accountability systems.

ALCOA's
Strategic Commitment to Safety

If you have ever driven in a car, flown in an airplane, scrunched up a beverage can, wrapped your dinner in aluminum foil, or watched your favorite team in a sports stadium, chances are you've had some contact with Alcoa. As the world's leading producer of primary and fabricated aluminum and alumina, Alcoa manufactures products and components that are used worldwide every day by millions of people. In 2002, the company employed over 120,000 people in forty countries and noted that it was six times safer to work at Alcoa than it had been in 1991. This statistic forms the backdrop for our analysis of how the company is putting its commitment to people into practice as part of its overall vision of being among the world's most profitable and respected companies.

Like most global companies, Alcoa has faced a deteriorating and challenging business environment since 2000, with all its major markets—aerospace, automotive, housing and construction, packaging, and industrial—affected by a slowing global economy. Over the past decade, however, the company has generally performed well against the S&P 500 Index and Dow Jones Industrials Index, and in the past five years it has outperformed its peers (other aluminum, metal, and broad-based industrial companies) in terms of total shareholder return, top-line growth, and return on capital. This financial performance is underpinned by a long-standing record of sound risk and crisis management, financial stewardship, and compliance. The company is cited as one of the world's one hundred best-managed companies by *Industry Week* magazine and as the world's most admired metals company by *Fortune* magazine.

At the same time, Alcoa has won international recognition for its environmental and social performance. It was the first company in the world to be awarded the United Nations Environmental Global 500 award in the 1990s. In 2001, its safety program won the Ron Brown Award for Corporate Leadership in the U.S., and in 2002, *Occupational Hazards* magazine listed Alcoa as one of the seventeen safest companies in America.[10] This safety record is not restricted to the company's North

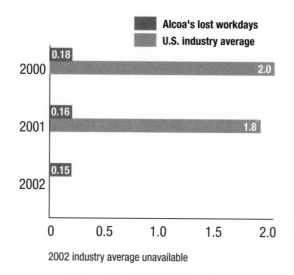

Alcoa's Lost Workdays against the U.S. Industry Average

Source: Alcoa, 2002 Sustainability Report

American operations—its facilities in Brazil, Australia, and Suriname have also received international recognition for being leaders in health, safety, and the environment.

In the minds of Alcoa's senior management team, the alignment among financial, social, and environmental performance makes sound business sense. As chairman and CEO Alain Belda stated in his 2001 letter to shareholders, "Alcoa has been able to capitalize on the global trend to privatize, often becoming a preferred bidder on government-owned assets because of our reputation for cultural sensitivity, values-driven management and community involvement."[11]

What does this values-driven management look like in practice? How does the company "walk the talk" with over 120,000 employees in some forty countries?

Alcoa's global safety process offers some useful insights into what is possible when a company makes a strategic commitment to translate values into practice. To give some idea of the progress that has been made—since 1988, the company has reduced its lost workday injury rate by more than 90 percent from 1.86 injuries per every 200,000 hours worked to 0.15. In the twelve-month period ending May 31,

2003, 75 percent of Alcoa's 487 locations had zero lost workdays, and more than 98 percent of the company's employees went home injury free. These results have been achieved despite growth in the output and the geographic spread of the company's operations and its acquisition and integration of other companies with less impressive safety records.

Alcoa's safety record demonstrates impressive performance against the U.S. industry average, as illustrated in the figure on page 134, but from the company's perspective, there is still room for improvement. Its target is zero work-related injuries and illnesses. Some may argue this is unreachable, and Alcoa itself had a sharp reminder of the challenge in 2002 when one of its employees and one of its contractors were fatally injured. Yet the company is convinced that the goal of zero is achievable. Indeed, its goal is to improve further, as William O'Rourke, vice president for environment, health, and safety, states: "We have to go past zero. We have to send employees home healthier than when they came to work. We do that through wellness and fitness programs that give them physical, emotional and work life support."[12]

What is the company doing to strive toward what would seem an unreachable goal to most corporations operating globally? The following factors stand out:

- Passionate leadership from the top

- A clearly articulated vision and values

- Effective accountability structures

- Simple and unambiguous targets

- Performance metrics and measurement systems

- Learning from internal and external stakeholders

- Community outreach

Passionate Leadership from the Top

When Paul O'Neill became chairman and CEO of Alcoa in 1987, he made safety his number-one priority and performance measure. Whether he was speaking at internal or external meetings, it was rare not to hear the word *safety*. He made it a priority item on the agendas for management and board meetings, hard-wired it into operational reports and performance appraisal systems, and acted as the company's champion for safety, while calling on every other employee to do likewise. As he stated in an interview at the time, "Safety is the most important performance measure that I use to drive the business. It's lost workdays. I believe this number is a leading indicator of whether you're leading or managing."[13] When O'Neill left the company, he publicly stated that one of the measures of his success as a CEO would be whether the company's focus on safety continued after he left.

The focus has not only continued but been further strengthened under the leadership of current chairman and CEO Alain Belda, with the support of a global health and safety management system that is increasingly embedded in the way Alcoa goes about its business.

This very public leadership commitment to safety has been a key factor in Alcoa's reaching toward the seemingly unreachable goal of zero injuries and illnesses. Yet, in a company of over 120,000 people operating in over 480 locations, individual leadership from the top, no matter how passionate, is not enough.

Clearly Articulated Vision and Values

The company's vision and values have also been critical in placing people and their safety at the heart of Alcoa's business proposition. The company's vision is unambiguous. Alcoa states: "Our vision is to be the best company in the world." As Alcoa executive Randy Overby observed in a recent speech, "Idealistic? Maybe. But it's useful to us in that it forces us to compare ourselves not just to the other players in our category, but to the world's best companies as well. It doesn't let us rest on our laurels as the world's leading aluminum maker."[14] Equally clear to the company's employees and its other stakeholders are the following seven Alcoa values, each of which is backed by a set of explicit business principles: integrity; environment, health, and safety; customer; excellence; people; profitability; and accountability. Alcoa was also one of the first major companies in corporate America to establish an explicit public statement on human rights, further indicating that it is serious about putting people at the center.

The company's values and business principles are distributed in sixteen languages to its employees and long-term contractors and supported by training. All of this has been crucial but is not sufficient to drive through real change and performance excellence. As Alain Belda noted to shareholders in Alcoa's 2002 annual report, "There is no amount of laws or regulations that will force a company to behave with integrity. The best line of defense is for integrity to be part of the living values of each individual member of the team. . . . Yet, as with everything we do, we are taking steps to further improve standards, controls, and account-abilities."[15] This same mind-set of accountability, standards, and mea-sures is applied to the company's other core values, such as safety.

Effective Accountability Structures

The Alcoa board plays a key role in ensuring accountability for imple-mentation of the company's core values. It is one of the most diverse boards in corporate America—with women, minorities, directors with strong environmental and human resource credentials, and directors with non-American perspectives from several continents. Apart from a brief period of CEO transition, the board has had only one noninde-pendent director, the CEO, since 1991. The board has a public issues committee, which among other things provides advice and guidance on public issues and reviews the company's reports regarding social and environmental matters. What is especially notable, however, is the fact that the board's audit committee, in addition to its vital oversight of financial auditing and control functions, "review[s] the company's en-vironmental, health and safety audits and monitors compliance with Alcoa's business conduct policies."[16] This is a strong statement that em-phasizes the company's commitment to auditing its social and environ-mental performance with a rigor not normally accorded these issues in most companies.

The board-level overview is backed up by the company's indepen-dent Internal Audit Department, which is responsible for undertaking financial, information technology, environmental, and health and safety audits in all Alcoa operations across the world. A Self-Assessment Tool adds a further level of rigor to enable business managers to take an in-tegrated and holistic view of their nonfinancial, as well as financial, risks and the resources and processes needed to manage them.

Performance Metrics and Measurement Systems

Alcoa has established clear targets for its safety performance, backed up by performance indicators that can be applied in all its operations around the world. It initiated a process almost fifteen years ago to collect and display data on safety, which is available to all employees. This system is still used today as a tool to develop action plans, set goals, measure progress, and take corrective action where needed.

At the same time, safety performance is an integral element of the Alcoa Business System (ABS). The ABS is the company's overarching operating system, aimed at serving customers better by safely delivering what they need, when and where they need it, by eliminating waste, and by actively engaging employees in problem-solving and transfer of knowledge around the company. It provides an integrated framework for performance, accountability, and continuous improvement in a range of business activities, including safety, quality, time and cost efficiencies, and customer satisfaction. "People issues" such as the safety and participation of employees, and the safety and satisfaction of customers, are placed at the heart of the company's management systems and tools.

Learning from Internal and External Stakeholders

In support of its management and accountability systems, Alcoa offers about three hundred safety-related training programs a year through its Pittsburgh headquarters on topics ranging from safety on the road and community safety training to the Safe Babysitter Certification Program. The company has established an annual award program for employee excellence on environmental, health, and safety performance. Many of the teams that are eligible for this award become a source of internal good practice that is shared more widely throughout the system.

Safety is also a key element of product development, and a number of Alcoa's products are directly focused on increasing user safety or security. In response to requests from its customers and suppliers, the company also conducts workshops and benchmarking sessions for external partners on its environment, health and safety programs and standards. This offers a good example of how large companies can share their expertise and international business standards with other partners along their global supply chain, thereby helping to raise industry standards more generally.

Another way of raising the bar is through the work of industry associations. For example, Alcoa is a participant in the chemical industry's worldwide Responsible Care program, which we profile under our Principle #6 (governance). An important element of this program is regular consultation between Alcoa's operating facilities and their neighboring communities on safety issues and accident prevention. In the United States, Alcoa is actively involved in the federal government's Voluntary Protection Program, which recognizes sites with exemplary safety and health programs that can serve as a benchmark and source of learning for other companies. Of the four million industry sites regulated by the Occupational Safety and Health Administration (OSHA), only about six hundred have received this recognition—several of these are Alcoa sites.

Community Outreach

Alcoa's focus on safety doesn't end at the factory gate. The company's safety program encompasses not only the health and safety of employees and contractors at work, but also employee and retiree families at home and citizens in Alcoa communities throughout the world. Almost half of Alcoa's locations have established community-level advisory boards or other mechanisms to enable the company's local managers to meet with community leaders and share issues, concerns, problems, and ideas for the health and progress of the wider community. The Alcoa Foundation, which has been in operation for over fifty years, has identified four core areas of excellence on which to focus its grant-making and its support for employee volunteer activities. One of these is "Safe and Healthy Children and Families."

Clearly, safety is a common thread throughout Alcoa. It is one of the company's core values and an integral part of its corporate strategy and business performance management system. It is audited for and monitored at the board level. It is integrated into executive performance appraisals and highlighted in awards for excellence. Safety is seen as both a moral, values-based imperative and a commercial, value-driven risk management and business opportunity for the company. And it is managed accordingly, with effective results.

The company sees a clear business value in being ahead of compliance, whether it is on health and safety, the environment, human rights, or other ethical, social, and environmental aspects of its business. As it states in one of its reports, "At Alcoa, sustainable development is a critical component of our 21st-century business strategy. Alcoa has done business in three centuries by always thinking beyond what laws require today. We take a leadership focus and try to anticipate where society will be decades from now."[17]

In summary, putting people at the center means establishing relationships with people—employees, customers, investors, suppliers, contractors, community neighbors, government officials—that are responsible, transparent, and accountable and that strive toward mutual understanding, respect, and trust. It means building relationships—especially in the workplace—that are based on a sense of shared community and compassion. The level of leadership attention and business discipline that is applied to the way a company approaches the health and safety of its employees, its customers, its contractors and suppliers, and the people in its local communities is one of the best possible indicators for assessing the quality and integrity of its management.

Simply put, great companies are passionate about people. This may not always translate into worrying about their safety, although in today's world, employee and customer safety is an issue for almost every company. It does translate, however, into caring about their well-being and ensuring that this care goes beyond nice words to become embedded in the company's management systems, accountability structures, and corporate culture. As Paul O'Neill, former U.S. Treasury secretary and Alcoa's former chairman and CEO describes it, "If you can connect with people and show them that their organization cares about them first as human beings, and everything else is second to that, then you have a chance of being a great organization. . . . You need to find a way to demonstrate that the belief is real, and not just some syrupy sentiment that everybody puts in their annual report."[18] Taking such an approach can help to ensure that those affected by business feel more respected, thereby turning potential alienation into constructive engagement. This in turn can help to build the confidence, trust, and commitment that is needed to increase the human capital and to sustain the social capital that enables business to survive and succeed.

Putting People at the Center

One: Identify key stakeholders and what matters to them.

Two: Understand the emerging human rights agenda.

Three: Protect basic health, safety, and quality of life.

Four: Enable people to participate in the company's structures and success.

Five: Build personal potential by enhancing skills and employability.

Spread Economic Opportunity

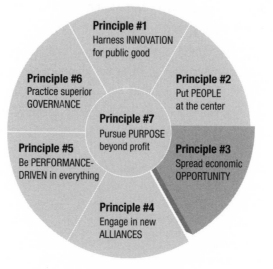

One of the best investments that business can make to create and protect long-term shareholder value is to spread economic opportunity to as large and diverse a group of people as possible. This helps to build better stakeholder relationships and can open up business opportunities for new products and markets, improve the productivity and reliability of suppliers, build the skills of future employees, and open companies to the new ideas and diverse perspectives that fuel innovation.

Companies can spread economic opportunity through activities in the workplace, along the supply chain, and in host communities. Key areas for action include creating employment; investing in small enterprise development; helping communities to build their economic assets; promoting e-inclusion; and supporting education and youth development.

Why Economic Opportunity Matters

Some of America's leading corporations are investing in community economic development as an innovative strategy for meeting business challenges and achieving competitive advantage. Corporate executives are building win-win relationships with residents of low-income communities and discovering they are bound together in the quest for wealth creation and sustained prosperity.

SUSAN BERESFORD, PRESIDENT, FORD FOUNDATION

Economic opportunity—in the form of access to jobs, education, training, credit, technology, and business opportunities—is a crucial foundation for prosperous communities and societies. It makes sound business sense for large companies to help provide people with access to such opportunities. Doing so can lead to the development of new markets, better-skilled and motivated employees, and more productive and reliable suppliers. This in turn can help companies to reduce their costs and risks, enhance their productivity, improve quality, and build their corporate reputation.

In undertaking such activities, companies can create new business opportunities for themselves while leveraging their capacity to give people now at the margins an opportunity to enter the economic mainstream.

Profitable companies spread economic opportunity as a direct and indirect outcome of their regular business activities. The "economic multipliers" that result from a healthy business include the payment of salaries, dividends, capital gains, and taxes. Some of this gets cycled back into society to fund further economic growth, investment, and public services, creating a virtuous cycle of value creation and employment opportunities. All profitable and responsible companies, regardless of their industry, make this contribution. Some, however, are more strategic and systematic about it than others.

Most companies can take further steps to spread economic opportunity, especially among people and communities who have been marginalized or excluded from such opportunity for historical, ethnic, or cultural reasons. Multinational companies can play an especially important role in spreading economic opportunity via their national and international supply chains. These supply chains are among the most effective conduits for spreading new ideas, technology, and economic opportunities to small businesses and microenterprises.

Some of the most useful analysis on how companies can spread economic opportunity in the United States and internationally has been undertaken by the Ford Foundation's Corporate Involvement Initiative.[1] The goal of this initiative has been to improve participation of low-income communities and individuals in the benefits of the market economy by influencing business attitudes, strategies, and practices. The program is an action learning network involving some fifty organizations that are at the cutting edge of the corporate responsibility and community economic development fields. In its report *Win-Win: Competitive Advantage Through Community Investment,* the initiative identified the following business models and benefits for spreading economic opportunity[2]:

■ *Develop untapped markets:* Low-income communities and minority populations in America comprise the fastest-growing customer base in the country. Well-established community organizations can offer companies improved access to these potentially lucrative untapped markets. Companies can secure competitive edge by selling to this expanding new customer base at a time when suburban markets are intensely competitive while the demand for goods and services in underserved inner-city and rural markets is largely unmet. Our profiles on the Initiative for a Competitive Inner City and FleetBoston later in this chapter illustrate the potential of this strategy.

■ *Tackle human resource challenges:* The demand for qualified employees has increased more quickly than the supply. Even in a period of economic downturn, the need to build skilled and loyal workforces remains paramount to corporate success. Companies can work with community organizations, employer trade associations, and training and education institutions to help provide workforce services that train and recruit previously disadvantaged people. Welfare-to-Work and similar programs have demonstrated that companies undertaking such activities can achieve high levels of employee morale and loyalty, productivity gains, and lower employee turnover. The Corporate Involvement Initiative has studied a variety of companies and industries that actively recruit and train people from low-income communities. They range from those in high-tech industries, such as DreamWorks, the film and television production company, Gateway, the computer manufacturer, and financial services leader Salomon Smith Barney, to service sector enterprises such as Marriott International, McDonald's, and Home Depot.

■ *Manage real estate and other physical assets:* There is untapped potential for companies to work with community developers and socially responsible fund managers to revitalize abandoned industrial sites and inner-city communities in a way that makes sound financial sense and enhances corporate reputation and relationships. In 2001, for example, Pfizer opened its new $300 million research facility in the distressed port town of New London, Connecticut, bringing substantial investment, local taxes, economic multipliers, over two thousand job opportunities, and new energy to the area. In the 1990s, Pfizer made a similar commitment to retain some of its key operations in Brooklyn, New York, rather than relocate in the face of rising crime and poverty. The company worked with local authorities and other partners to build new housing, establish a pioneering public charter school, and invest in better transport and security facilities. Together they have been able to create a more economically vibrant and safer neighborhood.

Another example is Home Depot, which works with community-based developers and volunteer groups such as Habitat for Humanity, investing corporate resources to secure safe and affordable homes in the communities where it does business and where its employees and customers live. Such investments in real estate, either for a company's own operations or to build physical infrastructure in the communities where it operates, can lead to real corporate gains.

■ *Purchasing and procurement:* Minority- and women-owned business enterprises are emerging as high-quality, low-cost competitors across a range of industries in the U.S., generating over

$500 billion in annual revenues. They form a growing component of corporate supply chains, driven by a combination of market imperatives and government regulations and incentives. Bob Dunn, president of Business for Social Responsibility, comments in the *Win-Win* report, "Doing business with diverse suppliers not only enhances the operation of the corporate supply chain, it opens doors to new market segments and business opportunities. No matter what industry sector, these businesses have access to reliable, cost-efficient sources and competitive, quality deals."[3]

In short, spreading economic opportunity matters. It matters to the individuals and families who are empowered through gaining access to such opportunity. It enables many of them to become entrepreneurs and earners rather than welfare recipients and dependents. Economic opportunity matters to the communities and countries where these people live because it creates more stable, secure, and prosperous societies. It matters to all companies that need healthy operating environments, whether in the United States or globally. And it matters, in particular, to the companies that have the vision to see the business potential of untapped markets, unemployed people, and undeveloped supplier relationships.

Making It Happen

One: Create Employment Opportunities

In today's competitive and ever-changing labor markets, people with good qualifications, skills, and experience are at a premium. But what about people who don't have these assets? For these people employment opportunities are often nonexistent, scarce, or at best badly paid and a poor alternative to welfare. Yet if effectively trained, they can become productive and loyal employees. Companies can play a key role in supporting such a transition by diversifying their recruitment and training activities to hire more minorities, women, and disadvantaged or unemployed people. Our profiles of Avon and Marriott International illustrate how such practices can lead to clear business benefits as well as societal gains.

Avon: Supporting Women's Empowerment

American women have been given opportunities for economic independence by selling Avon products since 1886—over thirty years before they earned the right to vote. Since that time, millions of women around the world have been Avon Ladies—acting as independent direct sales representatives for the company and often recruiting, training, and mentoring others. Today, independent sales representatives number about 3.9 million. They sell Avon products in over 140 countries.

In recent years, chairman and CEO Andrea Jung and president and COO Susan Kropf have embarked on a major transformation aimed at creating a more efficient, streamlined, and globally integrated company, updating product lines and reinvigorating and modernizing selling methods. Throughout this process they have sustained a clear commitment to diversity and to spreading economic opportunity, especially among women. The company has thrived. As of 2003, it had experienced fourteen consecutive years of sales and earnings growth, excluding special charges and unusual items.

Empowering women is not simply a "feel good" issue for Avon; it is crucial to understanding and meeting diverse customer needs from Tulsa to Tokyo. By listening to women and investing in the things they care about—in health, families, and economic independence—Avon is building a network of loyal independent sales representatives, employees, and customers for the future. Two examples:

Sales Leadership: First launched in the United States and currently being tested in twenty-five other countries, this initiative gives its participating representatives an opportunity to significantly increase their earnings potential by recruiting and training other independent sales representatives. In addition to higher earnings and opportunities to build their own skills and leadership qualities, this initiative gives women the opportunity to reach out and empower others, and creates a community of salespeople who are more connected and committed. It also helps the company to grow its sales force and customer outreach capability in a cost-effective, efficient, and personal manner. Any company with a sales force can adopt this approach.

Women's Health and Empowerment Beyond its mainstream business activities, Avon is focusing its philanthropic and public policy efforts on women's issues, from health concerns such as breast cancer to efforts to support women leaders in developing countries. Its Women of Enterprise program, for example, recognizes exceptional Avon sales representatives who have overcome personal and professional challenges to build successful direct-selling businesses. The company currently has breast cancer programs in over fifty countries and the Avon Breast Cancer Crusade has raised more than $250 million worldwide.

Marriott: From Welfare and Dependency to Work and Dignity

One of America's most enduring and frustrating problems has been its traditional system of welfare. After years of debate, Congress in 1996 enacted sweeping reforms, replacing Aid to Families with Dependent Children (AFDC) with the Personal Responsibility and Work Opportunity Reconciliation Act—in former President Clinton's words, "ending welfare as we know it." Several decades of ineffective governmental support of mothers on welfare was deemed to lock in a cycle of dependency and despair. A new paradigm sought to free welfare moms from the shame and dependence of the dole and to replace it with the prospects of a job and the dignity of financial independence.

Many U.S. businesses and the organizations that represent them in Washington lobbied in favor of the change. Thousands responded by joining the national *Welfare to Work Partnership.* Marriott International was one of the companies that led the way, and it continues to pursue an aggressive and successful corporate program, called *Pathways to Independence*.[4] This initiative seeks to create job opportunities for former welfare recipients and to give Marriott a source of competitive advantage in the marketplace for low-skilled employees. Marriott's involvement precedes passage of the Welfare to Work legislation. Since 1979, it had experimented with an innovative corporate training program designed to train welfare recipients and other underutilized segments of the workforce to become entry-level employees. With passage of the reform package, Marriott was poised to scale up its program.

Why would a hospitality business venture forth as a corporate pioneer in training and hiring some of the most vilified and seemingly least qualified groups in society? Partly it was a question of Christian concern and values. Led by chairman and CEO Bill Marriott, son of the company's Mormon founder, Marriott is driven by a culture and philosophy that places a strong priority on treating employees with respect. The company's entire ethos is built around a vision of "The Spirit to Serve." But it was also a business opportunity—even a business imperative. Marriott operates in a highly competitive, low-margin, cost-conscious service business, where the ability to deliver good quality at outstanding value is crucial to success. This makes the company highly dependent on the loyalty and talents of relatively low-skilled employees. At the time that *Pathways to Independence* was launched, Marriott faced difficulties in attracting and retaining the ninety thousand hourly workers it needed. Turnover was high, the labor market was tight, and the company faced a growing demand for competent and loyal entry-level workers, especially in its growing urban locations.

Pathways offered an opportunity to meet a pressing business need and, at the same time, make a difference in people's lives. With help from federal subsidies and in partnership with many community-based referral networks, Pathways was designed as part of the business operated with demanding discipline and performance metrics. Involving 60 hours of classroom training and 120 hours of on-the-job occupational skills training, Pathways training focuses on three key themes—accountability, dependability, and self-esteem. Participants are usually public assistance recipients.

In an industry with high turnover, Pathways has shown impressive results. Participants graduate at a rate of more than 80 percent and over half remain in the job after a year, comparing competitively with conventional hires. In its *Win-Win* report, the Ford Foundation observes, "The continuity of these employees contributes to the hotel's quality of service; and service offers a competitive edge in the hospitality industry."[5]

Despite challenging economic conditions, Marriott's long-standing commitment to spreading economic opportunity throughout its service chain is likely to remain a core element in its strategy. Corporate self-interest, long-held values of service and involvement in the community, proven success, and competitive advantage have all combined to sustain Marriott's commitment to see that Welfare to Work works.

In addition to Marriott, some twenty thousand companies throughout the United States were involved in the Welfare to Work partnership after its launch in 1997. They included large companies such as UPS, Burger King, United Airlines, TJX, and Bank of America, which each hired between fifteen and forty thousand people. They also included thousands of medium- and small-sized companies. Regardless of their size and industry sector, many of these companies have demonstrated higher retention rates, improved staff morale and loyalty, greater productivity and quality, and reduced recruitment and training costs.

Two: Invest in Small Enterprise Development

The vast majority of people in America and around the globe earn their living as self-employed small-scale entrepreneurs or as workers in small- and medium-sized enterprises. Many of these companies lack access to the necessary credit, markets, skills, and technology to be successful. Large corporations can play a vital role in improving their access to these assets through building links with small- and medium-sized enterprises along the corporate value chain and through investing in community economic development partnerships.

What are leadership companies doing to support minority business development in the United States?

In the United States, institutions such as the National Minority Supplier Development Council, the U.S. Chamber of Commerce, and Business for Social Responsibility offer useful guidelines, models, and best practice examples for working with minority-owned business partners. The National Minority Supplier Development Council, for example, has about thirty-five hundred corporate members, which it matches with over fifteen thousand minority-owned businesses around the country. The corporations purchase more than $54 billion annually from these enterprises. According to NMSDC, "This is accomplished not by lowering corporate purchasing standards—in fact, these standards have gotten much tougher in recent years—but by sourcing qualified minority firms and giving them business on a competitive basis."[6]

What can large companies do to support small and medium-sized enterprises along their global supply chains?

Many of the activities identified in the box on page 152 can be replicated on an international basis. Peter Brew, a director at the International Business Leaders Forum, observes:

Effective business linkages between multinational corporations and small-scale enterprises can create clear mutual benefits. They help to transfer world-class technology and spread international business standards, creating more competitive, productive, and quality-driven business sectors in many countries. They develop the pool of local skills, create market growth opportunities, and decrease procurement and other input costs for multinational companies.

Some Ideas to Spur Minority Business Development

▪ **Offer small contracts**—consider breaking contracts down into smaller parts that make it easier for smaller enterprises to participate.

▪ **Provide additional capital**—sponsor or participate in venture capital, credit, or investment programs aimed at minority-owned enterprises.

▪ **Get online**—encourage B2B opportunities. Develop a database for minority suppliers and extend it throughout the company and beyond, as Johnson & Johnson has done with its Supplier Outreach program.

▪ **Host networking events**—bring together major customers, minority suppliers, and business and community leaders on a regular basis to build new relationships.

▪ **Create a learning environment**—invite your company's minority suppliers to join you on calls to major customer accounts, offer work exchanges, produce educational materials, provide scholarships and grants for study visits and management training, sponsor business plan competitions and feasibility studies. UPS, Bank of America, Citigroup, and Staples are four companies that help to create a learning environment for their suppliers and other small enterprises.

▪ **Mentor and coach**—establish creative mentoring programs staffed by fast-track managers as part of their leadership development, or by retired employees with skills and time to offer. Use these programs to share management and technical training; offer financial, legal, operational, and marketing advice; and spread world-class quality and business standards.

▪ **Communicate success**—sponsor awards and other recognition programs for the company's "best-in-class" suppliers. Encourage publicity through membership and supplier networks and through local media coverage.

▪ **Set clear sourcing policies, guidelines, and stretch targets**—make minority supply initiatives a core element of your corporate mission and diversity programs, not just one-time transactions. Set key performance targets for all your business units and keep raising the bar. Require other major suppliers and business partners to set their own standards for working with minority-owned enterprises.

Source: NMSDC; BSR; U.S. Chamber of Commerce; and companies

They help to build trust with local business communities and government bodies and to ensure a "license to operate."[7]

Many corporations support small enterprise development through their global supply and distribution systems. They do this through a variety of franchising and licensing agreements, venture capital funds, equity financing, fair trade initiatives, special credit arrangements, and programs to share technology, training, marketing, and other services. Any company with a global supply chain or distribution network can implement such programs to support small, medium, and micro-enterprises.

DaimlerChrysler, for example, is forming innovative supply chain partnerships that aim to be both anti-poverty and pro-environment while developing high-quality raw materials for the company's premium-brand cars. In South Africa, the company's research team is working with local suppliers to grow and process good-quality sisal as a component in its Mercedes-Benz C-Class vehicles. Other car manufacturers in the region are following suit, creating a lucrative market for local sisal producers. In Brazil, the company has worked for ten years with Brazilian research institutes and communities in Amazonia to build economically viable fiber-producing farms. Not only are the fibers, such as coconut, used as recyclable materials in automotive components, their production in planted woodland also offers a carbon sink for greenhouse gas emissions—a double win for the environment. At the same time, the company and its suppliers get low-cost, high-quality raw materials, and the small-scale farmers and their communities earn a steady source of income and receive technical support and access to credit.

McDonald's is another example of a company aiming to spread economic opportunity along its value chain. It operates over 30,000 restaurants serving some 47 million people each day in over 118 countries. More than 70 percent of these are independently owned and operated by some 5,500 franchisees and partners, rather than by the company. The company only franchises to individuals, not to other corporations, partnerships, or passive investors. In the United States, minorities and women currently represent over 30 percent of the company's franchisees and some 70 percent of all applicants in training. In other countries, despite the fact that the Golden Arches are both applauded and vilified by supporters and critics of globalization, McDonald's franchisees are usually local residents, and the restaurants are in essence neighborhood businesses. The company also estimates that 80 percent of a typical restaurant's supplies come from the local country, with the balance usually coming from bordering countries or the same continent.

Our profiles of the Coca-Cola Company and Starbucks offer different perspectives on two other consumer brands that have started to systematically support small enterprise development along their global value chains. The Coca-Cola Company is over one hundred years old, Starbucks less than thirty years old. They have very different business models, but both are focused on a value proposition that aims to provide a unique and enjoyable consumer experience, offering quality-assured brands that are driven by a strong emotional connection with the consumer. The global expansion and competitive strategies of both companies rely fundamentally on building trust-based, mutually beneficial relationships with their suppliers, customers, retail partners, and other business partners.

The Coca-Cola System: Spreading Economic Multipliers

The success of Coca-Cola's business model relies not only on the company's legendary brand-building experience, its ability to innovate, and its marketing creativity and expertise, but also on the quality and strength of its diverse bottling partners and on other relationships along its global supply chain. The company's family of brands, from the famous Coca-Cola brand to a portfolio of some three hundred other products, is manufactured and distributed by a local business system consisting of about 300 bottler ownership groups in more than two hundred countries. Most of these bottlers are independent or are not majority management controlled by the Coca-Cola Company, and they are typically staffed by people from the countries in which they are located. The connection between these bottling partners and the Coca-Cola Company is seen as one of its "most valuable strategic assets."[8]

Linked to this core business system is a wider, multifaceted network of business relationships. These include primary and secondary suppliers, ranging from small-scale farmers to large packaging manufacturers, and millions of distributors and retailers, from large, highly capitalized supermarket and hotel chains to tiny microenterprises owned and operated at the community level.

Coca-Cola's ability to drive profitable and sustainable growth is crucially dependent on the quality of these local relationships in countries and communities around the world. Building the management skills, marketing capacity, and business networks of local entrepreneurs and small-scale enterprises is therefore important to the company's long-term strategy of continuing to build market share and serve a growing number of consumers around the globe. At the same time, this process helps to spread economic opportunity and build more prosperous enterprises and communities in the countries where the Coca-Cola Company operates.

What does the concept of spreading economic opportunity through local business linkages look like in practice? Studies by the University of Cambridge and the University of South Carolina[9] show that the Coca-Cola system supports six to thirty jobs in the local economy for every direct job it creates. It has generated substantial investment and income in some of the world's poorest countries. It has invested in programs to improve the quality standards of local farming and manufacturing processes in many countries, enabling these enteprises to be more productive and competitive. In countries such as China, Russia, and Poland, for example, joint ventures have helped to reform state-owned enterprises by upgrading technology, investing in structural changes, and introducing international management standards ranging from better financial accountability to quality improvement systems.

In China, a study by the universities of South Carolina, Beijing, and Tsinghua concluded that "over 400,000 jobs are associated, directly and indirectly, with producing and distributing Coca-Cola products. This is one of the most extensive multinational-local business systems in China. As a result, the enterprise system spreads advanced marketing know-how and production expertise to many regions of the country."[10] Elsewhere, the Coca-Cola system has trained and supported tens of thousands of individual entrepreneurs from Morocco to Mexico, Venezuela to Vietnam. Many of these people have been previously unemployed or marginalized from the formal economy. The Coca-Cola system has enabled small businesses and microenterprises to access credit, technology, and capital equipment and helped them to start supplier and retailing businesses. These businesses distribute not only Coca-Cola products, but usually other products and services to what are often remote communities. In several countries, such as China and South Africa, the Coca-Cola system has also entered into formal training agreements with the government to provide training beyond its own workforce, suppliers, and distributors.

The company has faced some financial and reputation challenges in recent years, which have emphasized the linkages between its commercial and social performance. Consumer and public perceptions are crucial in any industry that depends on local relationships, intensive marketing, and emotional connections with its brands. Sustaining trusted relationships and spreading economic opportunity are therefore key strategies for building long-term competitive advantage. Such relationships and networks are also immensely valuable intangible assets, which must be protected and enhanced in the same way as any other valuable corporate asset.

Starbucks: Working with Coffee Growers

In less than thirty years, Starbucks has grown from a small private enterprise in Seattle to a global brand listed on stock exchanges in America and Japan, with over 7,500 company-owned stores serving millions of customers in thirty-three markets. Sales have climbed an average of 20 percent annually, and profits have grown an average of 30 percent per year since the company went public in 1992. At the end of 2002, Starbucks had enjoyed 123 consecutive months of positive comparable store sales growth.

Mutually beneficial relationships along the company's value

chain have been crucial to its impressive growth. Business partners include Barnes & Noble bookstores, the Starwood and Marriott hotels, PepsiCo, Dreyer's Ice Cream, Kraft Foods, and United
Airlines. These relationships are innovative and important but not
that different from most successful corporate alliances. What is different are the business-driven relationships that Starbucks has
been creating since 1991 with nonprofit and community development organizations such as the international relief and development organization CARE, Conservation International, TransFair
USA, and Magic Johnson's Johnson Development Corporation.

These relationships have been established not simply from a
philanthropic perspective, but also from the perspective of helping
the company to better manage its global supply chain, reach underserved markets, and spread economic opportunity. With Magic
Johnson, for example, Starbucks has created a joint venture called
Urban Coffee Opportunities, with the goal of opening stores in low-
income neighborhoods in the United States. Other relationships are
focused on reaching backward along the company's supply chain to
hundreds of small-scale coffee producers who produce the beans
that Starbucks purchases from Latin America, Asia, and Africa.

Over half the world's coffee is produced on small family farms,
and many of these small enterprises struggle to be economically viable and sustainable. They face low and uncertain commodity prices
in a highly fragmented and volatile global market. They often lack
access to credit, modern technology, and environmentally sound
farming methods. Most of them have to go through middlemen to
reach major coffee companies that convert raw coffee beans into
consumer products. As a result, some of the world's most successful corporations are sourcing from some of the world's poorest producers in the global supply chain. It is unfair to place the blame for
this gap in economic fortunes on large corporations. But the large
corporations have an important role to play in finding solutions and
in spreading economic opportunity more fairly and widely.

Starbucks purchases only 1 percent of the world's coffee supply,
but this is enough to make a difference in the economic conditions

faced by the small-scale growers who produce this coffee. Selling premium-quality coffee is central to the company's value proposition, and as a result it has long paid good prices in order to obtain the finest coffee beans available. It has also been a pioneer in thinking about economic, social, and environmental conditions in coffee-growing regions. Initially this arose from a philanthropic and cause-related marketing mind-set, rather than strategic supply chain management. Today all of these motives play a role in the company's increasingly strategic commitment to spread economic opportunity and sound farming practices in coffee-origin countries. What are some examples?

Sourcing guidelines: Starbucks has worked with Conservation International to develop the coffee industry's first set of Green Coffee Sourcing Guidelines. These guidelines have been piloted for the last two years and will be formally introduced in 2004. Their central commitment is to pay coffee producers a premium price if they meet agreed quality, labor, and environmental standards.

Technical Assistance: The company has also opened the Starbucks Coffee Agronomy Company to help farmers in Latin America improve their farming methods so that they can grow better quality, sustainable coffee.

Fair Trade Certified coffee: In 2000, Starbucks formed an alliance with TransFair USA, which certifies Fair Trade coffee and helps farmers to obtain fair and more stable prices. Starbucks now offers Fair Trade Certified coffee in all its company-owned stores in the United States, with plans to extend this to all its U.S. licensees, and ultimately to all its stores globally.

Community development: Since 1991, Starbucks has been the largest annual North American cash contributor to Atlanta-based CARE, raising over $1.5 million for community development projects that have reached some 2.7 million people in developing countries. It has achieved this through a combination of cause-related or social marketing, employee volunteer efforts, and other innovative approaches to fund-raising.

In less than thirty years, Starbucks has created one of the world's most valuable brands out of one of its most ubiquitous commodities—coffee. In doing so, it has created impressive value for its owners and employees, including being one of the first companies to offer a stock-option program to part-time employees. At the same time, it is starting to spread economic opportunity as well as environmental, social, and quality standards along its global supply chain. The central challenge for the company over the next decade is to maintain the winning formula of *valuable brand + values = value creation* while it continues to grow in terms of size, global reach, and relationships.

Increasingly the commercial success and societal acceptance of these and other highly branded companies depends on responding to the concerns and critiques of a new generation of activists. In recent years, McDonald's, Coca-Cola, and Starbucks have all borne the brunt of the rising antiglobalization movement. This has ranged from physical damage to their premises to media exposés, activist campaigns, and litigation targeting the companies on issues such as woman rights, labor, and environmental impacts. Strategic efforts by the companies to demonstrate that their business models genuinely spread economic opportunity along global value chains will not answer all these criticisms. But such efforts can make a contribution to building trust and protecting brand value and reputation.

Three: Help Low-Income Communities Build Their Economic Assets

In addition to employing people from low-income communities and supporting small enterprise development, companies can also help low-income communities to build their economic assets by increasing access to financial products, improving financial literacy, and supporting community development organizations and think tanks.

Economic assets can be described as the financial and other economic resources that enable people to exert greater control over their lives and create sustainable livelihoods for themselves and their families. Federal Reserve chairman Alan Greenspan observes: "In our economy, the three principal means for household asset accumulation are through home ownership, small business ownership, and savings. As important as these are for the individual, they also represent distinct and important benefits to the broader economy, and therefore, play prominent roles in the operation of our financial markets and the priorities of our public policy."[11] The following examples illustrate how some financial service companies and the Initiative for the Competitive Inner City are helping low-income communities build their economic assets.

Increasing Access to Financial Products and Improving Financial Literacy

Over the past decade, leading financial corporations have started to move beyond compliance with the Community Reinvestment Act to offer finance, savings, and mortgage products for previously underbanked or unbanked enterprises and communities.

■ *Deutsche Bank's* Microcredit Development Fund illustrates how a bank can mobilize its own community investment dollars and banking skills, with donations from progressive private bank clients. Jointly the bank and its clients have created an investment vehicle to catalyze durable banking relationships between micro-finance intermediaries and local commercial banks in developing countries.

■ *Fannie Mae,* through its American Dream Commitment, has made an unprecedented $2 trillion financing pledge to increase home ownership rates and serve eighteen million targeted American families by the end of the decade. To deliver this ambitious target Fannie Mae will rely heavily on its relationships with lending partners and community organizations.

JPMorgan Chase has been another pioneer in community banking and funding real estate development in low-income communities. One of its innovations has been the creation of a group of bank professionals described as Street Bankers. Their job is to provide a bridge between the bank's businesses and community leaders, nonprofit organizations, and governmental agencies in the localities in which they work. They become active participants in community activities, serving as advisors and board members to local organizations, offering advice on financial needs, and acting as leadership role models.

Goldman Sachs has established an Urban Investment Group. Launched in 2000, this group aims to provide investment capital to underserved ethnic minority businesses and urban real estate ventures. The Wall Street firm believes that these markets offer sound growth opportunities and untapped potential for capital appreciation.

The Initiative for a Competitive Inner City: Showcasing the Market Power and Economic Assets of America's Inner Cities

Professor Michael Porter of the Harvard Business School is widely renowned for his groundbreaking work on competitiveness. Applying his penetrating analytical lens to a previously neglected and overlooked market, Porter produced a startling set of findings in 1995 about the competitive advantage of inner cities in America. Previously viewed by many—and certainly by the vast majority of business leaders in America—as dangerous and dysfunctional, the inner city, Porter revealed, in fact possesses many positive economic attributes and assets. He argued that the conventional governmental approach of costly subsidies and special-purpose aid, focused on inner cities as social welfare problems, often deepened the marginalization of the poor and their economic isolation. Instead, Porter called for a radically new strategy driven by building on the existing and latent assets of inner cities as markets and business locations, supported by government creating a healthy business environment, and grounded in new data about the potential economic advantage of inner-city communities.

Building upon his research, Porter created a vehicle for testing and disseminating his message and putting it to work—the Initiative for a Competitive Inner City (ICIC). Corporations such as PricewaterhouseCoopers, Merrill Lynch, Bank of America, and the Boston Consulting Group (BCG) offered early support, in the form of both funds and the skills of their consultants, as did the Bill and Melinda Gates and Kauffman Foundations. Since then, ICIC has mobilized numerous other companies, business associations, city mayors, business school students, and, above all, inner-city companies themselves. Together, they have succeeded in popularizing the business case for investment in inner cities, they have provided valuable technical assistance to a score of cities, and they have used their reputations and world-class business expertise to help shape a new market-based agenda for inner-cities.

Since 1996, ICIC has leveraged more than $16 million in pro bono research, and in 2001, the Boston Consulting Group announced a commitment to supply $3.5 million a year in free support services for inner-city business growth. ICIC has also established, in partnership with Inc. magazine, a prestigious "Inner City 100." This lists some of the fastest-growing companies in inner cities. It has become the definitive list of entrepreneurship in these cities, with 7,000 company nominations for the 2004 list. For many, the Inner City 100 list is their first positive impression of inner cities. ICIC has also brought this model to the United Kingdom, resulting in public policy changes and the UK Inner City 100 awards program. Most important, ICIC and its varied partners have helped to propel more businesses to invest and grow in areas they previously ignored or deliberately avoided, by laying out a sound business rationale for investing in the inner city. Among their findings:

■ The retail purchasing power of inner-city residents in America is $85 billion, slightly higher than that of Mexico; 25 percent of that demand is unmet, and retail demand per square mile is some two to six times greater than in surrounding metropolitan areas.

■ Inner-city grocery stores outperform the regional average by 39 percent. The compound average growth rate for the Inner City 100 is 44 percent. Over the next ten years, 54 percent of workforce growth in America will come from minority communities, heavily concentrated in inner cities.

■ There are over 800,000 business enterprises in America's inner cities, representing 8 percent of U.S. employment. Contrary to popular perception, the start-up and failure rates of inner-city companies is the same as the national average, as is the average size.

Porter's research and writings and the work of ICIC have contributed enormously to reversing a seemingly downward spiral of expectations about America's inner cities. Many other factors, of course, have contributed to this reversal, including a tight national labor market, declining inner-city crime rates, a new generation of hands-on, can-do mayors, the proliferation of thousands of community-based development corporations, and Congress's enactment of the Community Reinvestment Act, which encouraged and ultimately required commercial banks to open branches in and extend credit to previously cut-off and redlined inner-city neighborhoods. The net effect has been an encouraging tale of the ability of business, in conjunction with government and civic organizations, to tackle one of the nation's most intractable problems.

Four: Promote E-Inclusion Initiatives

In today's global knowledge economy, access to information technology and the Internet is essential to spreading economic and educational opportunities, building new markets, catalyzing economic growth, and increasing national and corporate competitiveness. But the "digital divide"—the gap between those who have access to digital technology and the Internet and those who don't—is a reality for millions of people in America and even more so internationally. If young people fail to harness the potential of information technology, this will limit their own career options, hurt the quality of future employees, and undermine long-term corporate success.

Information and communications technology companies have a critical role to play in helping to bridge the digital divide. In doing so they can increase their own market share, enter new markets, experiment with and develop new products and services, and enhance their reputation. Most infotech companies now run some type of program to bridge the digital divide through their philanthropic and community investment activities. A few leadership companies have also started to invest in mainstream business solutions aimed at bringing information technology solutions to currently underserved markets. Hewlett-Packard offers one example of such a business-driven, socially responsible approach.

Info-technology companies are not the only businesses that can support e-inclusion. Any company that uses information technology can

HP's "e-inclusion": Delivering Technology Solutions to the Underserved and Building Future Markets

In common with many of the leadership companies profiled in this book, Hewlett-Packard has a long tradition of innovation and competitive performance driven by a clear set of business principles—"the HP Way." The company's legendary founders, Bill Hewlett and David Packard, helped to develop the HP Way in 1957. Its core tenets—including global corporate citizenship—have remained to this day.

In 2001, HP launched its groundbreaking e-inclusion initiative that aims to work with partners in the public, private, and nonprofit sectors to develop and deliver technology solutions that benefit poor people in developing countries. These technology solutions will be focused on addressing key economic and social needs such as health care, education, employment, access to markets, and access to credit. The objective is to offer solutions that over time will become economically viable rather than rely on philanthropic donations, and which have the potential to create future revenue streams and markets for the company.

HP cites four main motivations for its commitment to this multi-year, multimillion-dollar initiative[12]:

■ To establish HP as a leader in an exciting new technology growth area in a way that also demonstrates its character and commitment to social contribution

■ To create significant revenue and profit growth over time through the creation of new markets, products, and services

■ To provide a showcase to the world of the company's capabilities, in terms of devices, infrastructure, and services

■ To enhance current HP business in emerging markets

The company is targeting the four billion people in the world who currently live on less than two dollars a day. The long-term business numbers look compelling. From the company's perspective, e-inclusion is about developing new, sustainable ways to create and share value. If the incomes of the world's poor were increased by one dollar per day, this would account for over $1 trillion in economic growth per year, resulting in a variety of potential opportunities for business.

An e-inclusion business team has been established to drive the initiative through the company, moving it from a citizenship contribution to a business priority. This team will work with HP's research and development teams, its sales teams, its country managers, and other business units to identify promising solutions for problems in developing countries. One of the initiative's early investments has been in India, where it is working with a state government to build an HP "i-community" in a place called Kuppam. This will provide access to technology for a group of rural villages with over 320,000 people, offering opportunities to improve education, expand access to health care and government services, and create new jobs. Although still in their early days, this initiative and others like it have the potential to deliver long-term business benefits and new markets for HP, as well as socioeconomic development for previously unconnected and marginalized communities.

share its skills, networks, and equipment, especially used equipment, to help less advantaged or low-income communities to access these new technologies. Our following profile of the Digital Partnership initiative offers one example.

The Digital Partnership: Converting Used Equipment into Economic Opportunity

Over the next five years, companies in North America, Europe, and Japan will decommission about 600 million personal computers. Most of these PCs still have a useful life of five years. In many developing countries, especially in Africa, fewer than two people in every hundred have access to computers and the Internet. How can used computers from large companies be transported, refurbished, and reused to support education and Internet access in developing countries? It's too expensive, say many people. They can't be serviced. Or the poor can't afford the software. "It's not feasible, it's not possible"—this has been the all-too-common mantra of numerous development specialists and companies.

Robert Davies, chief executive of the International Business Leaders Forum, was convinced that a practical and simple solution to this challenge could be found. He saw innovative possibilities where other people saw obstacles. After a year of extensive consultation, he proposed a business model based on the following strategies:

■ A network of public-private partnerships between organizations that do not normally collaborate, both within countries and across national borders

■ Getting information and communications companies, with their immense technical skills and problem-solving capabilities, to provide technical support and software

■ Mobilizing companies with large computer disposal programs to donate the equipment and working with cross-border logistics and transportation companies to move it

Getting local companies to refurbish the equipment and install software

Involving the government to ensure national impact

Less than two years later a pilot program is under way in South Africa, with a target of establishing two thousand E-Learning centers in disadvantaged communities and training two hundred "master facilitators" by 2004. Companies such as ABB, Eli Lilly, Nestlé, and Shell are providing decommissioned computers, with twenty-two Japanese companies soon to follow. Exel is offering door-to-door logistics solutions. Microsoft is providing software under a pioneering zero-royalty licensing agreement. Oracle, Intel, and Vodacom, part of the Vodafone global network, are supporting training. Cisco Systems is facilitating connectivity. The World Bank has provided crucial seed funding, and the South African government is supporting expansion activities. Each partner offers core competencies and problem-solving skills, while addressing its own operational and reputation needs. The Digital Partnership offers a win–win model that provides innovative solutions and benefits to all its participants while promoting e-inclusion.

Five: Support Education and Youth Development

A good education is one of the best assets any person can have—but millions of young people are not given this vital start in life. This is mainly the responsibility of governments, but companies can also add value in this area. They have a clear interest in building a skilled workforce for the future and spreading economic opportunity more generally. What can companies do to help develop an educated and skilled workforce for the future?

They can provide philanthropic funding and equipment or management advice to support programs that aim to improve the quality and relevance of education. They can support on-the-job training programs and work experiences that enable young people to build necessary skills for successful working lives. They can offer financial, technical, and mentoring support for youth enterprise programs aimed at helping young people establish their own businesses.

They can also develop initiatives that are relevant to their own industry sector's needs. The American Express Travel and Tourism Program, for example, trains thousands of young people in ten countries. In 2002, the company worked with other industry partners to offer experience-based learning to over 11,500 school students in thirty-one states in the U.S. and over 85,000 students in nearly three thousand schools outside America. As the company contributes to youth development, it is also training young people specifically for its industry sector, and a number of them may join the company itself. Auto companies are supporting education and training programs for young people to develop their engineering and technical skills. Ford Motor Company in Canada, for example, operates the ASSET program—Automotive Student Service Educational Training. In Los Angeles, Toyota has worked with the Urban League and other groups to establish the successful Automative Training Center. Science and research-based companies such as DuPont, Dow, GlaxoSmithKline, Shell, Alcoa, Merck, and BP are supporting programs in schools and universities to improve science awareness and scientific skills.

A growing number of companies are also supporting youth enterprise initiatives, such as Youth Business International and Junior Achievement, that have been implemented in numerous countries. In all of these cases, the companies are engaging their core competencies and strategic business interests to offer practical solutions to youth development. They recognize that addressing these needs will contribute to skilled workforces and more stable societies in the future, both of which will influence their future competitiveness. The profile of Nokia starting on page 169 illustrates how one company is making a strategic commitment to youth development.

Our final profile on page 171 looks at BankBoston, now FleetBoston Financial and soon to be part of Bank of America, which offers an example of efforts to promote economic opportunity, while building consumer outreach, employee loyalty, and profitability.

Nokia: Make a Connection

Almost unknown outside its home country of Finland in the 1960s, by 2001 Nokia was the world leader in mobile communications and was ranked by Interbrand as one of the world's top five most valuable brands. Its share of the mobile phone market almost doubled from 19 percent in 1997 to 37 percent in 2001. At the same time, it sustained impressive operating margins and profitability in an industry besieged by plummeting results, corporate failures, and crisis. Although Nokia faces major challenges going forward, it remains well positioned as an industry leader.

Established in 1865 as a pulp and paper manufacturer, the company has always been in the business of communications—only the medium has changed. Much has been written about Nokia's passionate commitment to innovation, design, and envisioning the future. Continuous learning is one of the company's four core values. While the company's business units invest in their own R&D, the Nokia Ventures Organization takes a broader view, aiming to "push the frontiers past what we can do today to what we envision for tomorrow and beyond."[13] This commitment to innovation and investing in the future, together with an unrelenting focus on operational excellence and heavy investment in the company's brand, is widely recognized as driving Nokia's impressive growth. A systematic focus on stakeholder relations has been another important factor. The company explicitly defines its stakeholders as "employees, customers, suppliers, shareholders, governmental and nongovernmental organizations, the media, the communities where it does business, and other parties that have influence over or are influenced by Nokia."[14]

Given Nokia's leadership in future-oriented technologies, young people are an obvious and increasingly important stakeholder group. The company is establishing mechanisms to listen to and learn from this group, integrating feedback from young people into its innovation processes and future visioning. It also recognizes the importance of building life skills and opportunities for young people.

Youth and education have therefore been made the strategic focus of Nokia's corporate citizenship activities. According to the company's CEO, Jorma Ollila, "In the future that Nokia's business is shaping, people will have the technology to communicate anytime, anywhere. Helping young people improve their skills, knowledge and connections to society is a natural outgrowth of Nokia's business, vision and values."[15] Executive vice president Veli Sundbäck emphasizes, "It is not our intention to promote technology as such, even though this is our core competence. In a fast changing world, we want young people to develop the skills they are going to need—creative thinking, the life skills needed to make quick decisions, and simply an ability to think for themselves and take responsibility for what's happening around them."[16]

As a company that revolves around innovation, Nokia is keen to work with innovative social entrepreneurs in delivering its youth and education programs. After extensive consultation, Nokia decided that the International Youth Foundation (IYF), founded by social entrepreneur Rick Little, would be an effective and creative partner in helping it to implement its global commitment to youth development. IYF's programs seek to build young people's character, confidence, and competence and to connect them to their families, peers, and communities. This purpose fits strategically with Nokia's own mission of connecting people. It also reflects Jorma Ollila's message that young people will need competence and skills for a fast-changing world, and his belief that character counts, especially in difficult times.

In April 2000, Nokia and IYF launched a multiyear, multimillion-dollar partnership called Make a Connection. This global initiative focuses on locally driven programs that improve educational opportunities for young people and teach them life skills. Through its global alliance with IYF, Nokia deploys its youth programming through an extensive network of local partners in seventeen countries. These indigenous organizations identify local youth needs and develop and deploy locally relevant programs that stress the societal benefits of actively engaging youth in addressing those needs. In each of the seventeen countries, the company's local staff also provides volunteer and professional assistance to the program. Nokia's current financial commitment to "Make a Connection" is about $14 million over four years, with the aim of leveraging more money, ideas, and technology through innovative alliances with development agencies and other corporations, as well as employee-volunteer efforts. During this period of time, the initiative is expected to benefit some 1.5 million youths and adults.

The program aims to mobilize financial and in-kind support from Nokia, its employees and business partners, other companies, and nonprofit organizations. Not surprisingly, an important element is making effective use of information and communications technology. One example is YouthActionNet, an Internet site for youths interested in making a change in their communities. It provides information on events, resources, and issues that young people can get involved in and enables them to interact with peers around the world. The site was developed, with Nokia's support, by a group of young people from eight different countries.

As it enters the twenty-first century, Nokia recognizes that its commitment to strong growth, profitability, and responsible market leadership depends on striving to "keep a clear focus on human needs, managing risk, building reputation and integrating stakeholder expectations into the company's business decision-making."[17] In the long term its success also depends on building the skills and opportunities of young people—the next generation of consumers, employees, and investors.

FLEETBOSTON FINANCIAL

Spreading Economic Opportunity

The efforts of FleetBoston Financial Corporation and its Community Investment Group (CIG) are an example of leadership in the field of community economic development—the application of a company's core lines of business to low and moderate-income communities. Over the past 11 years, the $200 billion financial services company

has developed an innovative model to create jobs, build
small businesses, provide financial and investment programs
to low and moderate-income families and help bridge the
digital divide—all while making a substantial profit.

BUSINESS FOR SOCIAL RESPONSIBILITY

BankBoston, now FleetBoston Financial and soon to be part of Bank of America, is America's oldest commercial bank. From the China trade to the textile mills of the early Industrial Revolution, from the first movie studios in Hollywood and the birth of McDonald's to the high-tech revolution along Boston's Route 128, it has been a vital part of America's economic history. By the late 1980s, it had grown into a formidable regional and international presence and had been paying dividends steadily longer than any corporation in North America. But it had also grown complacent, self-satisfied, inwardly focused, bloated, bureaucratic, and even arrogant. And then, in 1991, like so many other storied U.S. companies, BankBoston almost went bust.

Burdened with a billion dollars in nonperforming loans to less developed countries as well as a roaring regional recession, BankBoston looked as though it might go the way of a hundred other banks that were seized by the FDIC. Its stock plummeted from thirty dollars to less than three dollars per share, and thousands of employees and a million customers held their breath to see whether their bank would survive.

Management knew that it had to act, and to act decisively—and it did. Layers of management were eliminated, scores of uncompetitive businesses were sold or discarded, demanding new metrics imposed a tight financial discipline, and a comfortable, conventional corporate culture was reinvented and transformed into a leaner, more flexible, market-driven and customer-focused company. The results were certainly impressive. By the late 1990s, BankBoston was producing record earnings and growth, its stock had soared to $118 a share, and its market value exceeded $15 billion.

Managing for Value with Values

The story of BankBoston's comeback is a fairly familiar tale for those major U.S. and European companies that responded to rapidly changing market realities over the last two decades and who "got religion," reinventing themselves with a vengeance to become globally competitive and successful. What's somewhat different about BankBoston's story is that its transformation was driven not only by an unyielding commitment to creating shareholder value, but also by a widespread commitment to corporate and societal values. In a sense, what Bank-Boston attempted was a prototype of what pioneering and principled companies can achieve in the future: profits with principles, corporate performance that delivers value to shareholders while advancing societal values.

In BankBoston's case, a key driver beyond the traditional management disciplines was a tenacious commitment to extend economic opportunity to those previously ignored and to become a leader in inner-city bank lending aimed at serving historically underserved and culturally diverse markets.

BankBoston "merged with" Fleet Financial in 1999 and today is part of the tenth-largest commercial banking company in the U.S, with 56,000 employees and $200 billion in assets. Its CEO from the 1990s, Chad Gifford, recently became the CEO of Fleet, and while the combined institution has its own unique culture and priorities, many of the distinctive attributes of BankBoston—attributes that helped to make it such an attractive merger partner in the first place—have survived. Soon Fleet will become part of Bank of America, and Chad Gifford will become chairman of the second-largest bank in the nation, which promises to retain many of the characteristics and values of its latest acquisition.

The BankBoston story illustrates how a corporate turnaround can take place not only with efficiency and bottom-line focus but consistent with values and a concern for purpose beyond profits. In the process, BankBoston became a more culturally diverse and innovative company, ready to serve previously underserved customers in creative and commercially viable ways, and to engage with its communities in a partnership-based rather than paternalistic manner that built capacity and spread economic opportunity. This values-driven transformation and turnaround strongly suggests that "profits with principles" is not an oxymoron; they actually can go together, and in a way that fuels performance, benefits society, and provides a strong bedrock for future competitiveness.

How did BankBoston not only manage for value, but also manage *with* values? What lessons can we tease from this case study of an old, proud, but tired company re-creating itself in the mold of a tough, market-driven competitor with a soul? How did they do it—and what can other companies learn from them?

Champions

Of course, a corporate turnaround has to be led by a leader at the top. But leadership of a principled company doesn't require charisma so much as consistency, and champions of change need to be found and encouraged throughout the company and down through the rank and file. Bank-Boston's turnaround was led over a decade by two CEOs with dramatically different styles and personalities, and it succeeded in large measure because they both encouraged others in the organization to assume responsibility for owning change. Here are some graphic examples.

Sending a New Message In the depths of BankBoston's worst year of financial performance, then CEO Ira Stepanian cancelled the traditional annual executive golf outing and instituted, instead, a day of community service. The work was hard and unpretentious, the effort required teamwork and coordination. Some date the beginning of BankBoston's turnaround to this simple symbolic commitment to do things differently. A dysfunctional group was becoming an effective team, an inwardly focused organization was looking outside of itself, and a company that was previously viewed as aloof and arrogant started to reveal that it had a heart. That initial Day of Community Service, limited to the top executive ranks of the company, grew to an annual ritual involving more than 250 top managers. Today, in the new Fleet organization, more than a score of separate business units have become champions of their own Day of Community Service. Altogether in 2002, 22,000 Fleet employees volunteered 120,000 hours of service on 1,200 community projects.

Establishing a New Paradigm Champions need to be consistent; they also need to accept responsibility and occasionally to demonstrate courage. That's what BankBoston's CEO did back in the early 1990s, when commercial banks across the country were accused of redlining and discriminating against inner-city, largely black residents. Asked to testify before a congressional committee and fearful of angry community activists and a skeptical press corps, the heads of many other major banks declined the invitation. BankBoston's then CEO Ira Stepanian accepted, testified, and used the opportunity to unveil a bold leadership commitment to positively address the legitimate concerns of society by putting the bank's strength to work in the inner city.

Required by law, through the Community Reinvestment Act, or CRA, to meet the credit and banking needs of low- and moderate-income residents, many banks complained for more than fifteen years about the regulatory burden, protested the cost of compliance, and resisted taking serious or innovative action in advancing the law of the land. Historically BankBoston had largely followed suit. But when preparing to testify, Stepanian and his team broke out of the conventional mind-set, applied some creative business acumen, and came up with a strategy that transformed the CRA from a compliance obligation into a business opportunity—one that held promise for doing good and doing well, simultaneously.

Before the cameras, the activists, and the Congress, Stepanian revealed BankBoston's plan to create a bank within a bank, called First Community Bank, to develop specialized products and services to meet the unique requirements of previously disenfranchised inner-city residents and first-time homebuyers, and to become a leader in meeting the community's needs, while doing so in a profitable, prudent, and sustainable way. Long viewed as condescending and patronizing, BankBoston repositioned itself as the community's ally, partner, and friend, and Ira Stepanian became a consistent and courageous champion of BankBoston's leadership in terms of the CRA.

Celebrating Employee Leadership But champions are not only found in the executive suite. When BankBoston received the prestigious Ron Brown Award for Corporate Leadership at the White House, the key team who created the company's economic opportunity initiatives was there to share the CEO's glory, and mass meetings were held for the hundreds of line employees responsible for the biannual recognition by federal regulators of BankBoston's "Outstanding" CRA rating. Celebrating success, and most important the employees behind the success, became a core element of the company's internal communications strategy.

Spreading Economic Opportunity

Fleet's Community Investment Group The commitment to inner-city banking survived Stepanian's departure and the merger with Fleet. Indeed, now led by an African-American woman, Gail Snowden, Fleet's Community Investment Group has grown to include a variety of community economic development initiatives building on the strengths of both Bank-Boston and Fleet. These cover retail banking, wholesale community development lending, Community Investment Act and Fair Lending compliance, a digital divide initiative, and community development marketing.

Fleet Community Bank has grown to 157 inner-city branches, with 1,500 employees in five states. It has $5 billion in deposits, a $14.6 billion commitment to mortgage and small-business lending—one of the largest by any bank—and an innovative inner-city investment bank. Building on Fleet's experience with e-commerce and its Fleet Homelink online banking product, the CIG has established CommunityLink, aimed at bridging the digital divide. It brings computers to families and Internet access and bill-paying facilities to consumers in low- and moderate-income communities.

The Community Investment Group is able to build on a long track record of making a difference in the communities it serves while also generating consistently profitable financial returns and the highest levels of customer satisfaction and employee morale in the entire company. The support of the company's CEO and its board of directors has been key, but equally important has been the close interaction with the company's lines of business. This has facilitated innovation and ensured that community banking is not simply a charitable sideline for the bank but central to its business. Fleet now joins Bank of America, which is halfway along in fulfilling an unprecedented $350 billion commitment over ten years to community development lending and investment. Gail Snowden remains passionately committed and is optimistic about the future: "What we started at BankBoston and have sustained at Fleet now has the chance of blossoming at Bank of America. I'm feeling good that our values align quite nicely and even if Charlotte is a long way from Boston, our hearts are in the same place and now we can really take things to scale nationally."

Going to School on Workplace Diversity As a company that had for many years been a first mover in emerging markets such as Argentina and

Brazil, BankBoston had always sought out indigenous talent that understood local needs and customs. With its newfound commitment to being a leader in emerging markets and inner cities in its own backyard, Bank-Boston instinctively understood that it would need to attract and retain talent that understood these markets and was broadly representative of the new populations it aimed to serve. In a world where new entrants to the workforce are increasingly nonwhite and female, the company reasoned that to attract the best and the brightest, it would need to be a welcoming environment. This meant that it would need to "go to school on" changing its traditional Brahmin corporate culture. And it did so, with gusto.

Diversity Training The weeklong diversity training program had new CEO Chad Gifford in its first class, and enrollment was a requirement for the top two hundred managers of the company. Diversity had become a new corporate priority, and with it came new metrics for performance, new benchmarks of success, and alignment of human resources with business needs. No longer just wishful thinking or "the right thing to do," diversity management became a skill set and a distinctive corporate competence.

Walking the Talk on Diversity Values For some companies corporate values can come to mean nothing much more than window dressing or whitewash, sometimes even a cynical veneer that masks an inner core of opportunism, ruthlessness, and corruption. In a company not only guided by corporate mottoes but driven by corporate values that are internalized into management practices, putting those values to work every day is a test of commitment and sometimes even of courage. BankBoston sought to be a leader and to gain competitive differentiation by embracing diversity for business advantage. But when the CEO was asked to allow BankBoston's gay and lesbian employees to march behind the corporate banner at the annual Gay and Lesbian Pride Parade, suddenly glib rhetoric faced the reality of choice and the acid test of credibility. The CEO decided to allow the use of the BankBoston banner; indeed, he ended up joining with his employees and marching in the parade itself. When they asked him to support an end to discrimination against employees based on sexual preference, he ended up testifying before Congress in support of the Employment Non-Discrimination Act—the only Fortune 500 corporate CEO at the time to do so.

Building Skills and Assets in the Community As part of its corporate turnaround and reinvention, BankBoston was determined to transform its traditional corporate giving program into a more strategic investment initiative. Instead of just giving out small grants to many community organizations as it had for decades, engendering little goodwill or recognition in the community and realizing little quantifiable benefit to society, the company decided to pursue a new approach—one driven by a desire to make a difference and to harness not only its philanthropic dollars but its other corporate strengths in advancing a limited number of community needs.

City Year As BankBoston began to think about this new approach to social investing and partnership, they were approached by two young Harvard Law School graduates, Alan Khazei and Michael Brown, who wanted seed funding to start a program called City Year. City Year was envisioned as a privately funded urban Peace Corps that would attract a diverse group of seventeen- to twenty-three-year-olds to do community service in central cities. At the end of the year, during which they would receive a modest stipend to meet basic expenses, City Year graduates would receive a $5,000 voucher for their continuing education. City Year's founders thought that young people could be tapped to be part of the solution to inner-city problems and that idealism backed by a disciplined and entrepreneurial approach could result in changed lives and vastly improved communities. BankBoston decided that the idea was promising, even if untested, and that City Year had the potential of becoming a transformational initiative through which the company's philanthropy, combined with its corporate resources, might really make a difference.

The only problem was that the organizers had no track record, no infrastructure or support system, and virtually no organizational capacity. BankBoston set out to help the founders fill the gap. The bank gave its "Good Housekeeping Seal of Approval" by funding the first City Year team and then helped line up five other corporate sponsors. It trained the first year-round corps in financial literacy, provided them with free checking accounts and ATM privileges, and allowed a middle manager to serve "on loan" as City Year's first director of corporate development and fund-raising.

And when City Year decided to expand into a national program,

BankBoston funded the first non–Boston-based team, introduced CityYear to bankers and prominent customers in other major communities, and hosted a breakfast with big-city mayors from across the country so they could learn about CityYear's promise.

Nearly fifteen years later, CityYear has grown and expanded into fourteen cities and has been embraced by Nelson Mandela in South Africa. Then governor Bill Clinton visited CityYear while campaigning for president in 1992 and was so impressed with what he saw and experienced that he modeled Americorps on the CityYear precedent. Americorps, in less than a decade, has attracted 250,000 young people to full-time national and community service, more than have served in the forty-year history of the Peace Corps. In 2002 alone, Americorps had seven times as many participants as the Peace Corps. CityYear's 6,500 alumni have completed 9.7 million hours of community service and have attracted $109 million from 271 private-sector partners, helping to leverage an additional $87 million in federal funding.

The Center for Women and Enterprise and The Partnership As part of its commitment to fostering economic opportunity for groups previously disenfranchised and cut off from traditional banking services, BankBoston actively sought out other potential partners in the community that, like CityYear, were at the cutting edge of new approaches to outreach and engagement.

One was a start-up nonprofit designed to train and empower marginalized women to start their own small businesses—the Center for Women and Enterprise (CWE). Another—The Partnership—was an organization dedicated to making Boston a more inviting and hospitable community for African-American professionals. Both needed start-up or investment capital to launch their efforts into higher gear. In the case of CWE, BankBoston stepped up with a $150,000 commitment, becoming its first corporate supporter and seeing the initial funding used to develop internal infrastructure and management systems. To date, CWE has served over five thousand women entrepreneurs, and The Partnership has 100 corporate members, 145 professionals and executives in its yearly programs, and 1,200 African-American alumni—1,000 of whom are still working and living in Boston, helping to make it a decidedly more interesting, diverse, and healthy city.

Investing in Children and Education

Success by Six In 1994, the United Way challenged the community to think outside the box and create an innovative mechanism to ensure that all children in Boston are ready to learn by the time they *enter* school. Building upon the example set by the corporate community in Minneapolis, Success by Six was launched in Boston, with a most improbable cast of characters and a truly daunting mandate. BankBoston's Chad Gifford assembled a leadership council consisting of fifty of Boston's most prominent business, labor, community, and academic movers and shakers—many of whom had never met one another, and had certainly never before banded together to advocate for public policy changes.

Improbable, perhaps, but the potential and power of bankers aligned with labor leaders, world-class medical experts, and credible community activists served to create remarkable results. Just three years later, the United Way had hired a seasoned child rights advocate and political organizer, a broad-based coalition for children started to mobilize, serious analytical research had been commissioned, and a mass-media campaign was on the air.

BankBoston's CEO worked arm in arm with the president of the state AFL-CIO, along with noted pediatrician Dr. T. Berry Brazelton and a slew of strong community leaders. He wasn't pleading for tax breaks for his industry, but for rational investments in kids. Breaking out of the mold, Success By Six, led by an unusual but united coalition, achieved what many skeptics thought at the outset was totally unattainable:

- The first-in-the-nation license plate for children

- Enactment of a fifty-cent increase in the cigarette tax to make virtually every child in Massachusetts eligible for health insurance coverage

- Creation of a model program that allows every mother under twenty-one to have access to critically needed home visitation services

- A health-care diary, provided to every mother of every one of Massachusetts' 84,000 annual newborns, complete with handy references to a wide array of services, a schedule of inoculations and medical checkups, and progress reports on their child's growth and needs—available in multiple languages

Public leadership. Coalition-building. Public policy advocacy. Hardly the everyday stuff for the CEO of a major commercial bank. But Bank-Boston's CEO put his corporate strength to work for young, vulnerable children. The results speak for themselves. And the dividends will be paid out to society for decades to come. Perhaps not surprisingly, Bank of America also saw value in the Success By Six model. In fact, last year it completed a $50 million five-year philanthropic commitment to Success By Six nationally, the largest gift the bank ever made and one of the most significant corporate grants in history.

Operating with Credibility and Integrity

For BankBoston, credibility wasn't a virtue so much as it was a necessity, and integrity needed to be practiced and demonstrated if its efforts were to be taken seriously. No company is capable of consistently doing the right thing every day and every time, but as BankBoston transformed itself from an insular, protected, and complacent company into an open, entrepreneurial, and values-driven competitor, it needed to prove the skeptics wrong by showing a degree of consistency, credibility, and integrity in matters large and small. The next example suggests how demanding and challenging this standard is to uphold.

When BankBoston acquired BayBanks for $2.2 billion, the stock market reacted favorably to the prospect of eliminating two thousand redundant positions and creating a leaner back office to support a larger number of customers. Federal regulators, who might have been expected to balk given the extraordinary concentration of deposits that the new institution would control, hailed the merger and, due to BankBoston's exceptionally positive reputation and commitment to the community, didn't even require public hearings for approval. But not everyone was thrilled by the prospect of eliminating jobs and closing offices. Challenged to put its values to the test, BankBoston's top management team took a hard look at the numbers, took a long look in the mirror, and decided to do what had never been done before.

Instead of laying off the two thousand employees, the first priority became to lessen the impact by managing turnover—and saving fifteen hundred employees from receiving pink slips. The remaining five hundred whose positions were about to be eliminated were offered a unique Transition Assistance Program (TAP) that offered generous severance benefits and free individualized career and financial counseling to every employee. After consulting with other major employers and several community organizations, TAP offered three additional voluntary options: additional partial salary for six months if an employee chose to change careers and work for a not-for-profit community organization; three months' pay as an incentive for other companies to hire any laid-off employee of BankBoston; and free legal and accounting services and an interest-free loan for any laid-off employee who wanted to start his or her own new business.

The net result? Employees proud of their company and of the way their colleagues were treated at a critical time. Gratitude from the community and from others who were pleased to see that capitalism can operate with a conscience. At a time when expediency could have easily and predictably produced very different results, the bank provided a powerful demonstration of credibility and integrity.

From Compliance to Creating New Value

BankBoston, like the other leadership companies we've examined, focused its efforts around a mind-set of creating new value. This included an ongoing commitment to compliance; ongoing and rigorous efforts to control risks, costs, and negative impacts; and an ongoing commitment to charitable contributions. But BankBoston went beyond these strategies to create new value through core business products and services as well as employee practices and community investments, which genuinely promoted new economic opportunity.

Fleet today is struggling with all the problems that other major commercial banks are facing. But it has something that few of its competitors possess: a strong track record of innovation and success in inner-city lending, an enviable record on diversity, a legacy of leadership in the community, and a ten-year track record of managing for value with values. Signs are hopeful that these strengths will be embraced and embedded within Bank of America, which has its own strong traditions of values-driven leadership. Indeed, subsequent to the announcement of the merger with Fleet, Bank of America unveiled an unprecedented $750 billion commitment to lend and invest in community economic development over the next ten years, the largest in the history of U.S. banking. Companies that create economic opportunity cannot alone eradicate widespread poverty. They can and do provide opportunities to millions who have previously been denied them, while also building corporate advantage for themselves.

Spreading Economic Opportunity

One: Create employment opportunities.

Two: Invest in small enterprise development.

Three: Help low-income communities build their economic assets.

Four: Promote e-inclusion initiatives.

Five: Support education and youth development.

Engage in New Alliances

New cross-sector alliances with nontraditional allies are crucial to future corporate success. These alliances are also key to engaging business, governmental, and civic leaders in a collaborative effort that has the potential to achieve better leverage of resources, greater economic efficiencies, and enhanced political legitimacy in addressing issues of public interest.

These alliances involve new types of cooperation in the commercial, philanthropic, and public policy spheres. They offer companies the potential to enhance their core business performance, manage supply chain issues, leverage their philanthropic and community investment efforts, and work with others to shape more progressive public policy and market frameworks.

Successful alliances depend on mutual benefit, clarity of purpose, rigor of process, and effective evaluation of progress.

Why New Alliances Matter

*More than ever, the international business community has
an opportunity and responsibility to enter into effective
partnerships with governments and other organizations to
spread the benefits of the global marketplace and deal with
the multifaceted challenges of an integrated global economy.*

MARIA CATTAUI, SECRETARY GENERAL,

INTERNATIONAL CHAMBER OF COMMERCE, 2002

Every two years, hundreds of business leaders from around the world
gather together at the World Congress of the International Chamber of
Commerce (ICC). The ICC is the world's business organization. Established in 1919, it represents the interests of the private sector in supporting an open global trade and financial system. For almost a century
it has been developing self-regulatory rules and tools that facilitate millions of daily international business transactions, large and small. Its
members are individual companies and business associations from over
140 countries. It is the voice of business at global bodies such as the
United Nations and the World Trade Organization and a sounding board
for new trends in the world's business community. The purpose of its
biannual World Congress is to identify and debate these new trends by
bringing together leaders from business and the public sector.

In May 2002, the ICC held its first congress in the United States for
nearly a quarter of a century. It was one of the largest international business gatherings hosted in the country since the September 11 terrorist attacks. Business leaders came from around the world to reaffirm their belief
in global business and in America. The title of the congress and the underlying theme of almost every workshop was "The Power of Partnership."

Topics ranged from the predictable business subjects, such as intellectual property, technology, transport, security, world financial stability,
competition, and investment, to the less predictable—poverty, young
people at risk, the digital divide, business in society, and global governance. In almost every case, the challenges and solutions were seen
through the lens of partnership. Much of the focus was on new types of
alliances between business and other sectors in order to meet commercial objectives *and* wider societal goals.

The emergence of new types of alliances, networks, and partnerships has been one of the most striking business trends of the past decade. These cover a broad range:

■ From multimillion-dollar cross-border mergers and acquisitions to public–private partnerships aimed at addressing social and environmental challenges at local levels

■ From new virtual Internet-driven networking structures spanning the globe—B2Bs, B2Cs, and B2Es—to physical location–specific industry clusters

■ From new types of strategic business alliance and joint ventures to more focused technology cooperation, licensing, outsourcing, and franchising arrangements, and a vast array of joint research, funding, marketing, and distribution mechanisms

They include new business-led "public purpose" coalitions where business leaders come together to address public policy issues beyond their own immediate commercial interests, such as the International Business Leaders Forum, the Global Business Council on HIV/AIDS, and the World Business Council for Sustainable Development. They involve partnerships among companies and government agencies, community organizations, environmental groups, and trade unions. They range from relatively low-risk, low-cost, low-management-intensity adjustments to doing "business as usual" to high-risk, high-cost, high-leadership-intensity transformations that fundamentally change business strategies and business models.

Alliances aren't new, but something fundamentally different is happening.
While successful companies have long engaged in partnerships with other businesses to build value along their value chain, this practice is increasing in terms of the number, variety, complexity, strategic intent, and often the size of such alliances. In addition to business-to-business (B2B) alliances, we are witnessing the emergence of *fundamentally new types* of dialogue and partnerships. A growing number of the world's leading companies are using cooperation and collaboration as core strategies to build both shareholder *and* societal value. They are continuing to invest in a va-

riety of strategic and transactional business alliances, but they are also forming new collaborative initiatives that go beyond business as usual to tackle wider social and environmental challenges. And these new collaborative initiatives are often with nonbusiness or nontraditional partners.

New alliances can help to build competitive edge and tackle societal problems.

It is increasingly apparent that companies don't simply sit in a comfortable slot along a vertical or horizontal "value chain." Instead they are part of complex, interlinked, and overlapping "relationship networks" that consist not only of business partners with commercial alliances but also a growing variety of nonbusiness organizations participating in social alliances. Many of these connections have direct and indirect impacts on commercial performance.

In its report *The Connected Corporation,* for example, Accenture concludes:

> *Corporations are beginning to appreciate the interdependent systemic nature of the connections between businesses, governments, unions, non-governmental organizations, cultural institutions, society and the physical environment which contains them all. . . . The connected corporation—with its approach that values connections before boundaries, both within and beyond businesses—is ideally placed to seize opportunity. Its networked nature and powerful set of relationships should mean it is able to shape the external environment. It will adapt quickly to changing circumstances, constantly creating and re-creating partnerships to capitalize on its strengths.[1]*

In another report, *Measuring the Future,* the Cap Gemini Ernst Young Center for Business Innovation concluded, "Although many believe alliances are relatively insignificant, analysis shows that companies with more joint ventures, marketing and manufacturing alliances, and other forms of partnerships have substantially higher market values."[2] Research by Booz Allen Hamilton and the Kellogg School of Management concludes:

> *Winning companies define and deploy relationships in a consistent, specific and multifaceted manner. Although some companies will*

*define any concluded business deal a relationship, top-performing
companies focus extraordinary enterprise-wide energy on moving
beyond a transactional mindset as they develop trust-based,
mutually beneficial and long-term associations, specifically with
four key constituencies: customers; suppliers; alliance partners; and
their own employees.[3]*

The reasons for the growing focus on alliances should be obvious. As the business environment becomes ever more complex, more competitive, and more global, companies will have few choices other than to develop new forms of dialogue and partnership. In today's knowledge-driven global economy, few, if any, companies can totally go it alone. This is the case on a purely commercial basis, let alone in terms of tackling some of the wider societal expectations and challenges that companies now face. In these circumstances, the ability to cooperate and build new types of partnership will be essential to corporate competitiveness and survival. In order to meet the growing expectations of shareholders and society, companies will have to identify other organizations—both public and private, for-profit and nonprofit—that can help them to leverage scarce technical, managerial, and financial resources.

Every company profiled in this book is engaging in these new types of alliance. Often these are with nontraditional allies, and many of them extend beyond business as usual. These companies are engaging in new alliances within their core business activities and more broadly as part of their outreach to communities and to the public policy realm. These new types of alliances are an increasingly important element of corporate strategy, competitiveness, and accountability. Most of them simply did not exist ten years ago, and they create a variety of new risks and opportunities for business. They are not easy to build and often incur high transaction costs in terms of the time and effort needed to establish trust. Many of them fail, or they fail at least to meet initial expectations in terms of predicted efficiencies, synergies, problem-solving potential, and impacts. This is the case for business-to-business partnerships with a purely commercial focus, let alone for those with a broader range of participants and a broader societal purpose. Despite this, these new types of cooperation are not likely to go away. There is a quiet but transformational "partnership revolution" under way. Any business leader ignores it at his or her peril.

Making It Happen

Where and how can these new types of cross-sector or multistakeholder alliances be most effective? The following three types of alliances between business and other stakeholders all have potential to benefit both business and society:

- Alliances that are directly focused on *enhancing the core business proposition of the company* and aimed at improving economic, social, and environmental performance in core business activities

- Alliances that are focused around the *company's philanthropic or social investment activities* and have the potential to transform traditional philanthropy and civic engagement in order to increase its leverage and effectiveness

- Alliances between business, government, and other actors in the *public policy realm* that have the potential to shape public policy, change the rules of the game, and improve governance structures and market frameworks

All three types of alliances can provide direct business benefits, as well as create societal and shareholder value. In the following pages we offer a few snapshots of all three categories in action. There are literally thousands of these new types of alliance emerging. Most of the examples we have profiled in other chapters of this book have new types of cross-sector cooperation as a central feature. There is enormous diversity in terms of participants, location, scope, and purpose. Sometimes the alliances are fully fledged, legally binding partnerships involving common governance and decision-making structures and shared resources, risks, and benefits. In other cases they are more of an ongoing dialogue than a partnership. In all cases, however, the aim is to build relationships that are cooperative and constructive and that involve mutual respect and a genuine two-way flow of ideas, information, and resources.

One: Build Alliances to Enhance the
Core Business Proposition

More companies are engaging in cross-sector alliances to improve the environmental or social performance of their core business activities in the workplace, in the marketplace, or along their supply chain. These alliances range from strategic partnerships at the heart of the company's business model to collaborative efforts focused on developing or improving a specific product or process.

Alliances at the Heart of the Company's Business Model Two examples of companies that have integrated an ethos of improved environmental performance into their strategic business alliances are Atlanta-based Interface, the world's largest commercial carpet manufacturer, and Geneva-based STMicroelectronics, the world's third-largest semiconductor manufacturer.

Partnering for Improved Environmental Performance

Interface Interface's corporate vision is "to be the first company that, by its deeds, shows the entire industrial world what sustainability is in all its dimensions: People, process, product, place and profits—by 2020—and in doing so we will become restorative through the power of influence."[4] A key element of this vision is to form strategic alliances with customers to develop new customer-driven solutions for "closed-loop" products—essentially the delivery of high-quality, high-value carpets that use less raw material and energy in their production and can be returned afterward to Interface to be recycled, ensuring that they send less discarded material into landfills and into the biosphere. In essence the customers are getting a full life-cycle service, rather than a one-time product, and Interface is building strategic relationships that benefit the bottom line and the environment.

Already the company can point to examples where its corporate philosophy has served to win it contracts. It states, "There have been numerous instances where we have matched our competitors in terms of price and quality, yet our efforts and leadership in sustainability have become the deciding factors."[5] In order to build these successful customer alliances, CEO Ray Anderson and his team have clearly defined what they mean by the term *sustainability*, set performance indicators for measuring their progress, and focused on building what they call "ferocious cooperation" among the company's 5,500 associates, who run manufacturing operations on four continents and offices in over one hundred countries.

STMicroelectronics STMicroelectronics is another company with a successful business model built on a foundation of strategic alliances and a performance-oriented culture that places Total Quality Environmental Management (TQEM) at its core. Created in 1987 as a merger between two loss-making state-owned enterprises in Europe, less than twenty years later ST is a leader in the semiconductor business. During this time it has excelled at customer-driven innovation and execution across a dispersed global network that consists of the company's own operations and its strategic alliance partnerships, which ST describes as "actual extensions of our own business." These partnerships are with some of the world's leading companies, Alcatel, Bosch, HP, Marelli, Nokia, Nortel, Networks, Pioneer, Seagate, and Siemens VDO among them. They are a major source of the company's revenues, its financial stability, and its growth opportunities, as well as a conduit for increasing its access to new ideas and innovation. They also play an important role in furthering ST's public commitment to environmental sustainability.

President and CEO Pascale Pistorio and his team first announced ambitious public targets and time lines for their environmental performance in 1995, in what they call their *Environmental Decalogue*. One of their current goals is to become a "carbon neutral" company by 2010, meaning that they will either cut all their carbon dioxide emissions or offset them to neutralize their impact. To achieve this, they recognize that they must work with their business partners to produce products that meet customer needs with less environmental impact. The company states in its 2001 annual report to shareholders, "Our approach to the environment extends well beyond our company, as we articulate clear sustainability criteria to our suppliers, significantly expanding our impact. Also, as we collaborate with our strategic partners, we make sure environmental implications are built into every innovation."[6]

To date, ST's environmental commitment has shown good business results. Based on seven years of investment experience in environmental improvement, the company calculates that average payback on such investment is 2.5 years. As an indication of what is possible when a global company commits to environmental excellence, in 2000 ST saved enough water for a population of 50 million people to drink in one year, while saving about $50 million in water and electricity bills. At the end of one of the worst years in the history of the semiconductor industry, Pistorio was able to report to the company's shareholders:

> When I reflect on ST's ability to navigate through the difficult market conditions of 2001, I conclude that once more the difference is in our execution, driven by our people and our corporate culture. This encompasses the Total Quality Management that we embraced several years ago, as well as ST's commitment to remain socially responsible citizens. I am very proud to say that ST has been, is, and will remain a champion of environmental responsibility and sustainable development, having proven that contributing to a better world can also enhance business performance and profitability.[7]

The company's strategic alliances with its customers and suppliers are an important element of this equation.

Alliances to Develop New Products and Processes or Enhance Existing Ones Many companies are developing new alliances to bring an environmental or social dimension into their R&D activities and their organizational and operational processes. Examples that illustrate this approach include DuPont, BP, FleetBoston, Ford Motor Company, and P&G, which we have profiled in other chapters.

Alliances to Deal with Difficult Industry Dilemmas In some cases companies are joining forces to tackle strategic dilemmas associated with the core business activities of their industry sector, which are either too sensitive or too difficult for any one company to address on its own. Joining forces with other companies or organizations in other sectors can help to enhance both business performance and accountability in relation to these tough issues. Major international drinks companies, for example, have formed coalitions such as the Portman Group and The International Center for Alcohol Policies to help reduce the abuse of alcohol, support dialogue with public health authorities, and establish industry standards for abuse prevention and marketing. Another industry alliance focused on improving business performance and accountability is the chemical industry's Responsible Care program, which we look at under Principle #6 (governance).

Alliances to deal with difficult issues can be even more effective and have even greater legitimacy when they involve nonbusiness partners as part of their governance structure. The U.S.-based Fair Labor Association (FLA) is one example that brings together apparel and footwear manufacturers and retailers in the United States with consumer and human rights groups. Their common goal is to improve working conditions and protect workers' rights in factories in the United States and abroad. The FLA has a charter agreement that establishes an industrywide code of conduct and an independent monitoring system to assess corporate performance against the code. Participating companies include Nike, Reebok, Eddie Bauer, Phillips-Van Heusen, Polo Ralph Lauren, Liz Claiborne, Levi Strauss, Patagonia, and Adidas-Solomon. Together, these companies contract with more than four thousand factories in seventy-five countries and represent over $30 billion in apparel and footwear sales. Over 170 colleges and universities have also affiliated with FLA to ensure that the goods they purchase are produced in accordance with FLA principles.

Alliances to Improve Supply Chain Management Some of these new cross-sector alliances are focused on supply chain issues—either improving the quality of supply chain management or ensuring the reliability and sustainability of supplies. Our profile of Unilever at the end of the chapter provides one example. The examples of Coca-Cola, Starbucks, and Vodafone in other chapters also illustrate new alliances aimed at enhancing supply chain management. In the following profile, we look at how Nike, together with other companies and non-business partners, is working with the Global Alliance for Workers and Communities to improve its operational performance and to increase transparency and accountability along its global supply chain.

Nike and the Global Alliance for Workers and Communities

Few brands in history have attracted such an array of passionate fans and activist critics as the Nike swoosh. Named for Nike—the Greek goddess of victory—the company and the brand have come to symbolize some of the greatest opportunities and some of the most daunting challenges of the global economy.

To millions of loyal consumers around the globe—from world-class athletes to the Sunday jogger—Nike is an innovation-driven, customer-focused corporation with an iconic brand and products at the leading edge of performance, reliability, and design. To many antiglobalization activists, it is an exploitative transnational corporation with products produced by poorly paid and badly treated workers along its global supply chain in developing countries. To the people who work for Nike or along its global supply chain, it is a company that has embarked on a challenging journey of change management, aimed at producing the best products under the best factory conditions while remaining profitable and ahead of the competition in research and design. This goal requires the company to meet the expectations of its customers, who want quality and value in the products they buy; respond to the concerns of its critics, who want quality and value in the lives of factory workers; and anticipate a new generation of customers, employees, and socially responsible investors who are calling for quality and value in both products *and* workers' lives.

It is not possible for any individual company to meet these expectations without working in partnership with others. This is especially the case for a company whose business model is based on supplier relationships in a wide variety of countries with independent contractors that the company does not own or directly manage itself. Some 660,000 people work in about nine hundred contractor factories in over fifty countries producing products for Nike, as well as for other apparel and footwear companies. Working with credible and independent partners is also important for a company that needs to rebuild public trust and credibility after facing activist campaigns, as Nike has done in the past decade.

In 1998, Nike embarked on a comprehensive change management effort. Among other goals, it aimed to integrate socially and environmentally responsible supply chain management and manufacturing processes into the company's core business proposition. Consulting with internal and external stakeholders and working in partnership with others to achieve this goal have been integral to Nike's journey over the past five years. One example has been the company's role in helping to establish the independently governed Global Alliance for Workers and Communities.

In June 1998, the Nike team met with the founder and president of the International Youth Foundation, Rick Little. He proposed that the company, with the help of IYF and other partners, "go back to school" in labor practices and learn directly from the workers, most of them young women. This would require Nike to consult with workers, learning what they care about, worry about, and hope for and then trying to respond with workplace and community initiatives that actively involve them in design, decision making, and monitoring.

On the surface Nike and IYF were unlikely bedfellows—a company under siege from young activists campaigning against its labor practices and a foundation whose mission is to empower young people. But by April 1999, Nike and the International Youth

Foundation had joined forces with the World Bank and other partners to launch the Global Alliance for Workers and Communities. Its mission is to improve the lives and future prospects of workers involved in global production and service supply chains, the majority of whom are young adults, and to promote collaboration among the private, nonprofit, and public sectors in support of these efforts.

Today, the Global Alliance is an independent organization. Nike has one seat on the Oversight Board, together with other business, government, and NGO partners. As with all social innovations and efforts to move beyond business usual, the alliance has faced criticism and cynicism. But in a world beset with problems, it has focused on finding solutions—practical, local solutions to improve the lives of workers. In four years of operation, the GA has interviewed over twelve thousand workers in almost fifty factories in India, Indonesia, Thailand, and Vietnam. This is the first time such a major consultation effort has been undertaken along a global supply chain. Based on the interviews and other research, in 2001 the Global Alliance started to implement worker development and health programs, as well as management training for factory supervisors. It also began work in China. According to the alliance, these now reach over 240,000 workers, supervisors, and their families. In some cases workers themselves are playing a role in helping to design and implement these programs through project teams and peer educators.

The Global Alliance has now embarked on a three-year independent evaluation project. There is anecdotal evidence that the initiative is leading to better worker–manager relations, higher productivity, improved quality, fewer rejects, and reduced absenteeism. One key impact has been to raise awareness among factory supervisors of the beneficial business effects of good management practices. Nike, Gap, and other corporate partners are themselves gaining a better understanding of their supply chains and identifying opportunities to move beyond compliance.

At the same time, the worker education, personal finance, and health programs are making progress toward improving worker protection in terms of workplace health and safety, as well as basic quality of life and health issues in the wider community. The programs are also developing frameworks for increased worker participation in decision-making structures and in the success of the factories, and helping workers develop their personal potential through training and development opportunities.

As the Global Alliance's chair and executive director comment, "We hope to illustrate that by working with global brands and contract factories 'from the inside out,' and by focusing on finding solutions rather than problems, we have been able to empower workers, supervisors and managers, while simultaneously improving the bottom line for factory owners and global brands."[8]

The Global Alliance is still in its early days. As with all complex relationships, it is being constantly tested as new issues surface and its disparate partners and new participants work to build trust and a common vision and mission. It offers a precedent, however, for how global multisector alliances with a commitment to local engagement and ownership by local partners can make a difference to both corporate performance and community prosperity.

Two: Harness Alliances to Leverage Philanthropy

New types of alliance are fundamentally changing the face of corporate philanthropy and community engagement. We are witnessing the emergence of many new coalitions of companies, corporate foundations, civic groups, schools, hospitals, churches, and government bodies that aim to leverage resources to tackle common societal problems, such as illiteracy, the digital divide, drugs, crime, environmental pollution, health care, and domestic violence.

The key point is that business has management skills, other core competencies, and resources that can effectively help to tackle these is-

sues. These are equally as important as philanthropic financial donations, and they are often best leveraged through partnership. We are not
referring to traditional philanthropy or charity, which usually involve a
stand-alone, one-way transaction between company and recipient. Instead, more and more companies are engaging in what is termed *strategic philanthropy, social venture philanthropy,* or *social investment.* The
emphasis is on achieving mutual benefit, a strategic relationship, and
quantifiable results.

Instead of an open checkbook, companies are looking at innovative
and accountable financing mechanisms with nonprofit partners and at
ways to measure both the business benefits *and* the societal impacts of
their programs. Instead of ad hoc sponsorship or donations, companies
are looking at how to mobilize their core competencies and resources, including the skills and energy of their employees, to address community
issues or social and environmental challenges. They are looking to proactively engage community and other social partners in dialogue, joint
planning, and implementation. Instead of charity, companies are looking
for mutual benefit, for issues that link to their own business challenges,
strategies, and interests. Instead of perpetuating relationships of dependence with local communities, more companies are looking at building
long-term capacity and sustainability. In a competitive world, where philanthropy budgets are constrained, these approaches can improve both
the efficiency and the effectiveness of corporate philanthropy programs.
Some of these trends are outlined in the box on page 199.

There are numerous options for companies that want to get more engaged in civic partnerships at the local, national, and global level. Much
has been written about the experiences and good practices of city-level
partnerships in America, with examples ranging from the Cleveland Tomorrow initiative to the Atlanta Partnership, ReBuild LA, and the New
York City Partnership.

We now take a look at some companies engaging in partnership-
driven initiatives that have an impact on a global basis, often in developing countries. These examples demonstrate the possibilities of
tackling what seem to be intractable global problems by leveraging government, business, and other resources to deliver solutions in specific
locations. Our first example is Cisco Systems on page 200, followed by
two profiles of companies and nonprofit organizations forming new

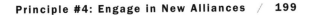

From "Checkbook Philanthropy" to Social Venture Partnerships

	Old-Paradigm Giving: One-way	New-Paradigm Partnerships: Strategic
Philosophy	■ Discretionary giving ■ Corporate obligation	■ New business discipline ■ Societal opportunity
Methods	■ Formulaic ■ Responsive ■ Conventional ■ Risk averse ■ Incremental	■ Entrepreneurial ■ Anticipatory ■ "Out of the box" ■ Risk-taking ■ Transformative
Decision-makers	■ CEO and their spouses ■ Board members ■ Department of good deeds	■ Line business managers ■ Stakeholders ■ Core strategic competence
Purpose	■ Conformity ■ Goodwill	■ Differentiation ■ Results and reputation
Recipients	■ The "usual suspects"	■ New social entrepreneurs and innovators
Reach	■ Local	■ Local and global
Impact	■ Minimal and not measured	■ Potentially high, leveraged, and measured
Employee Involvement	■ Minimal	■ Direct and intense
Relationship Management	■ One way ■ Arm's length ■ Bureaucratic ■ Paternalistic	■ Strategic partnership ■ Entrepreneurial ■ Mutual learning
Nexus with Core Competencies	■ Peripheral	■ Linked to core business purpose

partnerships with the support of the Global Development Alliance (GDA). Established by Secretary of State Colin Powell in 2001 as a new "business model" for the U.S. government's Agency for International Development (USAID), the GDA aims to leverage public and private resources to support international development goals.

Cisco Systems:
Delivering Networked Solutions for Customers and Society

Cisco Systems believes in the value of Internet Ecosystems, described by CEO John Chambers as, "complementary business alliances that create a unique set of interwoven interdependencies and relationships."[9] Despite a period of weak performance, this approach has enabled the company to survive the technology downturn and to help its customers make the productivity gains that are so essential to delivering profits. It has also enabled Cisco and its partners to build market leadership in a competitive industry by achieving greater efficiency, leverage, and effectiveness than each of the partners could achieve operating on its own.

Cooperation is also the ethos that underpins Cisco's wider societal relationships. While Internet Ecosystems are the company's value proposition for achieving one of its two core values—customer focus—the Cisco Corporate Citizenship Ecosystem enables it to achieve its second core value—corporate citizenship. Drawing inspiration from the company's business model, the Corporate Citizenship Ecosystem brings together partners to make a greater impact. Cisco's corporate citizenship strategy is focused on three key areas including basic human needs, access to education, and responsible citizenship.

In the area of access to education, Cisco's flagship initiative is the Cisco Networking Academy Program. First established in the United States in 1997, there are now over 10,000 academies operating in 50 U.S. states and over 150 countries—including an initiative targeted to reach the world's 49 Least Developed Countries (LDCs). Based in high schools, colleges, universities, technical schools, and community-based organizations, the academies are delivering a recognized blended-learning model that combines face-to-face teaching with the multimedia delivery of curricula and assessment over the Internet. It is reaching hundreds of thousands of students and teachers literally from Alaska to Afghanistan. The same core curriculum is shared on a global basis—allowing for economies of scale—but is delivered in different languages. The program enables many students to overcome the constraints of time, distance, and money to develop marketable skills in the networking and information-technology sectors or to prepare for further studies in areas such as engineering, computer science, and related fields. Data collected from the LDC Initiative consistently shows that 75 percent of its graduates are employed in-country after completion of the Cisco Certified Network Association (CCNA) curriculum. The academy provides leading-edge technology and training for schools and other education institutions often in disadvantaged or low-income communities. It also engages and motivates Cisco's employees and helps to build stronger relationships with government bodies and some of the company's business partners around the world.

Two of the strengths of the Cisco Networking Academy Program are its focus on developing countries and gender mainstreaming. The Least Developed Countries Initiative is one of the program's best models of strategic alliance development between the public and private sector. Since its inception in 2000, the initiative has brought together support and investment from different parts of the United Nations, as well as from the U.S. Peace Corps and the U.S. Agency for International Development. These partners have worked together to extend the Networking Academy Program to forty of the world's forty-nine least developed countries. Bringing the program to these countries has allowed their students educational opportunities that are offered to students in the developed world, resulting in assessment scores that are as high, if not higher. In 2000, Cisco Systems and the Cisco Learning Institute also partnered to develop the Gender Initiative, which aims to increase the access of women to IT training and career opportunities. As a result of this targeted campaign, 32 percent of the Networking Academy students in the LDC initiative are female, offering women in these countries the opportunity to develop marketable IT skills.

Alliances are a key factor in making the initiative so successful. Cisco has invested over $200 million in the Cisco Networking Academy Program over the last six years, consisting of money, curricula, equipment, and training. This investment has been leveraged many times by the different products, services, skills, and networks that its partners bring to the table. In addition to the public sector partners mentioned above, others who contribute to the initiative include companies such as Hewlett-Packard, Panduit, Fluke, Adtran, and Lands' End, helping the Networking Academy Program to provide more comprehensive and useful IT education.

ChevronTexaco and USAID's Angola Partnership Initiative

Africa's oil and gas reserves offer great potential for helping to meet the world's growing energy needs while underpinning progress and prosperity for Africa's citizens. Yet the African countries in which these reserves are located offer some of the most challenging political, physical, and economic operating environments anywhere in the world. All too often, oil wealth in Africa has exacerbated poverty and conflict rather than prevented it, and government oil revenues have been diverted from genuine development purposes to fund wars and the personal wealth of political elites. The central challenge for multinational oil companies investing in the continent is to work with governments and develop new types of alliances that will help to turn this negative spiral into a virtuous circle whereby oil production underpins national and community prosperity, as well as corporate profitability.

ChevronTexaco is one of America's largest investors in Africa and has a long-standing presence in Angola, one of the continent's most resource-blessed and yet conflict-torn countries. The company has a strong tradition of building partnerships and sees these as a hallmark of its success in a capital-intensive, technology-driven business that must often operate in difficult conditions. As chairman and CEO Dave O'Reilly describes it, "To us, partnership is not a legal or business term. It is a value. . . . Partnership transcends business—it governs our relationship with our employees, our communities, with governments and with customers. And it has served us well."[10]

In November 2002, the company announced a groundbreaking new partnership in Angola with USAID and the United Nations. The aim of this public–private alliance is to leverage the different assets and resources of the partners to help Angola restart its economy after years of civil war by investing in education, vocational training, and locally owned small and medium-sized business development.

The initiative, which calls for a $50 million commitment over the next five years, will involve the establishment of innovative funding mechanisms, technical assistance, and job creation mechanisms. A parallel partnership between ChevronTexaco and the Discovery Channel Global Education Fund, another example of leadership in responsible business, will provide satellite-linked video equipment and training to some thirty thousand Angolan schoolchildren, many of whom have never owned a book, much less been able to access interactive educational materials. The partners are working with locally based community organizations, business associations, schoolteachers, and government officials to ensure more effective and appropriate service delivery.

This public–private partnership is still in its early days, but it offers a model worth consideration by any large company operating in developing countries. As Holly Wise, the executive director of USAID's Global Development Alliance, observes, "A project of this size and scope lifts our efforts from philanthropy to true sustainable development."[11] For ChevronTexaco, which has invested close to $5 billion in Africa over the past five years, the partnership is another pillar, alongside the company's technological ability and operational expertise, in its efforts to build prosperity in addition to profitability. They will all be crucial in sustaining the company's long-term investment interests and ability to grow. They will also be crucial in ensuring that African oil and gas resources help to meet the development needs of Africa's people, in addition to world energy demand. There is much at stake in this effort, and it would be close to impossible without effective public–private partnership.

TechnoServe and McKinsey & Company

TechnoServe is a U.S.-based nongovernmental organization that aims to help entrepreneurial men and women in Africa and Latin America establish and grow businesses that create income and economic opportunities for their families, their communities, and their countries. McKinsey & Company is one of the world's oldest and most respected management consulting firms. TechnoServe has a staff of about 350 and focuses on those people on the bottom rung of the social ladder in poor countries. McKinsey has around five thousand professional staff and serves the world's largest corporations, operating at the most senior levels of business.

Yet, for the past few years, these two institutions have been developing an increasingly close relationship of mutual benefit, including direct partnering on projects in developing countries. TechnoServe is about bringing business solutions to assist the rural poor of the world—so why not get to the solutions with the support of those who excel in business strategy?

This support gives TechnoServe a significant edge in its work. A number of present and past McKinsey partners sit on its board, its management team includes five ex-McKinsey staff, and over thirty McKinsey consultants have undertaken studies as part of its volunteer program. In addition to helping McKinsey become a better corporate citizen, the partnership creates the opportunity for socially motivated consultants to work with a leading nonprofit in an increasingly familiar environment, and forms one of the core relationships for private-sector development work undertaken by McKinsey's nonprofit practice.

The relationship has also been of significant benefit to TechnoServe's clients in some of the world's poorest countries, who have accessed world-class strategic business thinking they could not normally afford. McKinsey consultants who have participated in the volunteer program agree that they have been exposed to more diverse challenges, been given greater responsibility, and have had a more direct sense of the worth of the work they are doing than at any other point in their consulting careers.

To support the relationship, funding has been raised from various public and private sources. One of the main funders has been USAID, through the provision of a matching grant arrangement to support the volunteers and through GDA funds to support a growing alliance in Mozambique that has recently developed industry strategies to support wood products and ecotourism industries.

As these examples illustrate, USAID and the United Nations are nontraditional but potentially valuable partners for multinational companies. Few companies or individual business leaders are able to emulate the $1 billion donation made to the UN by businessman Ted Turner in 1997, or the multimillion-dollar health partnerships that the Bill and Melinda Gates Foundation has established with the World Health Organization, but there are many other ways that corporations can engage with the United Nations. These range from support for the UN Global Compact, profiled under Principle #6 (governance), to community-based alliances such as those outlined above. We briefly illustrate four other models of engagement below. In different ways these mobilize corporate core competencies, customer relationships, marketing skills, and value chains to help tackle development challenges while offering mutual benefit to the companies and individual business people involved.

Mobilizing Corporate Technical Skills and Technology Microsoft has worked with the UN High Commission on Refugees and with some of its business partners, such as Compaq, Hewlett-Packard, Canon, Kingston Technology, Securit World Ltd, and ScreenCheck B.V., on the *Refugee Registration Project.* This was initiated in response to the Kosovo crisis in 1999, when the UN was struggling to list and reunite millions of refugees. Joined by the company's business partners, Microsoft volunteers helped the UN to design and deploy a refugee registration system. Within months it had enabled close to half a million people to register, making it easier for the UN to reunite families and manage the refugee crisis. The technology is now being used in other crisis situations. It draws on the different skills and resources of the companies and the UN system to deliver an efficient response to what seemed an unsolvable problem.

Harnessing Corporate Marketing and Distribution Expertise In June 2001, Coca-Cola launched a partnership with UNAIDS that mobilizes the company's extensive network of bottling partners and distributors in Africa to support local AIDS programs. The Coca-Cola system is one of the largest private-sector employers in Africa, with distribution networks extending into some of the most remote villages. Building on this extensive outreach and the company's marketing skills, Coca-Cola is working with the UN, governments, and other local partners to raise public awareness by printing and distributing pamphlets and testing kits and developing information campaigns. As a result of this program, people become more aware of Coca-Cola, and at the same time the company is able to help tackle an epidemic that poses serious risks for its long-term business growth in Africa.

Leveraging and Enhancing Customer Relationships Companies in the international airline industry have worked with the UN's fund for children, UNICEF, to develop the *Change for Good* initiative, which collects foreign currency from airline passengers around the world. It is currently run by thirteen airlines, with British Airways playing a leadership role. For the companies involved there is the benefit of improved employee morale, reputation, and customer relationships. Airline passengers are able to contribute with relative ease to a credible organization with coins that often end up at the bottom of a drawer when they get home. At the same time, UNICEF has mobilized over $35 million for children's issues in the past ten years through this program, as well as raised awareness of its brand and its work among international travelers.

Engaging Professional Volunteers in Civic Action Professional service organizations such as Rotary International and Lions, each of which has over a million business and professional members in over 160 countries, have a long-standing tradition of getting individual businesspeople engaged in their local communities. In the 1980s, Rotary made a decision to leverage its global membership network, together with its local presence in thousands of towns and cities, to help the United Nations address a global health challenge—the eradication of polio. Working in partnership with the World Health Organization, the UN's Fund for Children, and more recently the Bill and Melinda Gates Foundation, among others, Rotary established the *PolioPlus* program. This initiative mobilized funds, skills, logistics support, and products from thousands of companies and individual business leaders to fight polio. By the end of 2005 Rotary's financial commitment will be approximately $500 million, plus the support of thousands of Rotary members. In 1988 the polio virus circulated in 125 countries; today the number has fallen to no more than 20. Lions Clubs International has had similar success in programs to prevent blindness and to serve blind or visually impaired people in communities all over the world.

There are thousands of American companies and businesspeople operating internationally. To date, however, few have explored ways to cooperate with the U.S. government or the United Nations to more effectively deploy their social investment dollars, employee volunteer efforts, and other types of product and service donations. As the need to overcome anti-American sentiment grows in many countries around the world, such partnerships can be a cost-effective and efficient way to leverage resources and build trust and legitimacy with local communities many thousands of miles away from corporate headquarters. They can offer new ideas, skills, and resources to people in these communities. They can circumvent bureaucracy. They can reach directly to the people who will benefit most from support. By getting involved, American business can play a role in helping to make the world a more prosperous and secure place. And these programs can help build long-term markets and business relationships at the same time.

In recent years American business leaders have put their names and their companies' resources behind visionary initiatives such as *Business Strengthening America,* which aims to increase the number of businesses and employees engaged in service and civic activities, and the *Committee to Encourage Corporate Philanthropy,* which aims to lead the private sector to new, more strategic and measurable levels of corporate philanthropy. We believe the same levels of excellence and energy can be applied to mobilizing American and other multinational corporate philanthropy for more strategic impact in developing countries. There are already some encouraging models in networks, such as the Seattle Initiative for Global Development, the International Business Leaders Forum, the Corporate Council on Africa, and the Global Business Coalition against HIV/AIDS. Yet there is room for greater action.

We are not suggesting that business should be depended upon to solve international development problems. Clearly, governments and politicians need to take the lead. As Bill Gates has argued, "Foreign aid and foundation giving can achieve important advances, but the big examples of national success have all required political leadership."[12] Far and away the greatest contribution that business can make to developing countries is through mainstream business investment and trade. The private sector can still play a meaningful role, however, through partnership-based philanthropy, as Cisco Systems, Microsoft, McKinsey, Coca-Cola, British Airways, and others have demonstrated. These companies, together with individual business leaders like Ted Turner and Bill Gates and the thousands of businesspeople living in developing countries, offer an inspiration and model for others.

Three: Use Alliances to Shape Progressive Public Policy

New cross-sector or multistakeholder alliances can also have a major impact on public policy. Governments no longer have all the answers—if they ever did. As a result, business, academia, and civic organizations have much to offer in helping governments to shape more progressive and effective public policy. This partnership-based approach lends itself to tackling a wide range of public policy issues, many of which may not be crucial to an individual company's immediate business interests but have major implications for the long-term success of the private sector. Examples include education reform; tackling the digital divide; addressing Welfare to Work; health care; homeland security; smart growth; urban sprawl; crime; drugs; and a variety of environmental issues.

Business has always influenced public policy—both overtly and covertly, legitimately and less so. In a world where there are growing demands on companies to be more transparent and accountable in terms of both their own operations and their relationships with governments, there is a need for new types of partnership and governance structures. We profile some of these new approaches under Principle #6 (governance). Two other examples of partnership-driven approaches to public policy are illustrated below. One is aimed at policies to bridge the digital divide at the global level, and the second is aimed at policy innovations to improve corporate environmental performance at the national level.

The Digital Opportunities Task Force: A Global Public Policy Network

The Digital Opportunities Task Force (DOT Force) was jointly launched by government leaders of the United States, Canada, the United Kingdom, France, Germany, Italy, Japan, and Russia in 2000. Its aim was to review and make policy recommendations on how information and communication technology can bring opportunities to developing countries and help to bridge the widening global socioeconomic divide. The task force's structure was unprecedented. The governments agreed to create a group consisting of not only public officials, but also business leaders, academics, and nonprofit organizations. During the first year Vernon Ellis, international chairman of Accenture, chaired the private-sector delegation, which also included leaders from companies such as Hewlett-Packard, Siemens, Toshiba, Thomson, Telesystem, and Microsoft. The opinions and proposals of the corporate participants and other groups were then debated, and a consensus was built around a set of nine core recommendations for policy-makers.

These recommendations now have the potential to influence international policy-making, aid strategy, and even trade discussions. Accenture and other participating companies are now focusing their resources and efforts on helping governments and nongovernmental partners to implement, through practical on-the-ground projects, some of the key action points set out in the DOT Force implementation plan. For example, Accenture has worked with Hewlett-Packard and Telesystem to create a new nonprofit organization, Enablis, specifically to create digital opportunities. With initial funding from the government of Canada, Enablis supports entreprenurs and small- and medium-sized businesses that are developing or utilizing ICTs in their business. Accenture has, in partnership, provided the business and technical skills to make Enablis happen. In 2002, Accenture Development Partnerships was established. This group works with NGOs, foundations, and donor organizations, offering them the firm's management and technology consultation skills on a not-for-profit basis, aiming to help them achieve their social and economic development goals.

The potential for companies to get engaged on a pro bono basis in such new alliances at both the global public-policy level and the local project level is enormous. And there is a sound business case for doing so. As Vernon Ellis sees it:

> It seems to me that the increasing efforts being made by business to help build digital bridges actually reflect the emergence of a more sophisticated approach by both business and government. Governments increasingly recognize society's interest in having a successful business sector, and business recognizes that in the long term it can only pursue its own self-interest by ensuring that it is also serving the interests of the wider society. This new environment offers an unprecedented opportunity for a genuine partnership between government, civil society and business.[13]

The EPA's Partners for the Environment Program

Instead of simply lobbying against more regulation, the private sector can work in partnership with government to create a more efficient, and often more effective, enabling framework that includes some regulation but also moves beyond compliance to more collaborative ways of solving problems. Through its Partners for the Environment program, which includes some forty different initiatives, the U.S. Environmental Protection Agency (EPA) collaborates with over eleven thousand organizations, ranging from small and large businesses and trade associations to citizens' groups, local and state governments, and universities. Together these groups are using voluntary goals and commitments to achieve measurable results, both for industry and the environment. And they are doing so in a timely, competitive, and cost-effective manner.

Developing and implementing sound regulations remains central to the EPA's mission and its public mandate. At the same time, however, it is exploring new mutually beneficial and voluntary ways to work with business to improve environmental performance beyond traditional regulation. As the EPA states, "Innovation is key to environmental progress. From voluntary partnerships to market-based incentives to new technologies, we are testing a variety of ideas and approaches."[14] Among them are voluntary, performance-driven programs such as WasteWise, Energy STAR, and Performance Track, all of which assess and publicly recognize the top environmental performers in industry and encourage all companies to go beyond compliance with regulatory requirements.

The EPA's Performance Track program, for example, operates in a way that encourages competition for "best-in-class" performance, offers access to technical advice, keeps things simple, and lowers transaction costs. This partnership-driven approach makes sound business sense for the participating companies. It offers the leading companies strategic business opportunities. Companies that qualify for this and other programs, for example, not only benefit in terms of reputation and an EPA stamp of approval. They are also more likely to be suppliers and partners of choice and less likely to incur heavy costs from compliance monitoring and regulation. At the same time, the government is able to mobilize the skills, technologies, problem-solving orientation, and R&D capabilities of the private sector to advance national environmental objectives. This does not preclude the need for regulation, but it helps the leading companies to move beyond a compliance mindset, thereby freeing up public and private resources to create mutually beneficial and innovative results while enabling the regulators to focus their efforts on the corporate laggards.

Four: Focus on Purpose, Process, and Progress

Building cross-sector alliances is not easy. This is the case even when partners come from the same sector or country, let alone when a company is trying to build cross-sector, multicultural partnerships. Successful alliances require a difficult balance of idealism and pragmatism. They require a meeting of self-interest and mutual benefit. They require vision and a strong sense of mission, combined with practical and often frustrating hard work. They require demonstrable results if they are to survive, but at the same time persistence and patience when results are not forthcoming. Even if they are based on a strong commitment to principles, they must also reflect a willingness to accept, respect, and respond to other perspectives and different ways of doing things.

It is not surprising that many alliances fail to live up to expectations. Apart from the need for partners to overcome lack of knowledge about and in some cases mistrust of each other, there are numerous practical and cultural barriers. These include differing missions, management systems, governance structures, operating methodologies, communications mechanisms, time frames, and autonomy in decision-making. Different decision-making and accountability structures are also sometimes a problem.

Despite these challenges there are hundreds of examples—local, national, and global—to demonstrate that successful cross-sector alliances *are* possible. In most cases these successful alliances are built around a clear sense of purpose, with mutual benefit, a rigorous focus on process management, an ability to evaluate progress, and strategies for exit when necessary. These goals are not easy to achieve. Some will be more important than others, depending on the partners, their purpose, and their circumstances. There is no standard, one-size-fits-all blueprint. It is crucial to invest time up front—especially when pairing with nontraditional partners or past adversaries. Dialogue must be regular and constant. It is especially critical at the outset in order to build trust and establish a foundation for moving forward.

Our closing alliance example profiles Unilever and illustrates how one company is building new alliances to enhance its own performance and sustainability while also working with others to tackle global and local development challenges. The example conveys the management complexity and skills required to engage in constructive win–win partnerships. It illustrates as well the potential for business–government–civil society collaboration as a mechanism for tackling some of the major challenges facing society in the twenty-first century.

UNILEVER
Building Sustainable Supply Chains and
Meeting Consumer Needs Through New Alliances

Not all consumers are familiar with the Unilever name, but about 150 million people around the world choose its brands every day. These include Lipton, Knorr, Hellmann's, Ben & Jerry's, Bertolli, Skippy, Magnum, Dove, Lux, Pond's, and Vaseline, to name a few of the four hundred leading brands on which the company aims to focus its future growth. Unilever's strategy is to be multilocal, understanding and responding to local needs and cultures, and sourcing and manufacturing as much as possible within the regions where its customers are located. The company's statement of corporate purpose starts with its core mission to meet the everyday needs and anticipate the aspirations of its customers and consumers, with the goal of delivering creative and competitive branded products and services that raise the quality of life.

More than two-thirds of the raw materials used by the company are sourced from agriculture, and it is among the world's largest users of certain products such as tea, vegetables, vegetable oils, and whitefish. In order to ensure long-term accessibility of these critical raw materials, Unilever has started to integrate the concept of environmental sustainability and social responsibility into its core business model, in terms of both reducing the environmental impact of its own manufacturing operations and tackling these issues in the wider supply chain.

The company sees this in part as the right thing to do, based on its long-standing Code of Business Principles. These were revised in 2001 as part of the company's ongoing efforts to make them relevant to a changing world and embed them in the daily reality of its global operations. It also sees this approach to corporate responsibility as a hard-edged commercial imperative, one that is full of dilemmas, tough choices, and the growing need for new types of alliance. As cochairman Niall FitzGerald describes it:

> *Sustainability, that wedding between economic growth, environmental protection and social progress poses challenging questions for an enterprise such as ours. How can we procure fish from sustainable sources and at the same time promote the living conditions of small-scale fishermen in Spain or Greece? Can we apply gene-technology in products and at the same time protect the environment? Can we book economic growth in India and create jobs by producing and selling more detergents without environmental impact?[15]*

None of these questions is easy to answer, and most of them are impossible for any one company or organization to tackle on its own, no matter how global it is in terms of its operations and marketing reach. Unilever recognized at the outset that it needed to learn from and work in partnership with others. New types of alliance have been especially important in helping the company to manage environmental and social impacts along its global supply chains and in finding ways to serve low-income consumers in a manner that genuinely meets their needs, while building long-term markets and profitability for the company.

Unilever's leadership role in working with others to establish the independent Marine Stewardship Council is one example of how the company is aiming to meet the needs and aspirations of its customers in a profitable and sustainable manner not only today but into the future.

Partnerships to Support Sustainable Fisheries

The world's fish stocks are under threat. While global consumption of fish and fishery products has risen by 240 percent since 1960 and continues to grow, the catch of popular fish such as tuna, haddock, cod, and flounder has plunged by more than half during the past fifty years.[16] According to the United Nations, nearly three-quarters of the world's major fisheries are fully exploited, overexploited, or depleted. This has significant implications not only for the diets of millions of people around the world, but also for the environment and for the economic livelihoods of over 100 million people who work along the fish supply chain. Governments must take the lead in addressing this international challenge, but there is also an opportunity for consumers, companies, nongovernmental organizations, and fishing communities to work together in the search for solutions.

Unilever is one of the world's largest buyers of fish, and it recognized both the threat to sustainable fish supplies and the need for partnership in the early 1990s. Despite its size and market position, the company processes less than 1 percent of the world's fish catch and realized it could not tackle the challenge on its own. As a consumer-driven company, it looked at ways to mobilize market forces and consumer choice as one route toward more sustainable fishing. It figured that if consumers were given a choice about the fish they were buying and could be certain that labeled fish was produced in well-managed fisheries, it may be possible to use this information to differentiate between brands, attracting either increased loyalty of existing customers or increased numbers of new customers. Partnership was needed to take this idea forward.

In 1995, Unilever met with an environmental organization, the WWF—Worldwide Fund for Nature. The WWF had recently established the Forest Stewardship Council with the forestry sector, and it agreed to work in partnership with Unilever to set up the Marine Stewardship Council (MSC). At first glance, the MSC's founders seem unlikely organizations to form a strategic alliance. The WWF is one of the world's largest privately supported conservation organizations, with more than one million members in the United States alone and an active environmental campaigning program. Unilever is one of the world's major consumer goods businesses, with operations in over one hundred countries and food, household, and personal care products purchased by over 150 million people each day. Despite their different backgrounds and the contrast between the WWF's nonprofit motivation and Unilever's commercial nature, both are organizations with a clear sense of purpose and strong principles, combined with a shared interest in ensuring the long-term viability, quality, and sustainability of fish and other food supplies.

Their common goal was to establish an independent fisheries certification scheme that would offer supermarket customers a reliable, responsible, and high-quality option for purchasing fish sourced from sustainable fisheries. Unilever and the WWF brought different skills, knowledge, and networks to the partnership. Unilever emphasized its serious intent by making a public commitment to source all of its own fish from sustainable fisheries by 2005. Together they undertook a global consultation process. This included discussions with environmental and marine experts, scientists, fishing industry representatives, government officials and regulators, and consumer groups. At times it was difficult to get all the necessary players around the table. Some governments, for example, were initially wary of this private-led initiative. The partners persevered, and the process resulted in a set of broad principles and operating criteria that provide a framework for promoting environmentally and economically viable fishing.

In 1998, the Marine Stewardship Council became an independent accreditation body, separate from both Unilever and the WWF. Today it has its own governance structure, sets widely accepted voluntary standards, and provides a reliable marketing logo for sustainable fisheries. It is evolving into an innovative market-driven alliance that brings together—at times with some difficulty—a varied group of organizations operating at different stages and in different ways along the global fish supply chain. These range from fisheries and fishing fleets to manufacturers, retailers, and restaurants, as well as consumer groups, fish marketing bodies, and environmental organizations. Together they are helping to mobilize the power of the market and to influence consumer choice in tackling the serious decline in the world's fish stocks.

Certified fish products from the MSC first appeared in 2000 and now include fish from places as diverse as Alaska and New Zealand. The Alaska Salmon Fishery was the first U.S. fishery to be certified by the MSC and remains one of the largest. According to Rob Bosworth, deputy commissioner of the Alaska Department of Fish and Game, "Salmon processors believe the MSC label can provide Alaska salmon with a competitive advantage."[17] In turn this will help to maintain the small communities, fishing fleets, and family businesses that are at the heart of Alaska's fishing business.

At the retail end of the supply chain, in addition to Unilever itself, partners include major companies such as Whole Foods Market, the world's largest retailer of natural and organic foods, and Xanterra Parks and Resorts, America's largest park and resort management company. Over the past couple of decades, both of these companies have built a reputation for good quality, good value, and a strong customer focus, underpinned by missions that publicly commit them to achieving profitable growth in a manner that is environmentally sustainable. They have demonstrated impressive results despite the economic downturn and increased competition of the past few years and they are well positioned for future growth. At the same time, they have emerged as industry leaders in building effective and efficient partnerships along their respective supply chains. The MSC is becoming a valued partner to both of them, and they are now offering their customers MSC-certified Alaskan salmon. They are also supporting consumer awareness campaigns in partnership with the MSC, the WWF, the Alaska Seafood Marketing Institute, and the Chef's Collaborative, a national network of more than a thousand members of America's culinary community.

For companies like Unilever, Whole Foods Market, and Xanterra, involvement in the Marine Stewardship Council is spurred not by philanthropy or a "nice-to-do" mind-set but by hard-edged business logic. It is a logic that is driven by the need, on one hand, to secure sustainable sources of high-quality raw materials and food products from suppliers, and, on the other hand, to respond to changing consumer needs and aspirations.

From a consumer perspective, all three companies are poised to take advantage of significant demographic trends such as aging baby boomers and environmentally aware Generation Xers in their twenties, thirties, and forties. Both of these economically and numerically significant groups of consumers are driving increased consumer interest in health, well-being, and quality of life. This desire is turning natural and organic products, as well as other healthy food and beverage options, into one of the fastest-growing segments of the food retailing industry. It is also raising consumer awareness of the importance of ecologically sensitive and sustainable food chains. Fish products offer an excellent example of this equation between a growing consumer interest in high-quality, good-value, healthy foods and an interest in ensuring that the source of these foods is reliable and sustainable.

Thus the original dialogue between Unilever and the WWF has evolved into a worldwide, market-driven certification body supported by a multifaceted network of alliances among companies, environmental groups, government bodies, chefs, and educators. These alliances have started, in a small but progressive manner, to change the relationship between fish production and consumption. They have raised awareness, created new momentum among a group of diverse stakeholders from fish producers to fish consumers, and helped to foster practical standards that meet both economic and environmental criteria. More than one hundred fish-processing companies, traders, and retailers from over twenty countries now support the Marine Stewardship Council, and as of 2003 over a hundred products carried the MSC logo.

As for Unilever, it can demonstrate that it is buying more than a third of its fish from sustainable sources and some 6 percent from MSC-certified fisheries. The company remains committed to sourcing all its supplies from sustainable fisheries, but the complex nature of global fish supplies and a lower-than-expected response by consumers have made its original aim of realizing this goal by 2005 difficult to achieve. This illustrates the systemic nature of the challenge and the fact that no one sector or organization can solve complex global challenges without cooperation from others.

The Marine Stewardship Council is still in its early days, and neither the environmental nor commercial success of the initiative is assured. This will depend not only on its own efforts and ability to keep certifying and monitoring fisheries and building marketing and awareness-raising alliances, but also on the efforts of governments and the willingness of consumers to make purchasing choices that support a sustainable fish industry.

Both the WWF and Unilever agree that having clear ground rules was essential to the partnership's success. These included common working principles; transparent goals; agreed boundaries; an inclusive, participatory approach, which may be slow, but is essential when wider support is needed; and a coordinated rollout of initiatives, which discourages individual partners from seeking short-term, personal advantage outside the partnership.

Partnerships to Reach Low-Income Consumers

New types of alliance are also central to Unilever's growing commitment to deliver reliable, high-quality, cost-effective products to low-income communities, especially in developing countries. A variety of market-driven initiatives are under way to ensure that the packaging, pricing, and distribution of certain products makes them more accessible and provides genuine value for low-income consumers.

This approach is not simply about "doing good." Although it aligns closely with Unilever's statement of corporate purpose to responsibly "meet the everyday needs of people everywhere," it is about investing in the company's long-term competitive edge and market growth. Branded goods that respond to local needs and income capacities can offer low-income consumers reliable and safe choices and make a measurable difference in the quality of people's lives. At the same time, these people represent massive market potential, given that four out of five of the world's citizens live in the developing world.

As *Business Week,* among others, has observed, "Companies such as Unilever, Philips, Coca-Cola, and Motorola are finding that a focus on low prices, miniature sizes and simple to-use products may be the secrets to business success in developing nations where most of the world's population dwells. . . . All these efforts are aimed at what could well be the biggest source of economic growth in the coming decades: the two-thirds of the global population now making $1,500 or less annually."[18] In an August 2002 cover story, *Business Week* identified this trend—"small is profitable"—as one of the twenty-five best new ideas for a changing world. Unilever's deep-seated commitment to building local roots and its focus on serving the needs of consumers are helping it get ahead of the game, with the result that its business has almost doubled in developing countries in the past dozen years.

In India, for example, Hindustan Lever's sales in rural areas now represent close to 50 percent of its $2 billion-plus annual turnover. The company started its strategy of reaching out to rural communities back in the late 1980s. Since then it has worked with local communities and consumer groups to develop products that can be purchased in small units at a few cents apiece. Examples include low-cost tooth powder and fortified staple foods such as salt enriched with iodine and flour enriched with extra iron and vitamins. Hindustan Lever has innovated not only in terms of product development, but also in unconventional media and marketing techniques and creative distribution networks to reach rural communities, many of them located in India's 600,000 villages, which are difficult to access both physically and by the usual media channels. As part of the company's management trainee program, its Business Leadership Trainees, who include some of the country's most privileged and successful university graduates, spend four weeks living and working in low-income rural villages. The experience aims to challenge their assumptions, build leadership and teamwork skills, and encourage them to improvise, innovate, and collaborate. At the same time, they gain a better understanding of the opportunities and constraints of rural markets and low-income consumers.

This grassroots partnership-based approach to sales has the potential to benefit small business and microenterprises, as well as low-income consumers. In Tanzania, for example, Unilever has over 100,000 retail outlets in more than nine thousand widely dispersed villages. It has set up an innovative "bicycle brigade" of previously unemployed salespeople. These people are able to serve their local communities with products that are sold in small units for the equivalent of a few cents. A year after the launch of this initiative in 1999, its affordability and availability earned it an estimated 10 percent market share.[19] It also created new jobs, returning wealth back to local communities while building the company's value proposition and its outreach to consumers.

Building a Partnership-based Approach

Consistent and structured efforts at consultation, collaboration, and communication with a wide variety of stakeholders, including critics, lie at the core of Unilever's approach to building the partnerships we have outlined in this profile. This is underpinned by the company's ongoing efforts to increase the transparency and rigor of its measurement and public reporting of its financial, social, and environmental performance.

Unilever's commitment to partnerships is focused on its core competencies and business activities. Like most companies, it is active in community investment, mostly led and carried out at the level of the company's local operating units, but it sees its responsibility to society as first and foremost being about how it runs its core business. As the company states in its annual review of 2002, "We regard the very business of doing business in a responsible and sustainable way as the core of our corporate responsibility: selling products that meet local consumers' needs, investing in productive capacity, spreading our technical know-how, working in partnerships through the value chain and in local communities, and making environmental responsibility a central business practice."[20] Linked to this, the company emphasizes the crucial social responsibility of remaining profitable and viable as an economic entity in order to make a wider contribution to development.

Cochairman Niall FitzGerald concluded in his address to the company's shareholders at its 2002 annual meeting:

> Businesses really can help to tackle wider social, economic and environmental challenges—not least by providing professional, technical and scientific expertise. Governments, business and nongovernmental organizations need to work together—and to see business as part of the solution, not just part of the problem. . . . But in all this we remain aware of our commitment to our shareholders and our responsibility to increase your prosperity. Our authority in the area of social contribution and—more importantly—the resources can only come from running a consistently successful, growing and profitable business.[21]

Engaging in New Alliances

One: Build alliances to enhance the core business proposition.

Two: Harness alliances to leverage philanthropy.

Three: Use alliances to shape progressive public policy.

Four: Focus on purpose, process, and progress.

Be Performance-Driven in Everything

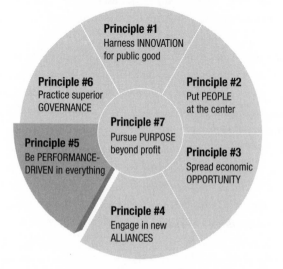

Great companies are performance-driven in everything they do. They implement management structures, systems, and tools to achieve excellence in all key areas of their corporate performance—ethical, social, environmental, as well as financial.

The performance-driven company has strong "buy-in" at the top from its board of directors and senior management team. It sets clear targets and rigorous metrics to drive and evaluate performance and makes a public commitment to achieving these targets. It reports publicly on progress and is committed to continuous learning as a way to drive improvement.

Performance-driven companies not only demonstrate corporate effectiveness, but also create a framework for improved accountability, thereby establishing a basis for greater trust between the company and its stakeholders.

Why Being
Performance-Driven Matters

We should ask whether a more multi-dimensional definition of success is required. Management should be evaluated on what it can control—the fundamental economic performance of the business and the institutional strength of the organization. It should set financial and nonfinancial goals and assess risks with an eye toward the long-term total value of the enterprise. A more balanced view of success, and the time over which it is measured, would ultimately serve shareholders and society better by encouraging more innovation and growth.

IAN DAVIS, MANAGING DIRECTOR,

MCKINSEY & COMPANY, 2003

Leading companies recognize that innovation and mutually beneficial relationships with their various stakeholders are critical drivers of value in today's competitive global economy. They see the potential to integrate ethical, social, and environmental considerations as well as economic and financial imperatives into their innovation efforts and their stakeholder relationships. They have a vision of what they want to achieve and clear values and principles that set the parameters for how they will achieve it. At the same time, they understand that no amount of good intentions or lofty aspirations will make a difference unless these are at the operational heart of the business and integrated into corporate strategy and performance systems. As Lou Gerstner, the former CEO of IBM, has argued in his book *Who Says Elephants Can't Dance?* "Vision statements are for the most part aspirational, and they play a role in creating commitment and excitement among an institution's employees. But in and of themselves they are useless in terms of pointing out how the institution is going to turn an aspirational goal into reality."[1]

Turning aspirations into reality requires having a clear strategy and the ability to execute it efficiently and effectively. It means setting ambitious public targets and then delegating the details and decision-making on how to meet these targets to the people closest to the action: those employees closest to the customers and the communities where the company operates. It requires the development of key performance indicators and metrics to measure progress against these targets. It means taking risks within clear parameters for what is acceptable behavior. It calls for the establishment of incentive systems that are aligned with what the company says it stands for, cares about, and aims to achieve. It means reporting progress to internal and external audiences, explaining where the company is going and why. And it requires an ability to learn from both failure and success, to adapt and to move forward. In short, visions need to be anchored by performance-oriented strategies and management systems that drive ethical, social, and environmental, as well as financial performance. The global telecommunications company BT describes its strategy as follows:

> *Our corporate strategy is a commitment to our shareholders, our customers, our people and the communities in which we operate. It makes plain how we plan to create shareholder value, how we will meet customers' needs and how we will manage and reward the people who work for the company. Our strategy defines us. It tells the world what we are about and what can be expected of us.*[2]

What are some of the specific steps and management tools that leading companies are adopting to become more performance-driven, not only in their financial performance, but also in their ethical, social, and environmental performance? What are they doing to "walk the talk" and build credibility among their stakeholders through delivering what they promise?

Making It Happen

Four of the key steps that characterize performance-driven companies are: getting commitment at the top of the company; setting clear targets and metrics to drive and evaluate performance; reporting publicly on progress; and committing to continuous learning.

One: Get Commitment at the Top

Individual champions and change agents are important at all levels of the company, but top leadership is crucial. A strategic commitment to deliver outstanding ethical, social, and environmental performance in addition to financial performance will never be part of the corporate strategy and culture unless it matters to the "top team," meaning:

- The board of directors

- The senior executive group

- The key operational managers—heads of business units and country or regional directors who have responsibility for specific geographic areas, businesses, product lines, or plants

Getting the steadfast commitment and serious buy-in of these groups is essential.

Put It on the Boardroom Agenda Almost without exception, the leadership companies profiled in this book have a board-level committee or a director with responsibility for addressing the company's wider societal performance and conformance. We look at some of these arrangements in our discussion of Principle #6 (governance). The names and mandates of these committees vary, but they play an increasingly important role. So, the first indicator of whether a company is serious about being performance-driven in everything is whether these issues are explicitly on the boardroom agenda.

Integrate It into Executive Structures In addition to a focus at the board level, credibility in terms of being performance-driven requires the senior executive team to take responsibility for addressing the following questions:

- How often does the team carry out a systematic assessment of the business risks and opportunities associated with the ethical, social, and environmental issues most relevant to the company?

- Can each member of the executive team readily identify these broader societal issues? Can they make a sound business case about why they matter to the company and its industry sector?

- Does the executive team keep updated and informed on key trends in these areas, especially those that are not currently on the corporate radar screen?

- What tools is the team using to keep ahead of the game? For example, is it using scenario planning, stakeholder dialogues, opinion-leader surveys, benchmarking, learning networks? How can these be made more challenging, more rigorous?

- Is responsibility for managing risks and identifying opportunities in these areas of ethical, social, and environmental performance integrated into the executive team's individual performance targets and appraisals?

- What role does performance against these issues have in succession planning, executive coaching, and executive development programs?

- How prominently and regularly are these issues featured on the agendas of executive team meetings and executive retreats?

- How often does the executive team revisit and critically test the company's statement of purpose, its values, and its principles or codes of conduct?

Make It Relevant to Key Operational Managers The business risks and opportunities created by ethical, social, and environmental issues are usually realized and managed at the operational level—by individual business units, product managers, country managers, and plant managers. Operational directors therefore have a key role in identifying and managing these risks and in identifying and capitalizing on opportunities. They also have ultimate responsibility for the day-to-day implementation of the company's business principles and codes of conduct. Together with the CEO they are often the company's public face to the world. They also serve as a vital source of information on local issues and trends and a source of new ideas and innovations.

Leading companies are putting various compliance and incentive systems in place to enable their operational teams to more effectively address the company's wider societal impacts and manage its wider stakeholder relationships. Here are a few of the good practices followed by the companies profiled in this book:

Letters of responsibility: Require country managers to sign an annual letter of responsibility or assurance for distributing and implementing the company's business principles or code of conduct, as Shell, Unilever, Anglo American, and Rio Tinto do.

Forums for debate: Provide opportunities for operational managers to rigorously debate the company's business code and principles and discuss how they apply these to their own functions, products, or locations, as Johnson & Johnson does.

Integration into existing systems: Ask line managers how they can integrate ethical, social, and environmental issues into existing management systems and tools, such as Total Quality Management and Balanced Scorecards, or how they can rethink management structures to better accommodate these issues, as Shell has done in developing its integrated Sustainable Development Management Framework or STMicroelectronics has with its Total Quality Environmental Management (TQEM) strategy.

Testing societal risks and opportunities: Encourage operational managers to test the societal risks and opportunities of new product development, sourcing, manufacturing, and marketing activities and integrate due diligence criteria into operating guidelines in each of these areas. Companies such as DuPont, Novartis, P&G,

and Starbucks are all doing this. Take a product life cycle approach for assessing social and environmental risks and opportunities, as P&G, Nike, GM, Ford, and Toyota are doing.

▓ *Stakeholder advisory councils:* Encourage country managers or plant managers to establish their own local or national stakeholder advisory councils as Dow Chemical and Alcoa are doing.

▓ *Internal markets and incentives:* Create internal markets or incentive structures for operational-level innovation, such as BP's internal emissions trading program, Suez Group's innovation awards, Nokia's venure capital funds, or the Siemens 3i program.

▓ *Employee engagement:* Encourage country managers and business unit heads to support employee engagement activities in local communities. American Express, Levi Strauss, IBM, J&J, Diageo, GE, and Microsoft offer examples of good practice in this area.

Two: Set Clear Targets and Metrics

Clear targets and metrics are critical tools for translating visions and strategies into action and results. There are two main reasons why a company invests time, intellectual capital, and money in setting targets and metrics for its wider ethical, social, and environmental performance:

▓ *Explicit targets and measurements help companies internally to drive toward meeting their strategic objectives and mission.* They provide managers with vital information for decision-making, planning, resource and asset allocation, performance evaluation, and continuous improvement.

▓ *Targets and measurements help companies externally to secure their legitimacy and acceptance with external stakeholders.* They help to provide investors and creditors with the information needed to attract capital. They provide governments with information to demonstrate compliance with laws and regulations; consumers with information to promote product quality, safety, and differentiation; and communities and the general public with information to gain societal acceptance and to protect the corporate brand and the company's reputation.

Despite their critical importance, targets and metrics are insufficient or inadequate in most companies. There is growing consensus that the business community faces major challenges and shortfalls in terms of the current measures used by companies to drive, assess, and improve their performance. This is the case even when it comes to driving financial performance, let alone wider ethical, social, and environmental performance.

The core measurement challenge that business faces can be stated as follows: Traditional financial accounting-based measures that look back at past financial performance are no longer sufficient to meet corporate information needs in a complex, knowledge-based, global economy where intangible assets and wider societal issues have a growing impact on corporate risk and performance. They are no longer sufficient to give corporate executives and managers the internal information they need to drive their business forward and act responsibly. Nor are they sufficient for external reporting purposes, which are crucial for building public trust and investor confidence. The challenge is not only a question of increasing transparency, honesty, and integrity in providing relevant information on company performance. It is also a question of what type of performance is reported and what measures are used.

These challenges have been outlined in research reports by business organizations such as the Conference Board and by international professional services firms such as KPMG and Pricewaterhouse-Coopers (PWC):

■ In its report *Communicating Corporate Performance,* the Conference Board identified the following shortfalls with traditional accounting-based measures of corporate performance: they are too historical; they lack predictive power; they reward the wrong behavior; they are focused on inputs rather than outputs; they do not capture key business changes until it is too late; they reflect functions, not cross-functional processes within a company; and they give inadequate consideration to items such as intellectual capital that are difficult to quantify.[3]

■ In 2001, KPMG carried out an extensive *Performance Management Study,* which surveyed senior U.S. and European executives. Among many useful findings was the following: "In addition to problems with technology, the organizational leaders KPMG surveyed believe their current measurement systems are: not aligned with strategic business objectives; dependent on lagging, not leading, indicators; poorly integrated with other information (internal and external); and far too reliant on financial measures."[4]

■ In 2002, PWC carried out a survey of 140 U.S. companies representing approximately $2.5 trillion in annual revenues. The results showed 89 percent of respondents believed that in five years there will be more emphasis on sustainable development issues than today, and 72 percent rated its importance to their business as 6 or higher on a scale of 1 to 10. Yet only 28 percent claim to incorporate the opportunities and risks associated with sustainability into their business strategies or project, investment, and transaction evaluation processes.[5]

There is little dispute among the world's major accounting and professional services firms and among leading companies that a new generation of performance measures and measurement tools is needed to monitor progress, improve performance, support competitiveness, and enhance accountability in an increasingly complex world. What these metrics and tools will look like in practice is the critical question. In the past five years, there has been an explosion in new measurement tools and management frameworks aimed at addressing some of these needs. A few of the approaches and tools that companies are using to assess and improve their nonfinancial performance are summarized in the box on page 231.

These emerging performance measurement tools have spawned hundreds of books and studies. They are driving numerous consulting practices and feeding into countless surveys and investor questionnaires that are being targeted at companies. The array of options and new ap-

Tools for Evaluating Performance

Performance Evaluation Approach and Tools	Examples
Investment-driven screening and rating systems	Dow Jones Sustainability Index; FTSE4Good; Domini 400 Social Index; Innovest ECO21; GMI Corporate Governance ratings; S&P; Moody's; CERES Principles
Certification standards and accreditation processes—usually undertaken on a specific site or physical location	ISO9000; ISO14000; EMAS; SA8000; Forest Stewardship Council; Marine Stewardship Council; Fair Labor Association; Ethical Trading Initiative
Process frameworks–to help companies develop management and reporting systems to integrate ethical, social, and environmental measures and stakeholder engagement into their mainstream business processes	The Global Reporting Initiative and the AA1000 assurance standards
Benchmarking and ranking—internal benchmarking against confidential data or external public surveys and rankings	Opinion surveys such as *Fortune*'s Most Admired Companies; FT Most Respected Companies; Business in the Community Corporate Responsibility Index; Boston College Community Benchmarking; London Benchmarking Group; stakeholder surveys, i.e., employee and customer surveys
Broader analytical frameworks	Kaplan and Norton's Balanced Scorecard; Skandia's Navigator tool and other systems for measuring intellectual capital; Stern Stewart and Co.'s Economic Value-Added model; KPMG's Value Explorer framework; PWC's ValueReporting framework; the Baldridge Quality Management framework; the European Foundation for Quality Management; the SIGMA project; and the Sustainable Business Value Model, developed by SustainAbility Ltd.
Learning networks—formal or informal networks within or across industry sectors that enable companies to share practices, lessons, and experiences, visit each other's sites, etc.	The UN Global Compact; the Conference Board's task forces; the Global Sullivan Principles; the Caux Roundtable; Society for Organizational Learning

Source: Updated from J. Nelson, *Building Competitiveness and Communities*, 1998

proaches can be confusing and frustrating for business, but they are unlikely to disappear. Companies that stay ahead of the game will be better positioned to drive continuous improvement in their performance
and respond to growing investor and stakeholder demands for more information. They will also be prepared for the mandatory requirements
for reporting on ethical, social, and environmental performance that are
likely to emerge from stock exchanges and governments in the coming
decade.

What are leading companies doing to address the challenge of identifying clear targets and metrics to evaluate their ethical, social, and environmental performance? What are the lessons for other companies?

Define What Issues Matter Most to You—and What Needs to Be Targeted and Measured

Ask what social and environmental issues are likely to create the greatest risks and opportunities for your company's shareholder performance and long-term competitive positioning. Focus relentlessly on
these, while still keeping your eyes on the radar screen for emerging issues. Leadership companies invest time not only in competitor analysis
and assessment of key market, economic, and political trends, but also
in analyses of key social and environmental trends. Shell's Scenario
Planning exercises offer a good example. Leading companies carry out
extensive stakeholder analysis, beyond just customers and investors, to
understand changing societal expectations and learn what key groups
expect of business and of their own company in particular. Examples
profiled in this book include Dow Chemical's Environmental Advisory
Council and DuPont's Biodiversity Advisory Council.

Once You Have Decided Where to Focus, Set Clear Targets and Make Them Public

Communicate these targets clearly and consistently through the company, along the value chain, and to the public. DuPont's "The Goal is
Zero" commitment and its metrics on shareholder value per pound (to
assess the environmental footprint of its core products) are examples of
setting public targets and metrics. As DuPont's chief financial officer,
Gary Pfeiffer, observes, "The progress we have made to date has been

driven by aggressive goals."[6] Other notable examples of clear targets include Alcoa's "zero injuries and illnesses" target, and BP's and Shell's public commitments in 1998 to cut greenhouse gas emissions from their operations in a set period of time. Also, there is Citigroup's $115 billion commitment to increase lending to low-income communities and Fannie Mae's 2001 American Dream Commitment, a $2 trillion public pledge to increase home ownership rates and serve eighteen million families by the end of the decade. Regardless of industry sector, any company can define what matters most in its societal performance and set public targets that commit it to achieving progress within a set period of time.

Identify Key Performance Indicators or Metrics for These Targets

Targets need metrics. The complexity of the issues that companies need to consider is growing almost by the day. As a result, there is a need for focus. Leadership companies set a defined and manageable number of targets and link these to a specific number of key performance indicators (KPIs). There is a danger of trying to do too much too quickly in terms of performance improvement and measures, which can raise unrealistic expectations externally and undermine morale and motivation internally. Shell's KPIs, illustrated in the case study beginning on page 245, offer a good example of how a global company with operations in over a hundred countries has been able to identify a set of sixteen KPIs that can be assessed through a combination of quantitative and qualitative methods.

Under Principle #1 (innovation) we illustrated the metric that has been developed by DuPont to measure shareholder value created per pound of product. The company uses this as a surrogate for evaluating its ability to meet growing consumer needs while decreasing its environmental footprint. The UK-based Corporate Citizenship Company has developed another useful metric called Cash Value-Added (CVA), which provides information on how a business distributes value to its different stakeholder groups. Companies such as Unilever, SABMiller, Diageo, Vodafone, Hong Kong Shanghai Bank, and Rio Tinto are now integrating this recognized, but rarely used, accounting technique into their measurement and reporting systems. It is a management tool that any company could use, drawing on information that is already available in most financial accounts. Unilever describes the metric as follows:

> *This calculates the wealth created in monetary terms through the value that our operations add to the raw materials and services we buy in, calculated as the difference between income from customers and payments out to suppliers. The value created is then available to be distributed to employees, governments, providers of capital and local communities. Some is retained in the business or invested for future growth—that is, for the benefit of stakeholders in the future.[7]*

Keep Ahead of Leading Industry Standards

ISO14000, SA8000, AA1000, DJSI, FTSE4Good . . . the list is daunting, and the "alphabet soup" of acronyms is confusing. But global companies cannot afford to ignore them. Any company that employs over a thousand people or operates across borders should keep updated on leading industry standards and voluntary guidelines. No company can follow them all, or should attempt to—but keeping updated is an important investment of time and effort.

Benchmark Against "Best In Class" Peers and Competitors

Most great companies benchmark their performance, either formally or informally. They benchmark quality systems, manufacturing processes, and marketing approaches. They benchmark human resource practices and boardroom performance. The same focus on observing the best, learning from the best, and aiming to beat the best applies in terms of the company's wider ethical, social, and environmental performance.

Three: Report Publicly on Progress

Once the company has evaluated its performance, the next key question is how to report it and to whom. Transparent and honest public reporting and the provision of credible, reliable, and relevant corporate information is a critical step for companies to build investor confidence and public trust in their performance. While investors are mainly interested in financial performance, they have a growing interest in the company's ethical, social, and environmental performance, especially where this may have a material impact on risk and other factors that directly affect financial performance. Other stakeholders are directly interested in the company's wider areas of societal performance.

Public reporting on these wider areas of societal performance is one of the most challenging and fastest-growing areas of management. As Andrew Savitz, a partner at PricewaterhouseCoopers, comments:

> *The mantra in today's business world is honesty in accounting, a natural and appropriate response to the scandals at Enron, WorldCom and a growing list of top tier U.S. companies. Tomorrow, however, we will be expected to go a giant step further—creating corporations that are sustainable, as well as accountable. Companies that take that step today, before it is mandated, will be rewarded by their shareholders, stakeholders, regulators, and perhaps most importantly, on the bottom line.*[8]

Some countries already have mandatory regulations for reporting on specific aspects of corporate environmental, health, and safety performance. This is especially the case in terms of product and process safety and toxic emissions, such as the U.S.'s Toxic Release Inventory reporting requirements. Very few countries, however, require comprehensive corporate reporting on ethical, social, and environmental issues. The French government was one of the first to make environmental and social reporting mandatory for publicly quoted companies, starting from the 2002 financial year. A number of other European governments are passing legislation on social and environmental reporting requirements, and stock exchanges in several countries are starting to explore more rigorous listing requirements in these areas.

Reporting on greenhouse gas emissions is likely to receive growing emphasis, given the increasingly clear financial, market, and operational risks associated with climate change. In 2002, a group of thirty-five major institutional investors, representing about $4 trillion in assets, launched the Carbon Disclosure Project. They contacted the world's five

---

The Global Reporting Initiative (www.globalreporting.org)

The Global Reporting Initiative (GRI) is a groundbreaking global coalition that includes companies, accounting firms, business associations, professional bodies, academics, nongovernmental organizations, labor, and the United Nations. Initially championed by the United Nations Environmental Program and Boston-based CERES, the GRI's mission is to develop globally applicable guidelines for reporting on economic, environmental, and social performance, initially for corporations and eventually for any organization. Some of the world's leading companies are already using or referring to its guidelines in their public reports. They include Johnson & Johnson; General Motors; Nike; Procter & Gamble; Bristol-Myers Squibb; Chiquita; Ford Motor; Siemens; Suez; Danone; Shell; BASF; Novo Group; and the BT Group.

The GRI Guidelines have been developed through an extensive process of consultation with thousands of organizations from all over the world. They are not a code of conduct, performance standard, or management system. They aim to outline reporting principles and content to guide companies in the preparation of corporate sustainability reports, enable them to present a balanced and reasonable view of their overall performance, and serve as a tool for stakeholder engagement. Over time the GRI aims to support comparability and benchmarking to help drive performance improvement. It is also working with different industry sectors to develop sector-specific performance indicators.

The GRI defines twelve reporting principles essential to producing a balanced and reasonable report on a company's economic, social, and environmental performance: transparency, inclusivity, auditability, sustainability, context, completeness, relevance, neutrality, comparability, accuracy, clarity, and timeliness.

They also provide companies with a framework for preparing their sustainability reports, consisting of the following outline of contents:

  I. Vision and Strategy
  II. Company Profile
  III. Governance Structure
  IV. Management Systems
  V. Economic, Social, and Environmental Performance Indicators

---

hundred largest corporations and asked them to complete a publicly available questionnaire on how their companies are addressing climate

change. According to their report, "While 80 percent of respondents ac-
knowledged the importance of climate change as a financial risk, only
35–40 percent were actively taking action to address the risks and opportunities."[9] Many governments, stock exchanges, insurance bodies,
trade associations, and nongovernmental organizations are also issuing
questionnaires and voluntary guidelines on how companies can report
publicly on their wider economic, ethical, social, and environmental
performance.

The reporting guidelines that are gaining the greatest traction and
influence around the world are those developed by the Global Reporting
Initiative (GRI). This unprecedented multicountry, multistakeholder,
multi-industry voluntary initiative is briefly outlined on page 236. It is
estimated that over two hundred major companies now use the GRI
guidelines to assist them in their reporting efforts.

Despite the lack of mandatory requirements for public reporting on
ethical, social, and environmental issues, there has been a marked increase in companies reporting on a voluntary basis. In its *2002 International Survey of Sustainability Reporting,* KPMG concludes:

> *The survey results show that there has been a significant*
> *increase in the number of companies issuing environmental,*
> *social or sustainability reports, in addition to their annual*
> *financial reports. In 2002 almost half of the Global Fortune 250*
> *companies (45%) produced these reports compared to 35% in*
> *1999. . . . sustainability reporting and the verification of these*
> *reports by the Global Fortune 250 companies is becoming*
> *mainstream business.*[10]

Multiple factors are expected to drive an increase in such reporting—from growing requirements by governments and stock exchanges
to growing demands from institutional investors and other stakeholders.

Some of the key practical questions that companies need to address
in terms of this broader reporting agenda are as follows.

Deciding What to Report How far should the company extend its
public reporting beyond legally mandated or stock exchange require-

ments when it comes to nonfinancial areas of performance and intangible assets? What are the most appropriate and comparable quantitative measures for these areas of the company's performance? There is a need to achieve a balance between gathering costly and excessive data that no one reads and producing glossy reports that are seen as superficial public relations exercises lacking in serious performance data and analysis. The GRI Guidelines offer a useful starting point and will be an increasingly valuable framework as they develop specific indicators for different industry sectors. Benchmarking against other companies in the same industry or country is also a useful way to decide what issues to focus on and what targets to set and measure. Useful research is being undertaken by the organization AccountAbility to help companies think through the concept of "materiality"—that is, what corporate information is "material" or important to the company's stakeholders. AccountAbility's CEO Simon Zadek, a pioneer in the field of ethical, social, and environmental reporting, comments:

> *Useful reporting is not about dumping ever-increasing volumes*
> *of data into the laps, and laptops, of unprepared investors*
> *and other stakeholders. . . . Effective public reporting must,*
> *in short, communicate what is important to targeted*
> *information users in ways that enable them to make coherent*
> *decisions and take planned and timely actions relevant to their*
> *interests in the company whether as customer, employee, neighbor,*
> *or citizen.*[11]

Deciding Whom to Report To Given that different stakeholder groups have different interests, who should receive priority in terms of public reporting and dialogue? Clearly there is the legal obligation to report to shareholders on financial performance. As the recent corporate governance crises have illustrated, there is much room for improvement even in this supposedly "tried and tested" area of corporate reporting. Beyond mandatory financial reporting and legal compliance on certain environmental and safety issues, however, who should the company target its reporting to? Should more efforts be focused on succinct site reports targeted at local authorities and community groups in the locations where the company operates, for example, versus large global reports? How important are employees as a stakeholder group versus the company's external stakeholders? It is important for companies to be clear who their key audiences are and what types of information they are interested in. For this reason, it is useful to make stakeholder identification and dialogue an integral part of preparing and distributing a report.

Deciding How to Report This question is related to both of the ones above: What is the most effective and efficient way for the company to provide information? Should it produce a specialized health, safety, and environment report, as an estimated two to three thousand international companies now do? Should it extend this to a more comprehensive sustainability report, also covering economic and social areas of performance, as the Global Reporting Guidelines recommend? How much information on the company's social, ethical, and environmental performance should be provided in its annual report to shareholders? If these issues are genuinely strategic to the company and its long-term prospects, surely this is where they belong, integrated with its financial statements. What role is there for Internet reporting and stakeholder dialogues?

Deciding How to Verify the Information In a period characterized by high levels of public distrust and a lack of confidence in big business, the issue of external or independent third-party verification takes on a new level of importance. How do investors and other stakeholders know that the information they are being given is accurate, material, and honest? This has proven hard enough to guarantee in the case of financial reporting, even after a hundred years of trial and error. So the challenge is that much greater when it comes to the more subjective aspects of a company's ethical, social, and environmental performance. Of the two thousand corporate environmental, social, and sustainability reports surveyed by KPMG in its 2002 survey, fewer than 30 percent had their reports externally verified, although the numbers have increased from 1999.[12] Of those that had external verification, over 60 percent used major accountancy firms. Some companies are also using specialized environmental, social, and community investment consult-

World-Class Reporters on Social and Environmental Performance

The social and environmental reports of the following companies have been highly rated on a consistent basis by the Association of Chartered Certified Accountants (ACCA), the largest global professional accountancy body in the world, and other organizations such as SustainAbility, Accountability, and CSRNetwork, which independently assess corporate reports. These reports provide useful models and benchmarks for all companies interested in improving their public reporting on their sustainability performance: Novo Nordisk, the BT Group, Chiquita, Ben & Jerry's, Unilever, BP, Procter & Gamble, SABMiller, General Motors, the Suez Group, Ford Motor Company, and Bristol Myers Squibb.

SustainAbility and ACCA have led the way in identifying what constitutes a world-class social and environmental report. Their recommendations include the following:

1. Tackle tough dilemmas and failures: This calls for a willingness by the company to address the key impacts and problems associated with its core business—not only areas such as philanthropy and eco-efficiency, but also some of the company's difficult dilemmas, strategic challenges, and past failures.

2. Engage stakeholders: The company should be able to publicly identify who its key stakeholders are and demonstrate how it is engaging them in its core operations and in the development of its performance and reporting systems.

3. Demonstrate meaningful CEO commitment: The report should indicate how seriously and strategically the CEO, board, and executive team take these issues and what leadership role they are playing in managing them, beyond a bland and pleasant introduction in the annual report.

4. Show links to financial performance and corporate governance: Social and environmental reports often fail to show a clear link to the company's financial performance, its wider economic value added, or its corporate governance framework. Equally, the annual report to shareholders often does not refer back to the company's social and environmental report, or demonstrate how performance in these areas is a relevant issue for shareholders.

5. Disclose public policy positions: Few companies disclose their public policy positions on key social and environmental issues relevant to their business.

6. Provide independent verification: External assurance or verification of data is still lacking in the majority of these reports, yet it is an important factor in ensuring their credibility.

ing firms, technical firms, academic institutes, certification bodies, or nongovernmental organizations. A number of the companies seen as leaders in the area of reporting are using a combination of assurance or verification processes, using both accounting firms and specialist organizations to assure different aspects of the company's nonfinancial reporting.

In summary, the issues of measurement and reporting are not easy ones, even in terms of financial accounting, let alone measuring and reporting on the company's wider societal performance. They are absolutely crucial, however, for any company that aims to be world class—first, they provide managers with information to make decisions, allocate resources, and plan for the future; and second, they provide stakeholders with information on the company that is needed to build the understanding, trust, and societal acceptance without which no company can survive long term. The companies that start reporting on a voluntary basis while there is space for experimentation and an opportunity to shape emerging standards and frameworks, will be ahead of the game and well positioned for the future.

In the box on page 240 we list some of the companies that have been consistently ranked as world-class reporters in terms of their social and environmental performance, and we highlight six key indicators of excellence in social and environmental reporting.

Four: Commit to Continuous Learning

The final step to being performance-driven is a commitment to continuous learning, especially across traditional boundaries and outside corporate "comfort zones." This not only drives continuous improvement in performance, but also increases the company's ability to anticipate new trends and be better prepared to respond to shocks and discontinuities. The companies best placed to welcome continuous learners are those whose executives and employees are cross-boundary thinkers—inquisitive, interested, and open to learning from unlikely sources and considering seemingly impossible ideas.

These are companies that encourage or even require their managers to participate in internal learning networks to share good practices across functions, geographies, business units, and age groups. They pull together eclectic task forces or action teams from different parts of the company to tackle specific challenges and establish incentives to encourage business units to share methodologies and ideas outside their own boundaries. These incentives include innovative award programs, internal venture capital and seed funding initiatives, challenge funds, team-based competitions, unusual mentoring and coaching programs, and integration of learning requirements into performance appraisals. BP, for example, has set up global learning networks around some of the key social and environmental challenges that the company faces, and Nike has established innovative cross-functional Environmental Action Teams.

Learning companies also invest time, money, and effort in experimental and sometimes risky stakeholder dialogues, often with critics and nontraditional allies. Examples include Chiquita's partnership with the Rainforest Alliance to develop more rigorous standards for banana production, Nike's involvement with the Global Alliance for Workers and Communities to improve working conditions along its global supply chain, and McDonald's relationship with the Environmental Defense Fund to help the company keep pushing the boundaries on its environmental performance.

One of the most important investments that any company can make toward continuous learning and readiness for the future is to develop the next generation of business leaders—not only those already inside the company, although this is crucial, but also those in business schools and universities.

Business schools in particular are multimillion-dollar enterprises that graduate over 100,000 people a year in the U.S. alone, and they are in danger of failing to keep up with a dramatically changing world. It took the crisis in U.S. corporate governance, for example, to dramatically raise the profile of ethics teaching and values-driven leadership, beyond a marginal requirement or poorly attended elective course. Ethics debates need to occur in every discipline taught in business schools—in finance, accounting, marketing, law, organizational behavior, operations—not as an add-on or elective course, but as integral to every aspect of doing business. As one of the major "clients" of business schools, companies can play a crucial role in driving change by demanding that values-driven leadership, corporate responsibility, ethics, and international development become more mainstream subjects in the business schools they support and recruit from.

There is no doubt that change is needed. In 2001, the Aspen Institute's Business in Society program conducted a groundbreaking longitudinal survey of over two thousand MBA students in thirteen business schools in the United States and elsewhere. The results were sobering: Over the course of their degree programs, students shift their priorities from "customer needs" and "product quality" to "shareholder value."[13] Students at all stages of their studies believe that during their business careers, they will experience significant stress by having to make decisions that conflict with their values. They believe they can't change company values—they either have to "put up" or "get out." The vast majority would like to better understand what corporate social responsibility means in practice and see it incorporated into core curriculum, not elective courses.

What can companies do to respond to these student concerns and to help build the next generation of business leaders? They can support the Aspen Institute's Business in Society initiative, which is working with business educators, business leaders, and students to increase the supply of future business leaders who understand and seek to balance the complex relationship between business success and social and environmental progress. Other initiatives include the European Academy of Business in Society and Net Impact, a student-led network in business schools throughout America that aims to build a new generation of socially and globally aware business leaders. The International Association of Students in Economics and Commerce (AIESEC) offers another opportunity for corporate partnerships and leadership. This is the world's largest student-led organization, bringing together some fifty thousand young leaders, mostly economics and business students, from over eight hundred universities in more than eighty countries. Through its members it runs corporate responsibility and values-based leadership projects in many of these countries and already partners with some of the world's leading companies to deliver them. The companies benefit from access to some of the brightest and most motivated students, while the young people learn from corporate executives about the dilemmas and opportunities of ethical business leadership.

Companies can also get more directly engaged with business schools themselves. They can fund research and teaching in ethics, social entrepreneurship, and sustainable development. They can support innovative programs that link students and their business skills with local communities and their social needs. They can support the development of case studies by opening their doors to business professors, and they can encourage their senior executives to visit business schools and universities as speakers and mentors and discuss the wider societal performance of business as well as competitive imperatives, and how to deliver both. Importantly, companies can also integrate these issues more systematically into their university recruitment activities. In short, there is enormous potential to build future business leaders who are performance-driven in all areas—financial, ethical, social, and environmental.

In summary, being performance-driven in everything is not easy, but it is a road that some of the world's most successful companies are starting to travel. This journey is increasingly difficult to avoid, especially for well-known companies with valuable brands to protect, and as institutional investors become more demanding in their requirements for greater corporate disclosure on nonfinancial performance. As Samuel Palmisano, chairman and CEO of IBM commented in IBM's first consolidated corporate responsibility report issued in 2003, "All businesses today face a new reality—more important and lasting, in my opinion, than the advent of any game-changing technology or global market trend. Businesses now operate in an environment in which longstanding societal concerns—in areas from diversity to equal opportunity, the environment, and workforce policies—have been raised to the same level of public expectation as accounting practices and financial performance."[14]

Our final example in this chapter looks at Shell, one of the world's oldest and most global multinational companies, and one that illustrates some of the challenges of aiming to be performance-driven in terms of nonfinancial, as well as financial results. Over the past ten years, Shell has faced a series of environmental, human rights and business prob-

lems. It has responded by undertaking fundamental changes in its man-
agement and governance structures. Part of this process has included a
public commitment to greater "triple-bottom line" accountability and
transparency—economic, environmental, and social. Despite progress
and gaining public recognition as a leader in corporate responsibility,
the company stunned its investors in early 2004 by announcing a major
downward revision of its proved oil and gas reserves. As a result, Shell
has faced angry investors, legal action, negative media coverage, re-
newed public censure, and regulatory investigations. This cautionary
tale illustrates that there are no easy solutions for high-profile compa-
nies, but equally there are few alternatives to being more accountable
and transparent on all aspects of performance in today's complex and
demanding global operating environment.

SHELL
Establishing New Performance Targets in Response to Changing Expectations

Despite global economic downturn and political uncertainty, Shell delivered robust profitability in 2002, having achieved its second best results in the company's 105-year history during 2001. It sustained its position as private motorists' most popular brand of gasoline for the sixth year running in the fifty countries surveyed by its brand tracker research and met its target of cutting greenhouse gas emissions from its own operations by more than 10 percent from 1990 levels. In a traditionally male industry, the company could point to women leading two of its five major business groups, as well as serving as its chief financial officer and heading up strategic planning and sustainable development. At its annual general meeting, Shell also delivered the sixth in a series of annual reports—*The Shell Report*—that detail its wider economic, social, and environmental performance and offer an externally verified review of how the group is living up to its business principles.

Yet at the same time the company received strong criticism from activist groups and some of its stakeholders. It was named by *Multinational Monitor* magazine as among the ten worst corporations of the year in 2002. It faced local community protests in some countries and a pending lawsuit in the U.S. related to its Nigerian operations. CorpWatch and Friends of the Earth awarded it a "Greenwash" lifetime achievement award for what they perceived as its double standards in being one of the world's leading environmental violators while marketing itself as socially and environmentally responsible.

Then, in early 2004 the company's senior management stunned the markets, its investors, and many of its employees, when they reported that Shell was reducing its figures for proved oil and gas reserves by 20 percent. Internal memos leaked to the press indicated that the company's senior management group had first been warned of overbooking of reserves in certain countries over a year previously, but had failed to disclose these concerns to the U.S. Securities and Exchange Commission or to investors. The chairman and the head of exploration and production were forced to resign. Less than two months later, following initial findings of an independent audit, the company again revised its figures downward, and postponed its annual general meeting and the publication of its annual report. Shell's share price and credit rating dropped, as did investor confidence and public credibility. Stakeholders expressed major concerns about the company's leadership, its governance, and its management structure.

Senior managers emphasized in their public statements throughout this period that during 2003, the company had delivered record cash generation, competitive returns, cost improvements, portfolio rationalization, and progress on some major projects and new discoveries for the future, all underpinning its dividend growth.

These contradictory results and perceptions of the company and its performance illustrate the strategic leadership challenges faced by many multinationals in today's world. This is especially the case for a company with the reach of Shell, which invested $25 billion and employed 115,000 people in 145 countries and territories in 2002, serving 25 million consumers every day and about one million commercial and industrial customers. Shell has some useful and hard-earned lessons to share, in particular the importance of candid reporting of both good performance and mistakes.

In 1998, during an earlier period of poor financial performance and high investor dissatisfaction, Shell's former chairman Mark Moody-Stuart observed:

> *Why bother producing a report on our contribution to sustainable development when the Group is under such harsh financial pressure? Should we not put all our efforts and resources into ensuring a profitable future? This, we believe, is exactly what we are doing. Our values, Business Principles, commitment to contribute to a sustainable form of development—and the candid reporting of our performance in those areas—are inextricably linked to our long-term commercial success.[15]*

In the mid-1990s, few people would have placed Shell on their list of performance-driven, innovative, or efficient companies, let alone described it as responsible. Despite a ninety-year history of global investment and technological excellence, the company entered the 1990s steeped in a hierarchical, bureaucratic, paternalistic way of doing business. Not only did it lack the agility and creativity needed in an increasingly competitive operating environment, but the company was ill prepared to understand and respond to changing societal expectations.

In 1994, Shell initiated a process of change that was its most thorough and far reaching in over thirty years—what it termed its Transformation. One year into this carefully planned process, the company was shaken to its foundations by two major reputation-damaging crises. They have been written about extensively, but a brief review follows to set the context.

An Environmental and Social "Wake-up Call"

The first crisis was environmental. In 1995, Shell was the target of a successful campaign in Europe by the nongovernmental organization Greenpeace. The environmental group attacked its plans to dispose of the Brent Spar, an offshore storage structure, in the Atlantic Ocean. Despite official government backing and solid scientific evidence that this was the best environmental option, Shell failed to engage widely enough with environmental groups and the public before announcing these plans. Activist groups throughout Europe led a boycott of Shell products and services, resulting in negative media coverage, a damaged reputation, and falling sales.

What had started as essentially a technical problem—and Shell was confident of its technical expertise and scientific findings—became a political and strategic nightmare. And it raised fundamental questions about the company's ability to read and respond to changing societal expectations. As Jeroen van der Veer, a member of Shell's committee of managing directors, has observed, "This event had a measurable impact on our company. We saw how easily consumers and customers can use the power of the marketplace, if they feel a company is not operating in an acceptable way. And we saw how enterprises must exist as part of a society, communicating and working with society—because outside society, there are no profits to be made in the long-term."[16]

The second crisis, which also occurred in 1995, was a human rights crisis, and it seriously affected the company's global reputation. Shell was accused by human rights campaigners of complicity with the Nigerian government in the execution of the world-renowned author, environmental activist, and community leader Ken Saro-Wiwa, together with eight of his fellow activists who had campaigned against the negative impact of the oil industry on the communities in which it operated. The Nigerian government, a military regime lacking democratic legitimacy, was failing to distribute oil revenues to its people and using military force against some of its citizens. Shell was the largest foreign investor in the country's oil industry. Although it claims to have made efforts to influence the government in private, the company's failure to play a more public and proactive role in trying to stop the executions was unacceptable to thousands of people around the world. As the ten-year anniversary of the killings approaches, Shell continues to face lawsuits and damage to its reputation as a result of this tragic set of events.

The crises faced by the company over Brent Spar and its Nigerian operations demonstrated forcefully that in an interconnected world, with global media and effective activists, there is no hiding place for a corporation that is deemed to "get it wrong" on environmental or human rights issues. No matter how remote its operations, in a "CNN world," local issues or crises can become global overnight. It also learned, as other major investors in developing countries are learning, that large and influential companies cannot set themselves apart from the actions of host governments. Nonetheless, no company can take full responsibility for a government's actions.

Determining exactly what the boundaries of a company's responsibilities are in practice and how these relate to building competitive edge and establishing trust among millions of stakeholders all over the world on a day-to-day basis are among the major leadership challenges many large companies will face in the twenty-first century.

In the case of Shell, this continues to be an ongoing dilemma. The company has aimed to address it by undertaking a series of fundamental governance, management, and organizational changes, which are still underway. These have been aimed at moving from an organizational structure of over 140 operating companies to one with four main global businesses, improving governance and control, and developing a more integrated "sustainable development management framework" to help the company better manage its wider economic, social, and environmental performance, as well as its financial performance.

Fundamental Management Change

While investors continue to have concerns about the company's complex and decentralized management and governance structure, and there are still many activists who place Shell and other oil companies at the top of their list of irresponsible multinationals, the management changes the company has made since 1995 go far beyond a superficial public relations exercise. As recent events have demonstrated, these changes are still a work in progress, but they offer useful lessons for other companies.

Values and Principles In 1997, Shell revised its General Business Principles, which were first produced in 1976. Two key revisions were the incorporation of explicit commitments to sustainable development and human rights. The new principles are among the most comprehensive frameworks developed by any company for its economic, social, political, ethical, and environmental roles and responsibilities. They also explicitly recognize the essential role of communications and the need for Shell to provide comprehensive corporate information about its ac-

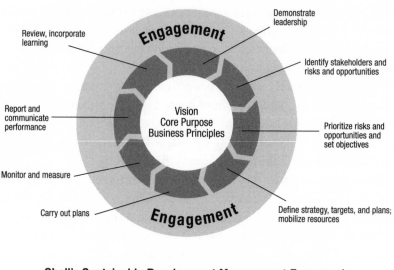

Review, incorporate learning

Demonstrate leadership

Identify stakeholders and risks and opportunities

Report and communicate performance

Vision
Core Purpose
Business Principles

Prioritize risks and opportunities and set objectives

Monitor and measure

Carry out plans

Define strategy, targets, and plans; mobilize resources

Engagement

Engagement

Shell's Sustainable Development Management Framework

Source: Shell

tivities to legitimately interested parties, subject to any overriding considerations of business confidentiality and cost. This commitment makes the company's failure to disclose its concerns about reserves in a more timely manner especially perplexing and damaging to its reputation.

In more recent years, the company has also established a set of seven *sustainable development principles* for use in business planning, performance assessment, and public reporting. These are: generating robust profitability; delivering value to customers; protecting the environment; managing resources; respecting and safeguarding people; benefiting communities; and working with stakeholders.

Standards and Compliance Shell has created a number of new standards and compliance systems to ensure that performance in accord with its General Business Principles is embedded in the company's core activities and taken seriously by employees and business partners. A key element of this has been to set clear and specific operating standards for different aspects of the company's performance. For example, it has established groupwide global standards on issues such as bribery and corruption, safety, biodiversity, minimum health management, diversity and inclusiveness, and security. Another key element has been developing a framework for independent third-party verification of the company's key social and environmental impacts and measures, as well as its financial results.

Management Systems The company has established the groupwide Sustainable Development Management Framework, which aims to integrate social and environmental issues, together with technical and financial analysis, into its core business planning, operational strategies, and investment decision-making processes. The ultimate goal is to take economic, environmental, and social considerations into account in all the company's strategic business decisions.

Strategic Planning The company has integrated sustainable development considerations, which it sees as an increasingly key part of its competitive edge, into its strategic planning processes. As a result of this integrated planning process, Shell has identified three major thrusts for its future strategic direction:

- *Optimizing current businesses:* learning from past lessons and aiming to improve the economic, environmental, and social performance of existing products and services

- *Gaining new business:* accessing new geographic markets such as China, as well as new markets created by changing societal expectations and demands, such as the growing market for cleaner transport fuels

- *Sowing the seed for radical departures* and *breaking new ground* by exploring new ways to produce energy and developing new business models

All three strategies emphasize the focus on creating value in a manner that uses resources more efficiently and lowers capital and material intensity, while increasing the knowledge intensity of products and services.

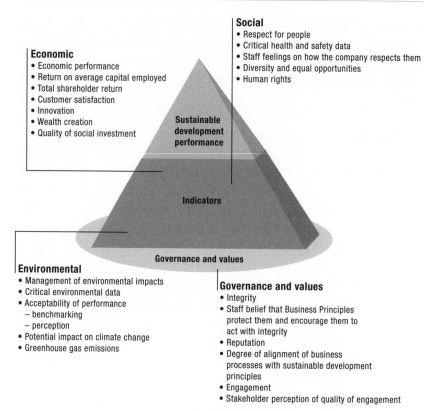

Economic
- Economic performance
- Return on average capital employed
- Total shareholder return
- Customer satisfaction
- Innovation
- Wealth creation
- Quality of social investment

Social
- Respect for people
- Critical health and safety data
- Staff feelings on how the company respects them
- Diversity and equal opportunities
- Human rights

Sustainable development performance

Indicators

Governance and values

Environmental
- Management of environmental impacts
- Critical environmental data
- Acceptability of performance
  - benchmarking
  - perception
- Potential impact on climate change
- Greenhouse gas emissions

Governance and values
- Integrity
- Staff belief that Business Principles protect them and encourage them to act with integrity
- Reputation
- Degree of alignment of business processes with sustainable development principles
- Engagement
- Stakeholder perception of quality of engagement

Shell's Key Performance Indicators

Source: Shell

Governance Structures The company has established an executive-level sustainable development committee, chaired by the group chairman and consisting of senior representatives from all the company's main businesses and corporate center functions. The committee is supported operationally by a sustainable development panel, consisting of functional experts and practitioners. At the board level, the company has established a social responsibility committee made up of external, independent board directors who review the company's policies and conduct against its Business Principles. Independent directors played a decisive role in calling for the resignation of senior managers and immediate remedial action on governance and controls in the wake of the 2004 revision of "proved" reserves.

Key Performance Indicators Critical to delivering on all of the foregoing public commitments has been the need to measure and verify progress. An important element of this has been the process of identifying and implementing a set of key performance indicators (KPIs) that can serve as targets and benchmarks for assessing the company's performance—both internally and externally. Indicators are used widely in financial reporting to illustrate how well or badly a company is doing—for example, return on capital and earnings per share—so why can't they also be developed to assess social, environmental, and governance performance? Shell has developed the KPIs shown in the diagram on page 252. Some of these the company already measures and it is testing the practicality of quantifying and reporting on others.

The company's crisis over the downward revision of its proved reserves illustrates how difficult it can be in practice to ensure accurate and timely information on nonfinancial assets and performance in a highly decentralized and global operating structure. As the *New York Times* commented at the time, "Calculating reserves can be as much an art as a science, and there can be debate about how to do it."[17] Yet, as the company's newly appointed head of exploration and production admitted in one of his first public statements after his predecessor's resignation, "This is not an exact science, but it is up to us to get it right. We can and should have done better."[18] It is one thing to identify key performance indicators in order to better monitor and manage a company's nonfinancial performance, but actually measuring and reporting on them, and doing so in a manner that maintains rock-solid consistency, integrity, and transparency, is easier said than done. This is increasingly important, however, to being a world-class company.

Shell's Key Lessons

What are some of the leadership and management lessons from Shell's experience over the past five years?

Consistent Consultation and Communications Learning from its failure in the mid-1990s to anticipate changing customer needs and societal expectations, the company has embarked on an extensive and ongoing program of stakeholder consultation and communications. After its 1995 environmental and human rights crises, Shell embarked on a series of conversations with people around the world to understand society's changing expectations of multinational companies and get feedback on its own reputation and standing. This involved 7,500 members of the general public in ten countries, 1,300 opinion leaders in twenty-five countries, and 300 Shell people in fifty-five countries.

Many companies have values or principles statements, but they are not always widely distributed to employees or accounted for in internal compliance systems. Shell's General Business Principles are available in fifty-one languages. Shell divisions in each country have a procedure to ensure that every new employee receives a copy. In over 120 countries, new staff are given specific training on the principles. An internal website has been established to share information, training, and ideas on the principles and a series of primers developed on key issues such as dealing with bribery and corruption, human rights, and child labor. Beyond their own employees, Shell companies in over a hundred countries, explicitly discuss the General Business Principles during negotiations with contractors and suppliers. In a growing number of countries, expectations about these principles are written into contracts, and screening for compliance is taking place.

The *Shell Report,* now in its sixth year of publication, is one of the company's most visible demonstrations to its commitment to be performance-driven in all aspects of its performance, not only the financial ones. It is now distributed to all investors together with every copy of the company's annual report and financial accounts. In 2002, some 2.5 million summaries of *The Shell Report: People, Planet and Profits,* were also inserted into international publications.

Shell's global "Profits and Principles: Is There a Choice?" communications campaign has been running for several years in print and broadcast media around the world. Although viewed by some critics as an empty public relations ploy and as evidence of double standards, this campaign has helped bring issues such as business and climate change, human rights, and biodiversity to public attention, as well as developing the company's brand identity. Developing marketing messages around societal issues or implementing cause-related marketing campaigns can be risky. This is especially so if the rhetoric doesn't match the reality or the external message doesn't reflect the internal modus operandi of the company. But if these external messages are part of an integrated and solid internal management system, they can be a useful strategy for communicating a company's overall commitment to corporate responsibility.

Credibility in Implementation Given the damage to its reputation resulting from the environmental and human rights crises it faced in 1995 and ongoing activist campaigns against the company combined with the negative investor, media and regulatory response to its 2004 restatement of proved reserves, Shell continues to face a challenge in terms of building trust and credibility. In a world where there is low public trust and investor confidence in financial reports, which have been audited for over a century in some cases, the challenge is even greater in gaining trust and confidence in social and environmental reports, where the issues are emotionally charged and the field of measurement and reporting is less mature.

Shell is working to address this credibility gap in ways that include:

- Offering independent, or third-party, verification of its social and environmental, as well as financial, data. This is done through auditors such as KPMG and PricewaterhouseCoopers and standards such as the International Organization for Standardization's environmental standard (ISO14001) and the Forest Stewardship Council's Guidelines.

- Providing both good news and bad news. For example, supplying information on situations where the company has failed to meet its commitments or performance targets, supported by an action plan for improvement or remediation. After being slow in disclosing its overbooking of reserves, for example, the company was quick to take remedial action, announcing new reporting structures, controls, and training requirements. It also announced that no top executives would receive performance-related bonuses for 2003.

■ Integrating sustainable development considerations into executive performance appraisal and reward systems. Social and environmental considerations now account for up to a fifth of the Shell scorecard, which defines how the company appraises its performance and determines the bonuses of all senior executives. Having said that, critics point to the fact that the booking of new reserves had constituted between 5 and 15 percent of the possible annual bonus of certain staff, possibly contributing to the 2004 "overbooking" crisis. Both points illustrate that incentives matter. In March 2004, the company announced that booking of reserves would no longer be a factor in determining bonuses.

■ Requiring that all new investment proposals meet not only financial criteria, but also social and environmental criteria. These criteria are clearly stated and publicly available. They include carbon costs of the new investment; social, health, and environmental impact assessments and plans; and plans for stakeholder engagement.

■ Ensuring a policy of zero tolerance when core business principles are violated. In 2001, for example, one hundred contracts were canceled because the operations of business partners or contractors were incompatible with the company's General Business Principles. In cases where investigations into bribery and corruption find employees or contractors to be responsible, contracts are either terminated or warnings given, depending on the nature of the case.

■ Shell's shifting business portfolio is another indicator of its progress toward meeting its commitment to sustainable development. As critics point out, the company remains heavily focused on fossil fuels and continues to increase oil and gas production. In a world where energy demands continue to rise, this is unlikely to change in the near future, but the company, like its peers Chevron-Texaco and BP, is making a measurable shift away from high-carbon fuels such as coal, which it no longer produces, toward lower-carbon sources such as gas. At the same time, it is starting to invest millions of dollars in renewable energies and innovative partnerships with the United Nations and others to deliver affordable, off-grid solar energy to some of the poorest communities on earth.

The company is demonstrating that it *is* possible to manage and measure economic, social, and environmental performance, but it is complicated, demanding, and exacting, and requires an unyielding commitment to consistency, integrity, accountability, and transparency across virtually every aspect of management and reporting. Continuous improvement needs to be at the core of a performance-driven framework. No company, no matter how performance-driven, can get it right all the time in all areas of performance. Equally, the types of management metrics and incentives that are set to drive performance can sometimes result in managers making decisions that are detrimental to either shareholder value or wider social and environmental responsibility, or both. For large, complex companies, being performance-driven requires an ongoing process of experimentation, assessment, and recalibration in order to drive results that create value for both shareholders and society, and that adhere to corporate values and principles.

Shell's restatement in 2004 of its proved oil and gas reserves demonstrates the ongoing challenge of accurate reporting in all key areas of corporate performance, and the reputation costs associated with real and perceived lapses in accountability. This is not the first time this great company has stumbled in terms of meeting stakeholder expectations.

Being Performance-Driven . . . in Everything

One: Get commitment at the top.

Two: Set clear targets and metrics.

Three: Report publicly on progress.

Four: Commit to continuous learning.

Presumably, it will correct, improve, and internalize the lessons, just as it has from previous mistakes, and go on to set a new, high standard for itself, stronger as a result of its adversity. Being transparent about areas of failure and taking demonstrable steps to address them is equally as important as telling the success stories. In an interconnected world, where increased expectations of large companies are supported by the Internet and 24-hour news, high-value, high-profile companies have little choice but to set performance targets and be accountable and transparent in reporting against them.

Practice Superior Governance

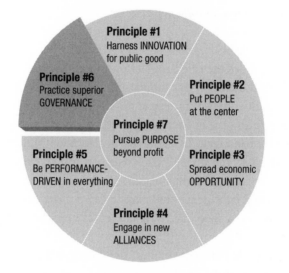

The governance agenda for business is being fundamentally reshaped. Key drivers include recent corporate governance scandals around the world, changing societal expectations, new government regulations, and voluntary industry initiatives.

This emerging agenda calls for more rigorous approaches to corporate governance. But more is required. Superior governance is also about the company's overall legitimacy and wider acceptance by stakeholders, including but not only shareholders. It is about increased transparency, accountability, integrity, and independent overview in *all* key areas of corporate performance, ethical, social, and environmental as well as financial—what is increasingly termed sustainability governance. And it is about ensuring a more transparent and noncorrupt interface between business and government everywhere that companies operate—what we have called public governance.

Why Good Governance Matters

*It is time to reaffirm the basic principles and rules that
make capitalism work: truthful books and honest people,
and well-enforced laws against fraud and corruption. All
investment is an act of faith, and faith is earned by integrity.
In the long run, there's no capitalism without conscience;
there is no wealth without character.*

PRESIDENT GEORGE W. BUSH, 2002

Governance includes the rules, regulations, relationships, and norms that determine how societies and organizations, including companies, are led and governed. Governance is essentially about power—about the distribution of power and the accountability, transparency, and integrity with which power is exercised. Governance is also about independent oversight to ensure that the people who have power use it responsibly. The quality of governance, at both a national and an organizational level, affects the trust and confidence that people have in our economic and political systems. It can also have a fundamental impact on prosperity and security.

From a corporate perspective, there are three types of governance that we believe are essential in determining the trust and confidence that shareholders and other stakeholders have in business:

■ *Corporate governance* is usually defined as focusing on the distribution of rights and accountability among shareholders, corporate boards of directors, and corporate executives or managers. In some parts of the world, definitions of corporate governance also explicitly encompass responsibility of the corporation to other stakeholders.

■ *Sustainability governance* goes one step, or several steps, further.[1] It is about applying the principles of accountability, transparency, integrity, and independent oversight not only to a company's financial performance, but also to its ethical, social, and environmental performance. It is about responsibility to stakeholders in addition to accountability to shareholders. Sustainability governance is also about systematically assessing and accounting for intangible as well as tangible assets and establishing board-level structures to address these issues.

■ *Public governance* relates to the evolving relationship between business and government, both nationally and globally, and to growing public demands for large companies to be more transparent and accountable in their interactions with government bodies and officials. Public governance also calls for companies to take more of a leadership role in tackling bribery and corruption.

There is growing evidence—both empirical and anecdotal—that bad governance in any of these areas over time will create higher transaction costs, undermine efficiency, result in increased human costs, and decrease the legitimacy and authority of leaders in both the public and private sector. The overall impact may be to lessen the competitiveness of individual firms and nations.

The Costs of Bad Governance

In recent years, we have been sharply reminded of the costs of bad corporate governance. These costs had been clearly demonstrated during the 1930s, when the 1929 stock market crash and the ensuing Great Depression led to the loss of countless large fortunes and small nest eggs, the failure of numerous banks and companies, the plummeting of global trade, and a period of economic depression and personal despair for many.

This period led to a number of critical governance and market reforms, including the Securities Acts of 1933 and 1934 and the establishment of the Securities and Exchange Commission, with the aim of protecting investors and maintaining the integrity of the securities markets. For almost seventy years this framework has been one of the foundations for the greatest economic boom in history. By the turn of the century over eighty million Americans were investors, either directly or through institutionally managed pension funds and mutual funds. The framework remains a crucial foundation today. But recent corporate governance failures have reminded us of the need for constant vigilance and diligence, for revised checks, balances, and controls, and for a renewed commitment to corporate ethics and integrity.

America's legislators, capital market institutions, and business leaders have rallied together to respond to the crisis. This response has resulted in the rapid passage through Congress of the Sarbanes-Oxley Act, a plethora of recommendations and guidelines as well as new listing requirements put forward by the New York Stock Exchange, the world's largest physical market, and the Nasdaq, the world's largest electronic stock market, which between them list over six thousand leading global companies. The Business Roundtable wrote a public letter to the American people on behalf of its members calling for more open corporate financial statements, independent corporate boards of directors, and greater fairness. Its members, major corporations that control revenues of over $3.5 trillion and employ over ten million people, vowed, "We will make changes to regain your trust as investors and co-workers."[2] In January 2004, the Business Roundtable launched its Institute for Corporate Ethics, which will draw on faculty from all over the United States to carry out research and teaching on applied ethics with input from the 150 CEOs who are members of the Business Roundtable. But it will take time and the sustained demonstration of superior corporate governance standards and integrity to restore public trust and investor confidence.

Bad corporate governance is clearly not an issue only for America. During the past decade, other parts of the world have also had forceful reminders of the costs of getting it wrong. The financial crises that rocked markets in Asia, Russia, and Argentina during the past ten years were in large part due to systems of weak corporate governance and inadequate market oversight, exacerbated by poor macroeconomic decisions and in some cases cronyism and corruption. Millions of investors and workers lost their savings and jobs, and thousands of companies failed, with high economic and human costs. The message is clear: good corporate governance and effective market oversight matter on a global basis. There is a need to share lessons and good practices between all the world's capital markets.

So much for bad corporate governance—what are the costs of bad sustainability governance? They include the legal costs, consumer boycotts, negative media coverage, damage to reputation, government fines, increased regulatory oversight, and in some cases lost market share incurred by companies that have been held responsible for major social or environmental crises. The large losses and corporate failures associated with asbestos claims offer one of the most notable examples to date of the financial costs of failing to take environmental and social risks into account. Recent research in the area of climate change suggests that failure by corporate boards of directors and institutional investors to take climate-related risks into account represents "a potential multi-billion dollar risk to a wide variety of U.S. businesses and industries."[3]

The costs of bad public governance have been demonstrated in many countries where there are high levels of bribery, corruption, and cronyism between political officials and business leaders. In such environments, it is difficult and sometimes impossible for principled companies to operate or to compete fairly against less-principled enterprises. In many key emerging economies, corruption and cronyism remain systematic and endemic, often leading to governmental collapse, which creates intolerably high economic costs for companies and citizens alike.

The Benefits of Good Governance

In the wake of recent corporate scandals, the business case for good corporate governance is irrefutable. As we outlined above, the costs of "getting it wrong" may include serious reputation damage, legal penalties, jail sentences, and, in extreme cases, corporate collapse. On the other hand, there are benefits to getting it right. In particular, a reputation for good corporate governance can be key to attracting new investors and the best workers and lowering the cost of capital.

In 2002, McKinsey & Company surveyed over two hundred institutional investors who are collectively responsible for some $2 trillion of assets under management and whose organizations manage an estimated $9 trillion.[4] The results make for compelling reading. An overwhelming majority of investors, over 80 percent, are prepared to pay a premium for companies exhibiting high governance standards. Financial disclosure was raised as a pivotal concern, and over 80 percent of investors supported the expensing of stock options in profit and loss statements.

This is not to suggest that good corporate governance automatically leads to competitive edge or better bottom-line results, but it can certainly do no harm. At a minimum, it gives potential investors and employees, as well as regulators, a greater sense of trust and confidence in a company and a willingness to invest financial and human capital in it.

The business case for good sustainability governance is also becoming clearer. A growing number of companies are reaping reputation benefits, and in some cases competitive edge, for demonstrating ethical, social, and environmental accountability. Admittedly, these efforts are still not strongly rewarded by the financial markets, beyond the relatively small socially responsible investment movement. Equally, few institutional investors are putting pressure on corporate laggards in sustainability governance. Having said this, as intangible assets become an increasingly important driver of corporate value and financial performance and as awareness grows about certain social and environmental issues, such as climate change, HIV/AIDS, and human rights, this situation is starting to change. At the same time, a growing number of voluntary industry-led initiatives, several of which we look at in this chapter, are starting to raise the bar on sustainability governance.

Good public governance is ultimately good for business, even if direct causal links are difficult to quantify. Individual companies may benefit in the short term from bribery and corruption, human rights abuses, weak implementation of laws and regulations, and low social, labor, and environmental standards, but eventually these will undermine national competitiveness and prosperity. Business thrives best in well-governed societies where there are clear and consistent rules of the game. Leading companies are recognizing this. They are getting more actively engaged in policy dialogue to help governments and civil society groups build good governance at the public level.

In summary, good governance matters. Whether we are speaking about corporate, sustainability, or public governance, the principles of respect for the rule of law, accountability, transparency, integrity, and independent oversight are all crucial pillars that underpin well-functioning markets and well-informed shareholders and stakeholders, all of which are needed for long-term business success.

Making It Happen

The emerging governance agenda is neither simple nor risk free. But no board of directors or executive management team can afford to ignore it, regardless of their industry or country of origin. At a very minimum, they need to understand and monitor the risks, opportunities, regulations, and capital market listing requirements that are associated with this emerging agenda. The leaders will be those companies that go further, with a publicly stated commitment and the implementation of effective board structures and management systems to deliver what we have termed *superior governance*. By this we mean accountability, transparency, integrity, and independent oversight in *all* three dimensions of governance—corporate governance, sustainability governance, and public governance. What are some of the practical implications and management challenges of committing to superior governance?

One: Master the Art of "And"

In today's complex operating environment, with its wide range of commercial pressures, regulatory requirements, and societal expectations, implementing superior governance increasingly requires boards of directors and executive teams who are able to address the following types of balancing acts.

Financial *and* Social, Ethical, and Environmental Performance Superior governance means being accountable and transparent with regard to the company's ethical, social, and environmental performance as well as its financial performance.

Tangible *and* Intangible Assets Measurement systems must be established to evaluate, protect, and enhance not only the company's tangible assets but also its intangible assets such as intellectual capital, brand equity, reputation, and relationships.

Accountability to Shareholders *and* Responsibility to Stakeholders Practicing superior governance means implementing structures and systems to strengthen the company's accountability and transparency to its owners or shareholders. It also means improving the company's ability to listen to, consult with, respond to, and be responsible for its impacts on other stakeholders, in particular its employees, customers, suppliers, and local communities.

Quantitative *and* Qualitative Assessment Measurement, reporting, monitoring, and incentive systems are needed that take into account both quantitative measures of corporate financial and nonfinancial performance and qualitative assessments. The latter are clearly more difficult to do but need to be integrated into governance frameworks as well as performance measurement systems.

Regulation *and* Self-Regulation Practicing superior governance requires adherence to both legally binding regulations and self-regulatory frameworks. Achieving the right balance between regulation and self-regulation will continue to be one of the most difficult and controversial issues when it comes to governing the financial, ethical, social, and environmental aspects of corporate behavior. There will always be critics who think there is either too much or too little regulation. It is clearly in the best interests of companies and their business associations to play an active role in this debate.

Rules *and* Values While superior governance requires adherence to rules, it also requires commitment to values such as honesty, integrity, transparency, and responsibility. As Federal Reserve chairman Alan Greenspan has commented, "I should like to emphasize that a market economy requires a structure of formal rules—a law of contracts, bankruptcy statutes, a code of shareholder rights—to name but a few. But rules cannot substitute for character."[5] So superior governance requires rules and regulations, but also people of character and personal integrity.

Conformance *and* Performance It follows that practicing superior governance involves a combination of control and incentives, risk management and risk-taking. It requires oversight structures and systems for risk management to ensure that executives are in conformance with external rules and regulations and with the company's internal rules, codes, and policies. At the same time, it involves advisory structures and incentive systems to inspire outstanding executive performance within the parameters of these rules and codes of conduct.

Individuals *and* Systems Individual boards of directors, CEOs, and management teams can do a great deal to ensure their own company delivers superior governance. But as the scandals of recent years have demonstrated, individual failure on the part of a few companies can damage public trust and confidence in all companies. Practicing superior governance calls for directors and executives who are accountable first and foremost for their own actions and those of their employees, but also understand the wider systemic linkages and have the courage to go public when cracks appear in other parts of the system. As Jeff Immelt, CEO of GE, has observed, "Trust is easily broken. It can be destroyed by a few. But trust can only be restored collectively, by all of us and the entire system."[6]

Independence *and* Teamwork At the individual board level, superior corporate governance requires directors who have no conflicts of interest and have the confidence and skills to offer independent opinions and ensure rigorous checks and balances against abuse of executive power. But it also needs boards that can operate as an effective team, with different perspectives and competencies, ultimately creating a whole that is greater than its parts.

Home *and* Abroad Finally, superior governance means meeting legal and listing requirements in the company's home country, but also understanding the international corporate governance agenda and the international standards and norms relating to ethical, social, and environmental issues elsewhere around the world. With today's global media and Internet access, it is increasingly difficult for major international companies to get away with applying high standards of governance in their home country and much lower standards abroad.

Two: Strengthen the Board of Directors

Corporate boards of directors have an increasingly crucial role to play in mastering the balancing acts described in the previous section and helping their companies navigate the emerging agenda of corporate, sustainability, and public governance. Despite differences in legal contexts, histories, and cultures, the boards of multinational companies in most countries face similar dilemmas and have broadly the same portfolio of functions to perform: ensuring oversight and accountability; selecting and remunerating the CEO; and acting as stewards for corporate values, policies, and strategic direction.

There is no one ideal structure for the high-performing board. Even if there were an ideal formal structure in terms of size, composition, number of committees, frequency of meetings, and so on, performance would still vary from board to board as a result of informal structures, relationships, and varying skills and human dynamics. It is possible, however, to identify broad characteristics or structures that define high-performing boards.[7] In the box below we list those that we think most define the type of board that is likely to be ahead of the pack in understanding the emerging governance agenda and practicing superior governance.

Characteristics of High-Performance Boards

1. Existence of written governance policies or board charters—A board needs statements that clearly define its roles, responsibilities, and boundaries, and those of its executive and nonexecutive directors and its committees. Some companies that have taken the lead in developing such publicly available board policies or charters include BP, Nestlé, General Electric, Alcoa, and General Motors. A publicly available corporate code of business conduct and/or ethics code covering the responsibilities not only of the board of directors but of all the company's managers and employees, is also key to delivering superior governance. Some companies, such as Pfizer, Baxter International, and Sunoco, have also established internal positions for chief governance officers, who act as internal advocates and champions for good governance practices.

2. Independence of oversight and opinion—This calls for the establishment of formal structures, as well as the selection of suitably skilled, confident, and independent directors able to act as effective "checks and balances" on executive power and as stewards of corporate values. Increasingly this means that a majority of directors are independent nonexecutives who chair crucial board committees such as audit, nominations, and remuneration committees, meet regularly without the CEO present, and meet with other managers and operational units in the company. Independence comes from the experiences and character of the directors as much as from any formal structure.

3. Diversity of perspective—In addition to independence of opinion, high-performing boards also need diversity of perspective and vision. Although there are growing numbers of women, minorities, and non–businesspeople on the boards of global companies, many are still largely homogenous—not only with regard to these groups but also in terms of multicultural representation that reflects the diverse regions in which these companies operate. In addition, most nonbusiness board members are "establishment figures"—such as civic leaders, heads of foundations, or academics. It is rare to find environmental or social activists, young people, or labor leaders on corporate boards in North America, the UK, or Australia, although labor representatives sit on the two-tier supervisory boards in continental Europe. Yet arguably, these are the types of people who are best placed to help boards anticipate and think through changing societal expectations and social and environmental risks and opportunities.

4. Good grasp of the business and industry—While boards need directors who offer diverse experiences and perspectives, it is important for all board members to have a good grasp of business and financial issues and awareness of the industry sector. This is more important in some industries and companies than others, but it is an issue for all. It is often cited as the main reason for having senior executives from other companies as the majority of independent directors. There are ways, however, that companies can help nonbusiness board members get up to speed on core business issues. This includes regular site visits and meetings with management teams and other stakeholders, in addition to formal director training.

5. Provision of accessible information—Companies that are serious about good corporate governance ensure that they meet not only legal reporting requirements, but also go to some length to explain their policies and procedures to the investing public and other interested parties. Shareholders and other stakeholders want access to corporate information that is accurate, timely, comprehensible, and credible in helping them decide which companies to invest in, lend to, work for, buy from, campaign against, and regulate. It is the role of the board to ensure such information is readily available.

Few companies, for example, make a connection between their investor web page and their corporate responsibility, citizenship, or sustainable development information, let alone discuss their corporate values or these wider aspects of corporate performance with their investors on a regular basis. Companies that provide regular and comprehensive information about their values and their broader governance and sustainability agendas to their investors include British Telecommunications, Timberland, BP, DuPont, Dow, Alcoa, General Motors, Novo Nordisk, Rio Tinto, and Johnson & Johnson.

6. Board appraisal—World-class boards have systems in place to assess not only CEO and executive performance but also the collective and individual performance of the board itself and the effectiveness of its formal structures and informal processes in achieving its core functions. In many cases this assessment is carried out through self-appraisals, but some boards are starting to integrate self-appraisal with external evaluation.

7. Board structures for sustainability governance—As corporate responsibility issues become more relevant to corporate strategy and governance challenges, it is increasingly difficult for senior executives to siphon them off to environmental, community relations, or public affairs specialists farther down the corporate hierarchy. Far from being marginal to the boardroom agenda, these issues are becoming integral to the board's role in monitoring risk and compliance, shaping strategic direction, and stewarding corporate values and principles. As a result, a growing number of boards are voluntarily establishing dedicated board committees or independent director positions to take responsibility for these wider sustainability, societal, or public policy issues.

A 2001 study by the Conference Board shows that 15 percent of the U.S. companies surveyed now have such committees, compared to fewer than 10 percent in 1980. These board committees are called a variety of names and have wide-ranging responsibilities, including: public issues and public policy; ethics; social and environmental responsibility; stakeholder accountability; and sustainable development.

Some of the most impressive, in terms of their independence, the scope of their mandate, and their link to overall corporate purpose, strategy, and accountability, include those established by Rio Tinto, DuPont, Ford Motor Company, GlaxoSmithKline, SABMiller, Merck, McDonald's, GM, Coca-Cola, and Unilever. Most of these committees are chaired by independent directors, and they meet two to six times a year.

8. External stakeholder advisory structures—Leading boards establish mechanisms, such as external advisory groups, to ensure regular and systematic dialogue with other key stakeholder groups and relevant experts on economic, ethical, social, and environmental issues of relevance to their company. Dow, DuPont, Verizon Communications, Interface, Coca-Cola, Unilever, British Telecom, Kraft, Novartis, and the Suez Group are among the companies that have led the way in creating high-level external advisory structures to improve their decision-making and the sustainability governance of their companies.

In some cases these external bodies focus on a very specific issue of strategic importance to the company. For example, DuPont has the Biotechnology Advisory Panel; Unilever has the Sustainable Agriculture Advisory Board; Kraft has the Worldwide Health and Wellness Advisory Council; and Suez has the Water Resources Advisory Group. In other cases, these external expert groups offer advice, guidance, and monitoring on a broader range of issues, such as Dow Chemical's Environmental Advisory Council, BT's Stakeholder Advisory Panel, Interface's Eco Dream Team, Coca-Cola's International Advisory Board, Verizon's Consumer Issues Advisory Panel, and the Ethics Advisory Board of Novartis.

Three: Implement Systems to Ensure Integrity

It may be true that the "buck stops at the board," but a company's ability to deliver day-in and day-out performance with integrity requires much more than a strong board of directors. It calls for honesty, fairness, and respect in dealing with all the company's stakeholders at all levels of the business. And it requires all the company's employees to take responsibility and be accountable for this. It calls for:

■ Clear and consistently applied *ethics policies* or codes of conduct, backed up by credible systems to ensure that unethical behavior is punished, even when it is committed by the company's top business performers, and ethical behavior is supported and rewarded, even when it results in lost business opportunities.

▪ *Operational guidelines,* distributed in as many relevant languages as possible and supported by training, dialogues, systematic reporting, and clear accountability structures.

▪ Genuinely confidential and easy-to-access *whistle-blowing mechanisms.* Despite all the rhetoric and the high-profile coverage of a few famous whistle-blowers, such as Enron's Sherron Watkins and WorldCom's Cynthia Cooper, most corporate whistle-blowers are still ignored, treated unfairly, or ostracized by their colleagues. Many end up leaving the company under duress.

▪ A commitment to operating with *integrity* both inside the workplace and beyond. This includes issues such as managing conflicts of interest, ensuring fair competition, and respecting other companies' assets, as well as protection and proper use of the company's own assets.

▪ Systematic policies and procedures to *combat bribery and corruption* in all countries and under all circumstances, ranging from the payment of unauthorized agency or facilitation payments and acceptance of gifts, to multimillion-dollar corruption on a grand scale.

▪ Compliance with local laws, rules, and regulations, but a commitment to strive for consistently high *international standards* everywhere the company operates around the world and in everything that it does, even if local laws are weak or poorly implemented.

Medtronic is widely regarded as a company that combines impressive financial performance with an unswerving emphasis on values and ethical conduct. It is instructive to look at the company's website. They clearly outline their values not only in English and Spanish, but in six major languages. The company also asks and answers the specific question, "Why does Medtronic have a Code of Conduct?" and describes the different practical steps it takes to align words with action. As president and CEO Arthur D. Collins recognizes, "No Code or Business Conduct Standards can cover every possible business situation which may arise in the complex regulatory environment in which Medtronic operates."[8] But by putting clear communication and compliance structures in place, the company has a better chance of helping its employees make the right decisions or ask for help when dilemmas arise.

Sara Lee has established what it calls a Global Business Practices program, which builds on its long-standing code of conduct. The aim of this program, launched in 1997, is to provide the company's 150,000-plus employees in over fifty countries a framework for ethical decision-making that goes beyond compliance to also emphasize values. The company has appointed over a hundred Business Practices Officers who oversee ethics and compliance around the world, including a hands-on ethics training process. About fifty Business Practices Committees add a further level of review and accountability.

Abbott Laboratories is also developing a management framework for ensuring organizational integrity that is rigorous in terms of compliance but aims to go beyond this. The company refers to "seven elements of an effective compliance program—leadership, standards, communications, training, accountability, assessment, and remediation."[9] It aims to integrate these elements into a continuous process of oversight, communication, and reinforcement that applies to its broader ethical performance, in addition to quality control and regulatory compliance.

Our profile that follows illustrates some of the ways that General Electric is embedding integrity throughout its management structures and responding to the governance concerns of its investors.

GE: Working to Implement Performance with Integrity

Few CEOs in history have faced the buildup of leadership expectations and the baptism by fire that Jeffrey Immelt handled when he took the helm at 120-year-old General Electric in September 2001 following the legendary Jack Welch. After years of carefully orchestrated succession planning and preparation, Immelt inherited a robust but complex company and then faced the business equivalent of a "perfect storm": a series of almost unimaginable events that no amount of planning could have predicted.

The economic boom of the 1990s was already showing signs of slowing, and it was clear that tougher times were ahead. Then, less than a week into Immelt's new job, the tragedy of 9/11 resulted in the deaths of several GE employees and multimillion-dollar threats to the company's insurance and airline-related businesses, followed by anthrax attacks at its NBC studio. The company rose to the challenge. Key GE businesses produced products and services to help meet the operational needs of emergency workers and cleanup crews, thousands of GE employees donated time and money to help victims of the attacks, and the company's diversified business portfolio kept revenues flowing. Then came negative media exposure over GE's legacy of responsibility for pollution of the Hudson River, followed in short order by mounting public disgust over executive remuneration and retirement benefits—and, of course, the unrelated but highly publicized accounting scandals at Enron, Global Crossing, Tyco, and others.

Angry investors started to focus their suspicion and skepticism on any company that appeared too complex, too large, or too successful. GE, one of the world's largest, most valuable, and most diversified corporations, fit the bill. At the end of 2002, although the company had weathered global economic downturn, delivered earnings growth of 7 percent, and been one of only seven industrial companies to retain a Triple-A rating, GE's stock was down 39 percent for the year, and the company was placed under a fierce media and investor spotlight.

As Immelt admitted candidly to shareholders in his 2002 report, "This was not a great year to be a rookie CEO."[10] Throughout this trying period, however, the importance of operating with integrity remained a central and consistent theme in Immelt's leadership statements and actions and in GE's management systems. It has also been a clear and important message in the company's efforts to reassure skeptical investors and sustain employee morale and motivation around the world. "Unyielding integrity" has long been one of GE's core values, along with performance and change. But the need to demonstrate how this commitment to integrity is put into practice in terms of corporate governance and daily operations has taken on new urgency in the face of recent events affecting corporate America. The manner in which Immelt is personally taking a lead in renewing and reinforcing the company's commitment to integrity, both internally and externally, offers a valuable example for other business leaders.

From America to China, he has stated clearly and consistently that "Nothing—not 'making the numbers,' competitiveness or direct orders from a superior—should ever compromise our commitment to integrity."[11] But, he admits, "One concern that keeps me up at night is that among the 300,000-plus GE employees worldwide, there are a handful who chose to ignore our code of ethics. I would be naïve to assume that a few bad apples don't exist in our midst."[12] It is for this reason that the company invests millions of dollars and extensive executive time in its compliance and auditing structures, its training systems, and its efforts to spread and reinforce ethical norms and shared values through a culturally and operationally diverse organization. A few of the practical steps it takes are the following:

Corporate Integrity Policy and Common Values Card GE has a globally applied integrity policy called "The Spirit & The Letter." Every GE employee signs a pledge to adhere to it when he or she joins the company, and all employees are given a values card. According to Immelt, "Our standards are resolute and absolute on a global basis. There's no country where we would go with convenience. And we've lost business because of that." But in the long run he is convinced that this commitment to integrity makes sound business sense, as well as being the right thing to do. He argues, "We have found over a long period of time that integrity is not only important for our reputation, but ultimately it helps you to be more successful as a business. It's a business asset. Countries and companies want to do business with people they think they can trust, where there's transparency and ultimately that leads to business success."[13]

That trust is subject to intense and ongoing scrutiny by a skeptical public and suspicious media. A *60 Minutes* report in early 2004, for example, entitled "Doing Business with the Enemy" identified GE as one of many U.S. corporations that, while complying with the law, maintains business investment through non-U.S. subsidiaries in "states that support terrorism." Even for a company that has established a sound internal system for upholding ethical standards the need to defend these standards and even perceived inconsistency is exacting.

Rigorous Compliance and Performance Systems The company has invested in a large internal audit team and continues to strengthen it, also increasing the rigor of its board audit committee, which meets at least seven times a year. In terms of performance, leaders within GE are measured with respect to business results and integrity. Immelt admits that assessment is easy when people demonstrate great results and good integrity but says, "It's always been a challenge to manage someone who gets good results, but has poor integrity, does it by abusing others, does it by cheating the system. My advice—and something I have learned in my career—is that you always have to eliminate those people. Even if they get good results in the short-term, they always poison the system; they always poison the work of other people."[14]

Training and Leadership Development GE's leadership development process is built around values. All new employees receive some form of integrity and compliance training when they first join the company. Immelt observes that one of the most important things GE has done is to have its operating leaders be responsible for this training: "in other words, we don't make human resources people responsible for integrity; we don't make the lawyer responsible for integrity. . . . the business leaders, the CEO, the general manager and the sales leader; those are the people responsible for integrity training."[15] Immelt estimates that he spends "at least 30 percent to 40 percent of my time interfacing with people . . . to spread [the] culture."[16]

Responsiveness to Investor Concerns The best internal systems and values-driven culture in the world aren't sufficient if investors don't believe in them or don't understand the company and how it operates. As GE faced the harsh media and investor spotlight of the past few years, the board came to recognize the need to respond rapidly and transparently to investor and public concerns. In responding to new corporate governance regulations and listing requirements, it has proactively announced measures to move beyond compliance.

The company has increased its investor communication sessions and the amount of information being made available about its integrity systems, its operations, and its long-term business vision. For the first time, the board has made publicly available its own governance policies and charters. *Business Week,* among others, recognized that GE "has raised the bar for disclosure and opened itself to an unprecedented level of scrutiny."[17] Requirements regarding director independence have been tightened. A presiding director has been appointed to guide the board's independence, the mandate and workload of the audit committee have been increased, and nonexecutive directors are required to visit a certain number of company operations each year. GE was one of the first companies to announce that it would start expensing its stock options; it also places restrictions on when its executives can exercise them to better align executive compensation with long-term results. At the same time, it has revised and in some cases phased out other executive benefits.

These actions may not immediately translate into a better stock price, but they strengthen the foundations for GE's long-term growth. The company has a diversified portfolio of leadership businesses, a proven business model, and a major effort under way to increase customer focus. It has a global presence with strong local roots, positioning it well for further global growth. Over 50 percent of senior executive hires since 1999 have been women, minorities, or foreign nationals. The company's state-of-the-art management tools include Six Sigma and its digital measurement systems, "digital cockpits." These enable every GE business to access fifteen real-time metrics online anytime, allowing for faster decision-making, reduced cycle time, and improved risk management.

Immelt and his team have learned that in today's world, customer focus and good business performance are no longer sufficient to build trust and keep the share price high. Greater transparency, increased communication, and demonstrating on a daily basis that it operates with integrity have never been more vital to the company's success. As Immelt has reported to his shareholders, "I believe that our reputation for integrity and honorable dealings is our most important asset."[18]

Four: Cooperate to Raise Industry Standards

We have looked at what individual companies can do to improve their corporate governance and sustainability governance and the systems through which they support ethical behavior and operational integrity. Leadership at the individual company level is necessary but not sufficient to improve investor confidence and public trust in business.

There is also a need to raise the bar for business more generally and to demonstrate industrywide progress in addition to individual progress. This is needed not only in terms of corporate governance, but also sustainability governance and public governance. Regulation has an obvious and important role to play, although it is not always the most effective or efficient approach to change corporate behavior. Voluntary self-regulatory or market-led accountability frameworks are also necessary to move beyond "the usual suspects" and to spur change toward superior governance.

Different Approaches to Self-Regulation

In order to encourage innovation and good practice and to avoid or minimize the heavy hand of regulation, more and more companies and business associations are seeing the benefits of self-regulatory governance structures. They operate in a wide variety of different ways and contexts. Three common approaches are as follows:

(1) Mobilize the power of the market to raise industry standards through market mechanisms such as eco-labeling, social labeling, and environmental trading permits, underpinned by independent certification and monitoring of corporate performance. We look at the examples of the Forest Stewardship Council and Home Depot.

(2) Use trade and industry associations to establish ethical, social, or environmental standards and make them an entry requirement for membership in the association. We look at the example of the chemical industry's Responsible Care program and the experience of the Dow Chemical Company.

(3) Establish multisector learning networks to discuss dilemmas, develop voluntary guidelines, and spread good practice regarding principles of governance—ethical, labor, human rights, and environmental. We look at the example of the United Nations Global Compact.

(1) Raise Industrywide Standards by Mobilizing the Power of the Market: The Forest Stewardship Council and Home Depot

Home Depot, established in 1978, is one of the most respected consumer brands in America. The company and its founders, Arthur Blank and Bernie Marcus, are credited with having revolutionized and dramatically grown America's home-improvement retail industry. They achieved this through an innovative combination of massive warehouses and economies of scale that offered wide selections of good-value and high-quality products, serviced by a motivated and customer-focused sales force and underpinned by a strong values-driven culture. The emphasis on values was a key factor contributing to high staff morale, motivation, and service levels—and these led to a growing number of customers and dollars in the till. Since 1978, Home Depot has grown to be the largest home-improvement retailer and third-largest retailer in the world, operating over 1,700 stores in fifty U.S. states, employing 300,000 associates, and stocking up to fifty thousand different kinds of products in some cases.

Although Home Depot now faces increasingly tough competition from other retailers, it remains committed to a value proposition that combines service excellence with a high-quality, price-competitive shopping experience, built on the foundation of clearly stated commitments to people and the environment. How does the company offer over a billion customers a combination of service excellence and value for money, with an assurance that the goods they are buying have been produced in a socially and environmentally responsible manner? How does it independently verify and account for the environmental sustainability, as well as the value and quality, of its products? How much do these issues matter to its associates and customers in an increasingly competitive retail market and weak, uncertain economy?

Arguably these questions are more important today than ever in ensuring that the company retains a profitable and respected leadership role in its industry. Finding answers to them, however, is more complex and demanding than in the past. Responsible sourcing of wood products offers one example of the challenge. Home Depot launched its early environmental efforts back in 1990. For almost ten years it played a pioneering role in "green retailing and sourcing" and was justifiably proud of its progress. Then in 1998 the company was targeted as part of a major consumer campaign led by the Rainforest Action Network. Using a combination of high-profile statements by Hollywood celebrities, newspaper ads, and guerrilla-style protests and stunts in Home Depot stores, Rainforest Action targeted the company for selling unsustainable forestry products, not because the company was guiltier than its competitors—in fact this was far from the case—but because it was the sector leader and the one company they knew had the power to influence the entire industry if it changed its own procurement policies.

As part of its response, Home Depot joined forces with industry as well as environmental NGOs to become part of an innovative fledgling market mechanism called the Forest Stewardship Council (FSC).

Founded in 1993 by a diverse group of representatives from environmental and social groups, the timber trade, and the forestry profession, the FSC envisioned bringing together all the players along the global wood-supply chain, from production to retailing, and then working with them to mobilize market forces aimed at ensuring greater sustainability of forests. By having a critical mass of key players on board, combined with a system for certifying responsibly sourced wood products, the FSC's founders believed they could change the way that forests products are grown and sold. And they could achieve this not through bureaucratic, government-led command-and-control regulations, but instead through harnessing the power of the market by providing consumers with the choice of buying forest products that have been independently and professionally certified. First established in Europe, with leadership from the World Wildlife Fund and UK home-improvement retailer B&Q, the FSC is now an increasingly well-recognized mechanism for improving environmental performance and governance in the international forestry industry.

Home Depot took a pioneering role in establishing an American market for wood products certified under the principles of FSC. It established a wood-purchasing policy for its own operations in 1999, and today the company is the largest supplier of certified wood in the world. It can also demonstrate that less than 0.15 percent of this wood comes from rain forests—the vital but fragile ecosystems that the world faces the greatest risk of depleting. At the same time, the company is using its purchasing power and dominant market position to encourage good practice along its wider supply chain. Through its vendor buying agreements and supplier relationships, it is influencing a growing number of its business partners to transition to more sustainable sources of forest products. Over the years, major competitors such as Lowe's and Wickes have followed suit in stocking more certified wood products, as have several large home builders such as Kaufman, Broad, and Centex.

Learning from its membership in the FSC, Home Depot helped to lay the foundation for the Certified Forest Products Council in the U.S., a nonprofit organization that promotes the increased purchase, use, and sale of independently certified forest products. Thus the company is using its position as an industry leader to work with others, including some of its leading competitors, to transform market frameworks and address a key environmental challenge.

Recent years have been tough for Home Depot. Competition has been relentless, and some business decisions have undermined staff morale and customer service. Under new CEO Bob Nardelli, and in the face of stiff competition from Lowe's, Home Depot has marketed more to women, invested $10 billion in the modernization of stores, and centralized merchandising functions. The company recognizes that it has to refocus on building the service excellence and sense of team spirit that made Home Depot great. Under these circumstances, a relentless commitment to good corporate governance and good sustainability governance will probably be more, rather than less, important in supporting the company's plans for renewed growth and reputation.

(2) Raise Industrywide Standards Through
Membership Requirements of Trade Associations:
The Responsible Care Program and Dow Chemical

In the early hours of December 2, 1984, a poisonous gas leaked from Union Carbide's pesticide factory in the Indian city of Bhopal. It became the worst industrial accident in history, killing several thousand people immediately and an estimated twenty thousand since that time. The human tragedy and environmental damage caused by the Bhopal disaster continue to this day—as do the lawsuits and campaigns against Union Carbide, now owned by the Dow Chemical Company, and the challenges faced by the chemical industry in regaining public trust.

Bhopal forced the chemical industry to start thinking beyond basic legal compliance to a more leadership-driven, collective approach to managing the human and environmental risks associated with its operations. It was a major driving force behind the establishment of the chemical industry's Responsible Care program. Initiated by the Canadian Chemical Manufacturers Association in 1987, Responsible Care has now spread to over forty-five countries around the world through national and regional chemical industry associations. It is a voluntary initiative that aims to increase the safety of chemical products from inception in the research laboratory through manufacture and distribution to ultimate disposal. It offers a good example of business-led collective governance aimed at raising standards across the entire industry above what is legally required in most countries. The program has ten core principles and six codes of management practice and measures of performance, and it provides a useful framework and model for other industry sectors.

It also has lessons to offer in terms of its governance framework. First, participation in Responsible Care is now a condition for company membership in many chemical industry associations. Other industry associations could require a similar responsibility-based approach to membership, but few do.

Second, in addition to members carrying out self-evaluations of their own operations under the framework, an external peer review process has recently been added to verify that participating companies have effective management systems in place. This external verification process not only increases accountability and transparency, but also helps to identify areas for improvement and spread good practice and awareness through the industry. In the United States every member will be required to disclose aspects of its performance to the public.

Third, the program calls for participating companies to involve the public more actively in their accident prevention programs and decision-making. This has resulted in many companies establishing community-level advisory structures and, in some cases, global advisory panels.

Responsible Care is certainly not without its flaws and critics, but it has played a key role in raising the bar for responsible business in the chemical industry. Since its inception, for example, releases of toxic chemicals and off-site disposal by the industry have decreased by some 50 percent. It has helped participating companies to decrease risks, improve stakeholder relations, and gain direct bottom-line benefits.

Dow Chemical is one of the founders of Responsible Care. Larry Washington, Dow's global vice president for environment, health, safety, human resources, and public affairs, argues the case for Responsible Care:

> *Fewer safety incidents mean healthy, productive employees. And fewer emissions mean your plants are running more efficiently and reliably. And that means you can deliver your product on time, on budget, and with the highest quality to your customers. . . . to be sustainable, to be competitive, our businesses must be accountable for their environmental and safety performance, the same way they are for profit and loss.*[19]

Dow offers a good example of a company that is using the types of sustainability board committees and external stakeholder advisory structures that we listed in our six characteristics of high-performance boards. The company's commitment to good sustainability governance starts with the board, where it has a long-standing environment, health and safety committee and a public interest committee. These are responsible, among other things, for reviewing the targets that Dow commits to on sustainability issues and reviewing the company's Public Report, which covers its performance against its triple bottom-line targets for economic, social, and environmental progress. At the other end of the governance spectrum, at the local site level, the company consults with its more than twenty community advisory panels in some twelve countries. In a growing number of countries it also produces local environmental and community reports. Dow publishes an annual corporate sustainability report that also includes twenty local reports from manufacturing sites around the world.

Dow's external Corporate Environmental Advisory Council also reviews its sustainability performance and reports. Some of its feedback, both positive and negative, is made public by the company. This council was established in 1991, when it was one of the first of its kind anywhere in business. According to Washington, "The council was formed to provide a credible outside perspective from thought leaders on current and emerging issues."[20] It meets two to three times a year and consists of about ten external experts, with members rotating to ensure fresh perspectives. Its recommendations are considered in decision-making, including discussions with Dow's board of directors. At the same time, the company is starting to work with auditors and consultants to develop an external assurance system to evaluate the processes that it undertakes and the data it produces on its sustainability governance and reporting.

(3) Raise Industrywide Standards Through
Learning Networks: The United Nations Global Compact

For over fifty years, the vast General Assembly hall in the United Nations building on the east side of Manhattan has been the exclusive preserve of nation-states, their heads of government, and their official ambassadors. In July 2000, Kofi Annan, the UN's secretary-general, hosted one of the most unusual meetings in the organization's history. Business leaders from over fifty major transnational corporations came together with leaders from the labor, human rights, and environmental movements to launch the Global Compact. The Global Compact is an initiative to spread international business principles and good practices, on a voluntary basis, in the areas of labor, human rights, and the environment. Kofi Annan's message was simple and clear: "Transnational companies have been the first to benefit from globalization. They must take their share of responsibility for coping with its effects."[21]

In particular, he urged the assembled business leaders to embrace a set of nine principles regarding labor rights, human rights, and the environment—all drawn from international agreements that have been ratified by most of the world's governments. Corporate participants agree to integrate them into their own operations and spheres of influence and to report on their progress, learning from their experience alongside the nonbusiness participants. The compact is not intended as a code of conduct or global monitoring body, but rather a values platform and learning network to encourage greater corporate citizenship and new forms of partnership. The Global Compact has its critics, ranging from activists who see it is a cynical ploy by business to avoid global regulation to corporate lawyers who are wary of the litigation implications if their companies participate. Despite this, some of the world's major companies, trade unions, and human rights and environmental organizations have agreed to take the risk of jointly exploring new approaches to global governance and raising international business standards.

The Pros and Cons of Voluntary Action on Governance

These three examples illustrate different types of voluntary mechanisms through which companies can work together, and with other partners, to raise industrywide standards and improve accountability and transparency on a collective basis. Some critics of these voluntary governance coalitions argue that they co-opt campaigning groups onto the side of "big bad business." Others argue that voluntary or self-regulatory frameworks are not nearly enough to influence the behavior of big corporations. They believe that only global regulation will do. While regulation is essential for preventing gross environmental, labor rights, and human rights abuses, it is rarely the best path to raising standards above the baseline and to encouraging innovation beyond legal compliance. The critical question is: What is the appropriate balance between regulation and voluntary or self-regulatory business-led frameworks?

Global companies cannot afford to ignore this debate. As author and columnist Tom Friedman has commented in the *New York Times,* "The best way to create global governance—over issues from sweatshops to the environment—when there is no global government, is to build coalitions, in which enlightened companies, consumers and social activists work together to forge their own rules and enforcement mechanisms. . . . It comes down to this: Do you want to make a point or make a difference?"[22]

Five: Clean Up Bribery and Corruption

Bribery and corruption represent the greatest challenges to good corporate governance, sustainability governance, and public governance. This includes both multimillion-dollar bribery associated with major projects and petty bribes associated with easing or facilitating day-to-day business transactions. It includes organized crime, money laundering, illegal or illicit facilitation payments, acceptance of unauthorized gifts and hospitality, conflicts of interest, fraud, contracting and procurement irregularities, and illegal information brokering. These activities continue to be a widespread and costly reality for many business-to-business and business-to-government transactions. They increase the costs and risks of doing business, undermine economic development in developing countries, create political scandals in some of the world's most advanced democracies, and destroy public trust in business everywhere.

Individual companies with antibribery policies often face a "first mover" disadvantage when they are competing with companies that continue to pay bribes. It is true that most large companies can shoulder the cost of lost business as a result of refusing to pay bribes. And as GE and others argue, there can be long-term business benefits to establishing a reputation for refusing to pay or accept bribes. For smaller companies, however, it is more difficult to compete effectively in the face of endemic bribery when less-principled companies are gaining undue and unfair advantages. So individual corporate actions are insufficient to turn the tide—collective or regulatory action is needed.

The record on legal frameworks is disappointing. Until recently there was no international legal framework for dealing with bribery and corruption, and even now it is still limited. America's pioneering Foreign Corrupt Practices Act of 1977, which makes it illegal for American companies to bribe foreign officials, has meant that in the past, U.S. companies have often been at a disadvantage compared to their competitors in Europe, where in some countries a company could even get tax breaks for facilitation payments in developing markets.

It was only in 1997 that the OECD passed a convention on bribery, which has now been signed by thirty-five countries. Although implementation is proving to be slow, it is hoped that American companies will reap some benefits as their competitors "play catch-up," establishing the no-bribery policies increasingly being called for by their governments.

At the same time, some of the leading American and European companies, together with counterparts in a number of emerging markets, are establishing the type of collective voluntary initiatives that we outlined in the previous section to raise the bar on tackling bribery and corruption. Examples include the development of business principles and guidelines against bribery and corruption by organizations as diverse as the International Chamber of Commerce, the world's major representative body for business, and Transparency International, a nongovernmental organization (NGO) dedicated to cleaning up corruption in both the public and private sectors.

There are also some innovative industry-sector initiatives emerging. Transparency International, for example, is working with a number of major international banks, among them Citigroup, Deutsche Bank, and JPMorgan Chase, to implement voluntary guidelines aimed at cutting down on money laundering and with other industries such as the construction sector. In 2002, the British government started to work with a group of major oil and mining companies and some leading NGOs to launch the Extractive Industry Transparency Initiative. The aim of this voluntary initiative is to establish mutual commitments between large companies and the governments of developing countries to improve disclosure of the taxes and royalties that exchange hands between the private and public sectors.

Six: Engage Transparently in the Political Process

A final critical element of practicing superior governance relates to the transparency and integrity with which large corporations manage their interface with politicians, political parties, government officials, and government bodies. This interface takes a number of forms, including lobbying; advocacy; political donations; business–government dialogues; business participation in governmental advisory panels; skills exchanges; and public–private partnerships to address issues ranging from policy reform to the delivery of public goods and services such as education, transport, water, and energy.

Making Political Contributions in the United States

One important question relates to growing public concerns about the potential conflicts of interest and undue influence associated with the long-standing tradition of corporate political contributions in the United States. These concerns have escalated dramatically in the wake of America's recent corporate governance scandals. As author and columnist Arianna Huffington argues in her bestselling book *Pigs at the Trough: How Corporate Greed and Political Corruption Are Undermining America*:

*The financial scandals of our time were made possible by an
unprecedented collusion between corporate interests and politicians,
that despite all the breast-beating about reform, is still going
strong.[23]*

Strong words, but they capture the mood of distrust among a sizable
and articulate group of American citizens when it comes to the political
clout of corporate America.

How should principled companies respond? Business for Social Responsibility has carried out valuable research on the "soft money" contributions and corporate donations companies make to organizations
that participate in "issue advocacy."[24] Citing the responsible policies of
companies such as General Motors, IBM, and Honeywell, BSR has sug-
gested the following practical framework for helping individual companies to minimize the litigation and reputation risks associated with
making political contributions:

- Establish clear written standards and policies.

- Include political giving policies in the corporate code of
conduct.

- Scrutinize the organizations to which money is given.

- Make political contributions transparent.

- Establish internal communication and controls.

- Consider alliances with other companies and their senior
managers.

Promoting Democracy in Transition Economies

When the United Nations was founded over fifty years ago, a full two-
thirds of the current member states did not exist as sovereign nations.
Today, many of these are fledgling democracies with market economies.
They offer great business opportunities, but also new risks for global
companies. Foreign investors in these countries face the challenge of determining the boundaries of their responsibility in helping to promote

open markets, democracy, and good government. This is clearly a highly sensitive issue, fraught with problems for even the best-intentioned companies, but it is difficult to ignore.

Established chambers of commerce and other intermediary business associations have a crucial role to play here. The U.S. Chamber of Commerce network, which operates in over eighty countries, offers a useful leadership model and a vehicle that foreign investors can get engaged with when they enter a new country. Other countries have similar networks or can support business linkages via their embassies. We look briefly below at the leadership role being undertaken by the Center for International Private Enterprise.

In summary, practicing superior governance involves first and foremost practicing good governance in the company's own operations—good corporate governance *and* good sustainability governance, underpinned by strong and independent boards of directors and effective management systems for operating with integrity. Second, it involves raising corporate and sustainability governance standards across industry sectors and geographic borders. This requires being compliant with laws, but also includes the creation of new and innovative voluntary governance structures

The Center for International Private Enterprise

The Center for International Private Enterprise (CIPE) was launched in 1983 as part of the National Endowment for Democracy. It is also affiliated with the U.S. Chamber of Commerce. It focuses on the interrelationship between democracy, free markets, and private enterprise and works with local partners, chambers of commerce, individual companies, and governments to help build the legal and institutional structures necessary to build market-oriented, democratic societies. It also supports programs to strengthen the entrepreneurial culture of the private sector and share international standards in business. Since it was founded, the CIPE has provided grants and technical support for close to a thousand projects in eighty countries. It often works with large foreign investors, leveraging their knowledge and skills. This offers a good example of how individual companies can make a contribution to building democracy without having to bear all the risk and cost themselves.

where companies work either collectively with each other or collaboratively with other sectors to raise the bar for their entire industry sector. Third, it involves adopting a responsible approach to the way in which individual companies and industry associations engage in the political process and public policy making, at both national and international levels.

These are all different types of leadership challenges, but they share four overriding common characteristics. First, they are about achieving greater corporate accountability—to shareholders and to other corporate stakeholders and regulators. Second, they are about ensuring better public access to information and increasing the transparency and clarity with which a company talks about itself and its performance to interested parties. Third, they require personal and organizational integrity. They require that individual business leaders and companies make a systematic and measurable effort to "walk the talk." And fourth, linked to all the above, they call for independent oversight by external directors, auditors, regulators, consultants, and advisors.

We finish this chapter by profiling General Motors and its efforts to practice superior corporate and sustainability governance in the face of enormous business challenges. We have selected the company as one of our corporate visionaries as we believe its management team has a clear vision of the future and how to get there, despite some major obstacles en route that could severely impede not only the company but its entire industry sector. The profile illustrates some of the dilemmas as well as the possibilities inherent in governing a responsible and profitable business in today's complex world.

GENERAL MOTORS
Building a Turnaround Strategy on a Foundation of Superior Corporate and Sustainability Governance

General Motors is on a publicly stated mission to regain productivity, profitability, and prestige after several decades of less-than-stellar performance—and to do so while facing relentless competition, cautious consumers, global economic downturn, geopolitical uncertainty, vocal and well-organized social and environmental activists, and a burgeoning pension and health care bill. This is no small task, especially for a company that employs over 350,000 people around the world, manufactures in some thirty countries, and sells its products in over 190, representing about 15 percent of the global vehicle market. In addition to this, the company's leaders juggle the governance and management challenge of not only being the world's biggest car manufacturer, but also operating one of its leading financial services companies and being one of its biggest corporate borrowers. GM is also the largest private purchaser of health care in the United States, providing coverage to some 1.2 million employees, retirees, and their dependents.

GM's management team knows that it must do all the usual things well—cut costs, eliminate inefficiencies, ban bureaucracy, increase teamwork, revamp aging plants, revitalize innovation, reenergize employee creativity, and refocus on consumer trends. The company must do all this to generate the cash that it will need in the coming years to fund its legacy of generous health care and pension benefits, let alone beat the competition by delivering better-quality, more appealing, and more reliable products.

Added to all of the above is the growing pressure from governments and consumers alike to ensure that these products are safer than ever and cleaner than ever in terms of their impact on the environment. Together with big oil, "big auto" sits at the heart of the evolving debates on both global climate change and national security. No other industry faced the almost surreal activist campaigns that targeted the American auto sector during 2002 and 2003. These ranged from television advertisements asking drivers "What is your SUV doing to our national security?" to an Internet campaign that swept many of the church halls of America, asking the question "What Car Would Jesus Drive?" In both cases, the campaigns urged consumers to stop buying SUVs and to opt instead for more fuel-efficient vehicles. There is debate about how effective these campaigns have actually been in influencing consumer attitudes and purchasing choices, but regardless of the immediate outcome, these are issues that are unlikely to go away.

In short, the company and most of its industry peers face a daunting set of economic, social, and environmental challenges. If they can overcome these challenges, they stand ready not only to achieve impressive and profitable growth, especially as markets such as China develop, but also to make an important contribution to addressing one of the greatest sustainable development issues the world faces: how to increase access to mobility, bearing in mind that less than 15 percent of the world's population currently own a vehicle, while doing so in a way that takes into account the risks of increased air pollution, global climate change, and road safety.

GM, together with other leading auto companies, is determined to demonstrate that it can be part of the solution to these challenges, rather than a cause of the problem. CEO Rick Wagoner speaks of "our commitment to integrate economic, environmental and social objectives into our long-term strategic planning, as well as our daily business decisions. We believe this can be a competitive advantage for us if we move fast and take a leadership role."[25]

Investment in new technologies and in product and process innovation sits at the heart of GM's goals to producer cleaner and safer vehicles, while doing so in a way that increases productivity and profitability. Leading-edge fuel-cell technology, for example, is already an increasingly important component of the company's innovation pipeline.

Another key element of taking a leadership role in environmental sustainability is the company's governance systems and standards. It has a long-standing reputation as a pioneer in the area of corporate governance and is now playing a similar role in the emerging area of sustainability governance. Some of the processes, practices, and partnerships it has put into place offer useful lessons for other companies, and we review a few of them here.

Corporate Governance

In 1994, the GM board of directors was one of the first in corporate America to voluntarily write and adopt a set of corporate governance guidelines. Since then, this influential twenty-eight-point set of guidelines has been studied and emulated by companies around the world, influencing good practice far beyond the GM boardroom. Revised in 1997 and again in 2003, GM's guidelines provide a clear mission statement and cover a range of practical issues in the following areas:

- Selection and composition of the board

- Board leadership

- Board composition and performance

- Board relationship to senior management

- Meeting procedures

- Committee matters

- Leadership development

Independence and diversity of board directors is also a long-standing tradition at the company. In 1971, the pioneering civil rights crusader the Reverend Leon Sullivan made history by becoming the first African-American ever elected to the board of a major American corporation. The board was GM's and he served on it for over twenty years. Today, the board is composed of eleven members, of whom ten are independent directors and two are non-American, which is still rare in corporate America. The audit committee, executive compensation committee, and committee on director affairs are composed solely of independent directors. GM stockholders are asked annually to ratify its external auditor. The board also has an investment funds committee, which acts in a fiduciary capacity for employee retirement benefits, and a public policy committee.

Some 53,000 GM employees worldwide hold stock options, and the company started to expense them in 2003. These structures and guidelines, among others, set the framework for GM's corporate governance, but as Rick Wagoner has commented in reference to the corporate governance challenge faced by all companies, "No single action is enough to restore investor confidence in the current climate of concern over corporate accountability. We have to earn investor confidence day in and day out by running our business with integrity and honesty."[26]

Earning the confidence of investors and other stakeholders also depends on increased disclosure and transparency from the company. As Wagoner states, "We place a high value on communicating clear, consistent, and truthful information about our performance to our employees, suppliers, dealers, investors and customers."[27] This is reflected in the fact that GM has one of the most comprehensive corporate governance websites of any company, including not only copies of its governance guidelines but also details of the purpose and meeting frequency of all its board committees and copies of its SEC filings.

Communicating with small investors is also seen as important, in addition to the more common focus by companies on their large institutional shareholders. GM has some one million individual investors and communicates with them via a biannual newsletter, a dedicated investor website, and regional forums. As a reflection of these practices, in 2003—for the second year in a row and during a period of enormous investor distrust in corporate America—GM was awarded top honors for communications with retail stockholders in the internationally recognized Investor Relations Magazine Awards. The company has recently launched another dedicated stakeholder communications website, called GMability, to increase transparency on its broader economic, social, and environmental performance. This forms part of its growing emphasis on sustainability governance.

Sustainability Governance

GM has also played a pioneering role in the area of sustainability governance, although like most companies it remains challenged to keep up with growing public and investor demands for greater disclosure and many activists question its commitment to tackling climate change. Back in 1977, Leon Sullivan's combined experience as a member of the GM board and a civil rights activist led to his creating the influential Sullivan Principles for American companies operating in South Africa. These played an important role in raising standards of corporate responsibility and providing parameters for institutional investors during South Africa's apartheid years. In 1999, GM was one of the first major companies to announce its support for the Global Sullivan Principles, which provide guidance for businesses on issues such as human rights, worker rights, the environment, community relations, supplier relations, and fair competition.[28]

In 1994, GM was the first Fortune 50 manufacturing company in America to formally endorse the CERES Principles for Environmental

Performance, developed by a coalition of investor, environmental, and advocacy organizations.[29] Among other things, these principles require participating companies to publicly report on their environmental progress on an annual basis. GM's relationship with CERES has sometimes been rocky, but it continues to raise the bar for the company's performance. Since 1994, GM has set performance targets and reported publicly, initially on its environmental performance and now more broadly. A few years ago, it was one of the companies that helped to establish the Global Reporting Initiative (GRI), which was described under our Principle #5 (performance).[30] The GRI is becoming an international framework for nonfinancial reporting by companies, and GM is one of the pioneers in testing and refining this methodology.

In addition to endorsing and publicly reporting on these principles and guidelines, GM underpins its sustainability governance with input from external advisory committees such as its Science Advisory Committee, European Advisory Council, Asia Advisory Council, and Supplier Environmental Advisory Team. The company's executives also get exposure to a diversity of opinions, including critiques, by engaging in other industry and multisector initiatives such as the EPA's Climate Leaders Group and the Sustainable Mobility Project, which GM has co-chaired with Toyota and Shell. GM is also a member of the World Resources Institute's Green Power Market Development Group. The Group is a unique commercial and industrial partnership aimed at building viable corporate markets for green power. Other participants include Alcoa, Dow, DuPont, IBM, Interface, J&J, Kinkos, and Staples. All of these activities provide a framework for increased accountability and transparency on the part of GM, but also for increased exposure to new ideas. As such, they have the potential not only to improve the company's governance standards, but also to be a source of product innovation and business development.

Public Governance

Research by the San Francisco–based organization Business for Social Responsibility cites GM as one of the leaders in being transparent and consistent in its policy on political contributions. In 1997, the company issued a written policy on political contributions. It still loans vehicles to major political conventions, which it sees as a promotional activity, and is happy for its executives and employees to be politically active on a personal basis or via the GM political action committee, which is employee run with contributions being voluntary and confidential. The company itself has chosen to stop using corporate funds for donations to any national political party or state political campaign.

While these types of commitment are still very much works in progress, the companies that are setting new standards in the areas of corporate governance, sustainability governance, and public governance offer tangible benefits to shareholders. They also offer a promising model for corporate engagement with other stakeholders who are demanding greater accountability, more transparency, and a clearer nexus between the private actions of firms and the public benefits of these actions to society at large.

Practicing Superior Governance

One: Master the art of "and."

Two: Strengthen the board of directors.

Three: Implement systems to ensure integrity.

Four: Cooperate to raise industry standards.

Five: Clean up bribery and corruption.

Six: Engage transparently in the political process.

Pursue Purpose Beyond Profit

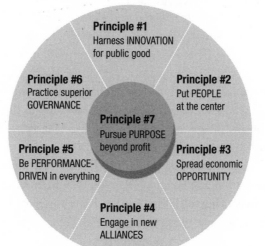

Principle #1
Harness INNOVATION
for public good

Principle #6
Practice superior
GOVERNANCE

Principle #2
Put PEOPLE
at the center

Principle #7
Pursue PURPOSE
beyond profit

Principle #5
Be PERFORMANCE-
DRIVEN in everything

Principle #3
Spread economic
OPPORTUNITY

Principle #4
Engage in new
ALLIANCES

Each company has the core purpose of providing goods or services that meet customer needs or aspirations and yield a profit. In great companies, purpose extends beyond short-term profit and the creation of shareholder value. It often encompasses a longer-term vision to make a contribution to improve people's lives and be a force for progress in the world. Together with principles and values, purpose is what a great company stands for and would stand by even if adhering to them resulted in a competitive disadvantage, missed opportunity, or increased costs.

Purpose, principles, and values are the bedrock of excellence. The manner in which they are articulated and implemented plays a key role in determining a company's strategic direction, its corporate culture, and the policies and incentive systems by which it operates and impacts the world.

Why Purpose Matters

No enterprise, no institution, perhaps no individual can really succeed without a sense of purpose—a purpose which explains and guides every step. Our purpose, our fundamental objective is to be one of the world's great companies. That means delivering results and doing our business exceptionally well day by day. But it also means aligning our activity with the world's needs, leading change and being a force for progress in everything we do.

JOHN BROWNE, GROUP CHIEF EXECUTIVE, BP, 2000

What is the purpose of your business? What do you stand for? What values or principles are nonnegotiable even if adhering to them results in a competitive disadvantage, missed opportunity, or increased costs? What is your vision for the future?

These are some of the most fundamental and important questions that anyone working in business, large or small, should be asking and should be able to answer. They are important in both a personal and organizational context. They are particularly crucial for anyone in a leadership role.

Companies exist to provide products and services. To stay in business they need to deliver a profit and reward investors with competitive financial returns. But profit, especially sustained profit, is a *by-product* of the enterprise, achieved by firms that deliver value in many other ways.

In recent years the unrelenting pressure for ever greater, and in some cases unrealistic, quarterly earnings has made it difficult for all but the most visionary and values-driven business leaders to think beyond the bottom line and beyond short-term performance. But an exclusively bottom-line, short-term focus cannot suffice for the future. This is especially the case for publicly traded companies. To renew public trust in business, meet changing societal expectations, and survive over the long term, companies in the twenty-first century will need more than ever before to be guided by a sense of purpose and values—one that extends beyond short-term profit and private gain.

Ask most people, however, "What is the purpose of business?" and the majority will reply "Maximization of profit or shareholder value."

There is a prevailing view that maximizing profit is the raison d'être of business and that it is not possible to be entrepreneurial and commercial while at the same time being driven by a sense of wider public purpose and benefit.

There is no doubt that corporations are legal constructs that have been designed to channel funds from and back to their owners in order to finance the efficient production of goods and services. But corporations are not only legal mechanisms or funding structures. They are also social constructs that are part of society, not separate from it. They are communities of people and complex networks of relationships. They are living organisms *as well as* legal mechanisms, and they have a soul *as well as* a structure.

Delivering shareholder value and profit are crucial objectives. In fact, they are the lifeblood of a healthy business. Viewed in isolation, however, they are paltry and uninspiring concepts for understanding the myriad impacts that companies have on our lives, whether we are investors, consumers, employees, citizens, or, as in the case of many of us, a combination of all of these. Profits are a *means* rather than an *end*—they're not the real reason that business exists, or the ultimate purpose for what it does.

So what does this have to do with operational and financial performance? There is strong evidence that purpose, based on a clear set of values and principles, enhances corporate performance.

A clearly articulated and credibly implemented corporate purpose and set of shared values form the bedrock on which long-term business success is built. They are the compelling reason why top-quality employees choose to work for a company, why patient investors choose to hold a stock rather than churn it, why customers remain loyal, why communities welcome a company as a neighbor, and why regulators work with rather than against it. They don't always "pay" in terms of immediate impact on the bottom line or on profits, but they are an integral component of solidly performing companies over the long haul. If anything, they are more important in times of economic downturn and individual corporate crisis or transition than they are in good times.

Purpose and values provide a compass for steering companies through the vagaries of short-term share price and market fluctuations and through the uncertainty of mergers, acquisitions, and other types of often painful restructuring. They offer a road map for harnessing new technologies and for navigating the development of new markets, products, services, and processes. They help to provide a screening and "matchmaking" mechanism when choosing new business partners, developing new alliances, and recruiting new people. They serve as a foundation in tackling the ethical dilemmas and difficult trade-offs that are an integral part of business life. They provide the clarity that helps companies to make difficult decisions, choose the right path, and do the right thing.

A number of highly regarded empirical studies demonstrate these points. Drawing on over twenty-five years of research in the field of organizational behavior, for example, Charles O'Reilly and Jeffrey Pfeffer of Stanford University, in their book *Hidden Value,* comment about companies that have achieved extraordinary results: "The most visible characteristics that differentiate the companies we have described from others are their values and the fact that values come first, even before stock price."[1]

Jim Collins and Jerry Porras, in their bestselling book *Built to Last,* conclude, "Great companies generate substantial wealth, but great companies do not let the pursuit of profit divert them from their central purpose."[2] And Jim Collins reinforces this message in *From Good to Great,* which analyzes a group of American companies that generated cumulative stock returns seven times greater than the general market over a fifteen-year period: "Enduring companies don't exist merely to deliver returns to shareholders. Indeed, in a truly great company, profits and cash flow become like blood and water to a healthy body. They are absolutely essential for life, but they are not the very point of life."[3]

Legendary business leaders, both past and present, have reinforced this message, as we see in the table on page 304. Plain common sense should make it obvious. Companies guided by a sense of purpose, principles, and values often outperform those that are not, especially over the longer term.

What Business Leaders Say About Purpose and Profit

Business must be run at a profit, else it will die. But when anyone tries to run a business solely for profit . . . then also the business will die, for it no longer has a reason for existence.

HENRY FORD, FOUNDER, FORD MOTOR COMPANY

I think many people assume, wrongly, that a company exists simply to make money. While this is an important result of a company's existence, we have to go deeper and find the real reasons for our being.

DAVID PACKARD, COFOUNDER, HEWLETT-PACKARD

Does our value system make good business sense? The answer is clear: Absolutely. It brings us the best people. It helps us make the best decisions. And at the end of the day it contributes greatly to a reputation that is, for us, an important competitive advantage. . . . The core values embodied in our Credo might be a competitive advantage, but that is not why we have them. We have them because they define for us what we stand for, and we would hold them even if they became a competitive disadvantage in certain situations.

RALPH LARSEN, FORMER CHAIRMAN AND CEO, JOHNSON & JOHNSON

The reason good people stay at a company is that it's a great place to work. . . . Secondly, people like to work for good leadership. So creating a culture of leadership that people like is key. And the third is, are you working for a higher purpose than an IPO or a paycheck? Our higher purpose is to change the way the world works, lives, and plays.

JOHN CHAMBERS, CHAIRMAN AND CEO, CISCO SYSTEMS

Making It Happen

The soul of a company is its purpose. Without this sense of purpose, backed by shared values and principles, written or unwritten, there is little evidence that companies can survive successfully over the longer term, let alone sustain profits and build competitive advantage. In a growing number of companies, corporate purpose, principles, and values are articulated in written statements. In the most successful companies, they are also embedded in the company's culture, traditions, and daily practices. From successful start-ups to enterprises over one hundred years old, they are part of the company's story, part of its corporate DNA.

Corporate purpose and values do not always have an explicit ethical or moral component. Common values in leading companies include customer service, innovation, creativity, originality, and quality. But in most cases, either explicitly or implicity, these statements also include ethical or moral values such as respect for others, integrity, honesty, fairness, compassion, and responsibility.[4]

What does pursuing purpose beyond profit mean in practice? How does it relate to vision, mission, culture, and codes of conduct? How does it translate from words into action? And how can it best be defined and embedded in your company's DNA?

Some companies have developed detailed general business principles, or public statements with titles such as "What We Stand For" or "How We Work"—BP, Shell, Unilever, and Rio Tinto all have detailed statements of this nature that are worth looking at. Others, such as Nokia, ChevronTexaco, and Danone, have emulated one of the most famous and often-cited values statements: "The Hewlett-Packard Way." Still others have built their principles along similar lines to the famous "Johnson & Johnson Credo," which focuses on the company's service to its key stakeholder groups. Nike has developed what it calls its "Maxims," Standard Chartered Bank its "Beliefs," and Dell the "Soul of Dell." Some companies' purpose, principles, and values statements cover several pages, others a few lines or paragraphs. Some are focused on different types of stakeholders, others on key issues or themes. Many combine both.

There is no perfect blueprint or one-size-fits-all approach. What every company has to address, however, is how to translate these statements of purpose, principles, and values into concrete practice and measurable performance in the daily operating reality of the workplace, marketplace, and value chain.

Many companies develop operational guidelines and codes of conduct to set ethical boundaries and to make the link between words and action. These are in turn driven by management systems—both compliance- and incentive-driven—and key performance targets, indicators, and measures. As Robert Kaplan and David Norton argue in *The Strategy-Focused Organization,*

In addition to communicating the grand purpose of the organization, managers also need to communicate what behavior and actions are unacceptable in pursuit of the mission. Companies need boundary systems that describe the actions that must never be taken. Boundary systems include legal constraints and codes of conduct that clearly identify forbidden actions. They are intended to constrain the range of acceptable behavior.[5]

What are some of the key lessons for putting purpose, principles, and values into practice?

One: Align Words with Actions

Most companies try to rally their employees around a set of principles or core values; indeed, few major public companies do not promulgate a vision statement or the equivalent. But too often these statements and the values that they espouse ring hollow: they are either so bland that employees and others treat them as meaningless, or they are so lofty that they don't have any saliency or connection to day-to-day reality. In too many companies these statements have become a source of cynicism and mistrust, rather than guidance and inspiration to employees and other stakeholders. They can be empty promises for corporate practices that don't match the rhetoric. They can fail to reflect the real corporate culture. Such lack of alignment leads to cynicism, low morale, and alienation among employees. Just check out *Dilbert,* the ubiquitous scourge of corporate hubris and insincerity, for the latest take from the troops about lofty vision and values statements from the corner office!

Statements are therefore important, but not nearly sufficient. "Walking the talk" or "practicing what you preach" is what really matters. The need to align words with action—in terms of the way senior management behaves and the way the company's management systems, structures, and incentives support the company's words and statements—is an obvious and crucial point. Yet in practice this is often lacking or insufficient.

The story of Enron has become a classic example of what can go wrong when there is a lack of ethical alignment among purpose, principles, and practice at senior levels of a company. When Jeff Skilling, Enron's former CEO, resigned on August 14, 2001, the share price stood at

$43.61. By December 2, 2001, it was 40 cents, leaving thousands of ordinary Enron employees without savings. The company and its thousands of stakeholders were failed by a handful of senior executives who did not live by its publicly stated values: "Respect, Integrity, Communication, and Excellence."

Instead of respect and integrity, there were serious conflicts of interest throughout the company. These ranged from the manner in which off–balance sheet partnership structures were established to the composition of the company's board and its relationships with politicians, regulatory authorities, and its auditors. Employees who had been encouraged to hold a large percentage of their savings in Enron stocks were advised by senior management to keep holding these stocks in the months before the company collapsed, at the same time that some of these same executives were offloading their own holdings. Instead of genuine communication, there was a serious lack of transparency and openness to consumers, investors, and the company's own employees. Despite the company's motto, "Learn the Power of Why," it became almost impossible for employees to question the actions of their profit-making colleagues. As the *Financial Times* reported, "The main factor that discouraged questioning of Enron's business practices was a ruthless and reckless corporate culture that lavished rewards on those who played the game, while persecuting those who raised objections."[6] And while there was undoubtedly excellence in innovation and execution, ultimately it was fatally undermined by the lack of alignment between the company's stated values and its actions. Enron attracted skilled and dedicated employees who drove this innovation, but this was not enough to guarantee the company's survival. Excellence in innovation and execution without an ethical compass, underpinned by operational checks and balances and a values-driven as well as value-focused management ethos, can rarely be sustained over the long term.

The rapid unraveling of Arthur Andersen, largely as a result of its association with the Enron scandal, is another salutary lesson on how the unethical actions of a small group of people can undermine, and in exceptional cases destroy, an otherwise strong firm. Once customers, investors, employees, or regulators lose trust in a company, that trust can be extremely difficult and costly to regain. In severe cases, it is now clear, corporate survival can be put at risk.

Two: Engage Employees

Edicts from the head office that are imposed from above without the active engagement of employees are rarely effective. CEOs and senior executives can say all the "right" words, produce all the "right" bits of paper, and even establish all the "right" procedures. If they fail, however, to genuinely motivate and mobilize their employees around a sense of common purpose and shared values, the company will achieve, at best, compliance and mediocre performance. Neither is sufficient for companies that aspire to be world class.

Developing a sense of *common* purpose and *shared* values is fundamental to success. This requires engaging employees in the process of defining, redefining, reviewing, and implementing the company's core statements of purpose and values. Companies need to invest in internal consultation, consistent communication, and training to ensure that every employee understands what the company stands for, knows the boundaries of acceptable behavior, and has the tools needed to make a contribution.

Johnson & Johnson is one company that offers valuable insights on how to engage employees in ensuring that the company's stated purpose and values become a living document that is embedded in the reality of daily business practice.

Johnson & Johnson: Engaging Employees Around Purpose and Values

We believe our first responsibility is to the doctors, nurses and patients, to mothers and fathers and all others who use our products and services . . .

These are the opening words of the famous J&J Credo, written in 1943 as a statement of corporate purpose and values by General Robert Wood Johnson, the chairman of Johnson & Johnson from 1932 to 1963. He believed that "industry only has the right to succeed where it performs a real economic service and is a true social asset." During the past sixty years, under his leadership and that of his successors, the company has evolved from a small family-owned business to become the world's most comprehensive and broadly based manufacturer of health-care products.

During the gravity-defying market growth of the past ten years, J&J didn't shine as the most exciting or dazzling performer on the block. Instead, it continued to produce steady, consistent performance, focusing on its customers, employees, communities, and then shareholders—in that order of priority, based on its Credo.

To put this consistency of performance into perspective: 2002 marked the company's seventieth consecutive year of increased sales, its eighteenth consecutive year of double-digit earnings increases, excluding special charges, and its fortieth consecutive year of increased quarterly dividends. Let's go back even farther. Johnson & Johnson has delivered consistently good performance with a compound sales growth rate of 11.6 percent since the company was founded in 1886. It has a strong balance sheet and maintains a Triple-A credit rating.

In 2002, the Economist Intelligence Unit, working with an advisory board of leading academics and business leaders, awarded the company first place for the Americas region in its Global Corporate Achievement Awards. In 2003, J&J was ranked as having the best corporate reputation in America for the fourth straight year by the annual reputation survey published in the *Wall Street Journal*.[7] It is also regularly listed in other surveys as a respected company that recent graduates, women, and minorities most want to work for, and is publicly recognized by government bodies and market-driven sustainability indices for its social and environmental performance.

What is the basis of the consistency and endurance of J&J's financial and societal performance over many years?

In their 2002 letter to shareholders, the company's chairman and CEO, William Weldon, and its vice chairman and president, James Lenehan, report:

We sustain our consistent performance through a culture that is based on a strong system of values. We expect the highest standards of ethical behavior throughout our global organization, achieved when each of us assumes responsibility for leadership and integrity. We are guided in that pursuit by our Credo, the embodiment of our values, which has now been in place for 60 years. This four-part strategic business model— broadly based in human health care, decentralized, managed for the long term, on a foundation of strong values—has served us well, yielding an enduring record of consistent growth and performance. It continues to light our way into the future.[8]

Engaging employees in debating and implementing the Credo is an integral element of the company's internal communications and leadership development processes. This helps them to embed it more effectively in their own daily activities, reinforce its enduring values, and sustain it as a vital, living document. The company keeps the Credo alive and relevant in a number of ways:

Integrating the Credo into Leadership Accountability The Credo has always been a central point for leadership accountability throughout the company. This is formalized through the company's Standards of Leadership model, which has the Credo at its core, surrounded by five major clusters of competencies:

- Customer marketplace focus

- Innovation

- Interdependent partnering

- Complexity and change

- Organizational and people development

The Standards of Leadership model is increasingly used as the basis for recruiting new employees, undertaking performance reviews, managing the company's 360-degree feedback processes, and even determining executive compensation.

Integrating the Credo into Top Management Gatherings Every few years the company holds a global meeting for its top executives. At this meeting time is spent "challenging" the Credo. According to former CEO Ralph Larsen, "We ask our top people from all over the world to test it. We open the door for them to question it, and to question our leadership at the very top. We consider whether clauses need to be reworded or maybe even deleted or added."[9] Substantive change has been rare over the past fifty years, but this process helps to reinvigorate the Credo and increase management ownership of it. It has also underpinned those changes that have been made, such as updating some of the language and adding sections on a few new areas, including the environment and balance between work and family. How many other companies bring their senior managers together with the explicit aim of debating and invigorating the company's statement of purpose, principles, and values?

Employee Credo Surveys Every two years each and every employee in over 200 J&J operating companies around the world is asked to complete a Credo survey. It seeks their opinions on how they as individuals, their management, their operating company, and the corporation overall are doing in fulfilling the responsibilities of the Credo in day-to-day operations.

Developing Performance Measures At a few sites across Europe J&J managers are working together on a project they are calling "Values into Value," developing business performance measures to encourage greater creativity, innovation, and leadership in operationalizing the values of the Credo. A key objective is to inspire operational managers in the company to think about the opportunities that the Credo offers for developing new products and services and building the long-term sustainability of their business.

Johnson & Johnson offers an excellent example of steady and reliable corporate leadership. It is a company anchored by its purpose and values, keeping its eye on building for the long term, while at the same time delivering sound short-term performance without being obsessed with managing quarterly earnings. The company's consistent and enduring performance over many years demonstrates that purpose and values do count, especially when they are owned and lived by employees, from the corner office to the factory floor and sales force.

Three: Learn from Outsiders

Getting employees actively engaged in developing and implementing the company's purpose, principles, and values is crucial but insufficient in today's world. Companies also need to engage with external stakeholders on these issues. There are two important elements to this external stakeholder engagement:

■ First, how companies *listen to and learn from their stakeholders* on matters relating to the company's purpose, principles, and values. Ultimately the board and senior management must decide what external feedback, advice, and criticism to integrate into their decisions, but being open to outside perspectives can play an important role in helping to shape a more widely accepted and credible statement of purpose or principles. We look briefly at the experience of Rio Tinto in this area.

■ Second, how companies learn from and *influence their external business partners,* such as joint venture partners, suppliers, contractors, and distributors, to adopt similar commitments to operate according to publicly stated purpose, principles, and values. We look briefly at the experience of Vodafone, a young and rapidly changing company that is developing its own clear sense of purpose and values while also engaging with suppliers to spread this commitment along its supply chain.

Rio Tinto: Engaging with Stakeholders
to Revise Business Principles

Rio Tinto is one of the world's largest mining and minerals processing companies, operating in one of the world's most environmentally and socially controversial industries. With an Australian and British senior management structure and almost 40 percent of its operating assets and 30 percent of global turnover in the United States, Rio Tinto's operations span the globe. It has been the target of some high-profile activist campaigns and reputation challenges over the past decade. At the same time, it is becoming a leader in shaping the emerging business agenda on more sustainable patterns of development.

The company has focused its efforts to define responsible operating principles first on its own direct operations, and second by working with others on an industrywide basis. Extensive consultation with external stakeholders, as well as employees, has been central to both approaches. One example was the manner in which Rio Tinto reviewed and updated its statement of business practice, "The Way We Work," in 2002. Using the first edition of the statement, developed in 1997, the management team first contacted the company's employees and asked for their feedback on the statement's practicality and usefulness, as well as ideas for improvements.

At the same time, it asked Business for Social Responsibility to carry out a global benchmarking exercise against industrywide guidelines and those of other leading companies. Over a hundred sources of feedback were then incorporated into a new draft. This feedback was shared with about forty of the company's hands-on business unit and line managers, as well as about fifty external experts in academia, NGOs, and government, and investors from around the world. It was also made widely available for employees' comments on the company's intranet. After a six-month period of listening, learning, and refining, the company's revised version of "The Way We Work" was presented to and accepted by its full board of directors.

Due to the complex challenges and high levels of public mistrust in its sector, Rio Tinto realizes that acting on its own isn't enough. There is a need to engage stakeholders at the industry level, not only the company level, in order to tackle some of the tough dilemmas and to agree on mutually acceptable standards of business principles and practice. As a result, the company took the lead in helping to establish the multisector Mining, Minerals and Sustainable Development (MMSD) initiative.

Over a two-year period, this initiative has consulted with thousands of individuals and hundreds of public, private, and community organizations all over the world. It has identified some of the tough issues facing the mining and minerals sector. It is now starting to focus on how public reporting and accountability guidelines can be established to gain and maintain higher levels of public trust in this important sector. The MMSD initiative is a useful model for any sector to consider as a mechanism for consulting external stakeholders on issues relating to industry purpose, principles, and values, and to the most effective standards of corporate practice and accountability.

Vodafone: Engaging with Suppliers to Share Values

Vodafone first launched a mobile phone service in 1985, becoming a listed company in 1988. Just over fifteen years later, Vodafone is now one of the world's largest companies, with operations in twenty-six countries, and Partner Network Agreements in eleven other countries. Arun Sarin, the company's recently appointed chief executive says, "We have over 130 million proportionate customers worldwide, €50 billion in revenues and a complex global supply chain. We're facing greater scrutiny, greater responsibility, and greater expectations from all of our stakeholders and we need to build trust with them through the way we conduct ourselves as individuals and as a company. When people talk about Vodafone, I want it to be positive, whether it's about our practices or processes or our supply chain or whatever it is. I want Vodafone to be complimented for doing good and for fulfilling our responsibilities to the world around us."[10] The senior management team are working to achieve the company's vision through a management system and accountability structure that ensures the company's values and business principles are embedded in daily operations.

Vodafone's chief operating officer, Julian Horn-Smith, has been responsible for driving forward the process of implementing corporate responsibility in the company. He comments, "As we have grown from being a portfolio of national companies to an integrated multi-national group, even greater emphasis has been placed on delivering our values. Over the past three years, we have been pursuing an increasingly systematic approach to issues of corporate responsibility."[11] Learning from best practice in its own industry and beyond, the company developed and publicly launched a statement of its vision, values, and business principles in 2002. It has also set a timetable for establishing management systems, and it has identified seven priority corporate responsibility areas on which to focus management attention, making public commitments and setting public targets for these priorities and giving the group's Operational Review Committee collective responsibility for their implementation. Importantly, each initiative is also led by an operating company CEO or a senior director. These actions are helping to put delivery on values and corporate responsibility right at the heart of the company's business model and line-management structures, rather than at the margins as a "nice-to-have" add-on managed by a philanthropy unit or a health, safety, and environment department. The company's corporate responsibility director and her team still play a key role, providing expertise, trend analysis, facilitation, and backup, but responsibility rests with the operating units.

Given the nature of its business model, Vodafone works closely with major suppliers around the world, and the quality, reliability, and service excellence of these suppliers is crucial to its own success. The company uses the cash value added metric that we described under Principle #5 (performance), and this metric shows that over half of its revenues go back to the many companies that work with or for Vodafone in its networked business model. The company has therefore made working with suppliers on corporate social responsibility (CSR) issues one of the seven priority areas described above. The aim is to promote CSR best practice and to identify related risks and potential opportunities in the supply chain.

In February 2003, Vodafone hosted an initial workshop on CSR for over twenty of its key global suppliers, which include other leading companies such as Nokia, Hewlett-Packard, Sony, and Ericsson. Building on the learning shared and the issues raised at this workshop, the company is now working with a smaller group of its suppliers to test the implementation of its code of ethical purchasing. Working together, these companies will have an opportunity to spread responsible business practices and values further along the global telecom supply chain.

Four: Have the Courage of Conviction

There has been much analysis of and debate on the business case for being a values-driven company—the argument that doing good equals doing well, or that "ethics pays." Indeed, in this book we cite numerous examples and empirical studies of cases where values-driven and responsible companies deliver world-class performance and good financial results. It is important, however, to be clear that there is not always a win–win scenario. There *will* be trade-offs between values and value—especially in the short term. Accepting and making these trade-offs is a critical function of good business leadership. Doing the right thing, not just the immediately profitable thing, is the ultimate test of values-driven corporate leadership.

In many cases there is a relatively straightforward alignment between a company's purpose, its core values, and its performance and profitability. At the very least, sound and widely understood values are unlikely to destroy value, and they often protect it or enhance it. In some cases, however, especially in the short term, values-driven companies have incurred costs, turned down potentially profitable opportunities, taken a risk, or taken a courageous stand in order to live their core values or to be true to their core purpose.

Sir Geoffrey Chandler, one of the former Shell executives who was responsible for developing Shell's first General Business Principles in 1976, argues:

> *I don't believe ethical behavior should depend on its*
> *paying. To suggest that doing right needs to be justified by*
> *its economic reward is amoral, a self-inflicted wound hugely*
> *damaging to corporate reputation. . . . Doing right because*
> *it is right, not because it pays, needs to be the foundation of*
> *business, with principle, not profit, the point of departure.*
> *There does have to be a choice about priorities. . . . If we are*
> *to preserve the most effective mechanism the world has known*
> *for the provision of goods and services—that is the market*
> *economy with the public limited company its main instrument—*
> *then it has to be underpinned by principle. Financial failures can*
> *destroy individual companies. Moral failure will destroy*
> *capitalism.*[12]

This is a message that today's business leaders increasingly need to articulate and implement if we are to rebuild public trust in the private sector. It can relate to a whole range of business decisions. These include entering or disinvesting from controversial markets; product recalls of unsafe or tampered products; development and distribution of new life-saving products that may not be big profit generators; and undertaking major environmental commitments and investments that may not have an immediate or even medium-term payback in terms of cost savings or other benefits.

Here are a few examples of business leaders taking a principled public stand that at the time may have undermined profits or drawn censure from their peers:

▓ BP's CEO John Browne speaking up publicly on climate change and political contributions, and voluntarily committing his company to address these issues ahead of his industry peers and regulatory legislation

▓ DuPont's CEO Chad Holliday, Interface's CEO Ray Anderson, and Pascale Pistorio, CEO of STMicroelectronics, publicly committing their companies to core business strategies and ambitious targets that embrace the concept of sustainability

▓ CEOs such as Niall FitzGerald of Unilever and David O'Reilly of ChevronTexaco taking a public stand on the need for the governments of developed countries to cut their agricultural subsidies and make their domestic markets more accessible to agricultural exports from poorer countries

Courage is also about collective leadership—for example, major oil and auto companies deciding to stand shoulder to shoulder with environmental campaigners such as Greenpeace in September 2002 to call on the world's governments to ratify the Kyoto Treaty on Climate Change. Or the sixty-plus companies that stood up to be counted in support of the University of Michigan's commitment to affirmative action when the case went to the U.S. Supreme Court.

We look next at the courage displayed by Merck in its groundbreaking decision to develop and donate the drug Mectizan for people who it knew at the outset would be unable to pay. Although many other pharmaceutical companies have since emulated this initiative, and in some cases gone beyond it with their own donation programs, Merck's courageous decision still serves as a benchmark today, and an embodiment of a company's leaders having the courage of their conviction and living their values.

Merck's Commitment to Eliminate River Blindness

Merck operates in a highly competitive industry where public suspicion is high, the hunt for talent and R&D discovery is unrelenting, and the market is unforgiving. Since its founding, the company has been driven by a publicly articulated commitment to improving the health and well-being of society. This "North Star" of values and purpose has helped to give it competitive advantage in recruiting and retaining top-notch researchers, gaining entry into new and emerging markets, and establishing a well-deserved reputation for brand integrity and corporate responsibility.

The story of Merck and Mectizan is a case study in putting a company's values to work for society and harnessing its core business competence to achieve breakthrough performance in terms of public–private partnership and positive differentiation in terms of public values and corporate value. It is a powerful illustration of how important it is to have a purpose beyond profits and act according to core values.

In a 1950 speech at the Medical College of Virginia, George W. Merck, the company's president for twenty-five years, stated simply and unequivocally: "We try never to forget that medicine is for the people. It is not for the profits. The profits follow, and if we have remembered that, they have never failed to appear. The better we have remembered it, the larger they have been." Flash-forward thirty-five years: Merck was being challenged to put its corporate values to the test, as an industry leader in the growing and profitable business of veterinary products to combat parasites in animals. In 1978, one of Merck's research scientists had stumbled upon a potential application for a variant of the drug ivermectin— an application that could possibly provide a treatment for the widespread disease river blindness, which severely crippled millions of rural villagers throughout Africa. The company's line management had to decide how to proceed.

Should they invest the twenty to forty million dollars needed to test the educated hunch of their top-notch researchers when they might possibly come up dry? Should they proceed to explore a human formulation of a compound originally developed for animal use that might cause unanticipated and risky public health consequences? Should they invest precious R&D expenditures in a drug intended for patients who had *no ability to pay?* Should they supply drugs to countries where the public health authorities were often unable to respond effectively to people's health needs? What would be the effect of saying no to their scientific staff, who felt that they might be on the verge of developing a breakthrough blockbuster drug that could improve the lives of hundreds of thousands of people every year?

There was internal debate and some disagreement, but ultimately Merck's senior management team, acting on its core corporate values, decided to invest in the development of Mectizan. Having proven its safety, soundness, and efficacy, Merck then proceeded to manufacture the drug, and working in partnership with the World Health Organization and other governmental and nongovernmental organizations, both domestic and international, it made an unprecedented commitment to donate Mectizan free of charge to combat river blindness "wherever it is needed for as long as it is needed."

In 2002, Merck's current chairman and CEO, Raymond Gilmartin, visited Africa and celebrated the fifteenth anniversary of the Merck Mectizan Donation Program, delivering the 250-millionth free dose of the drug to a woman in a small rural village in Tanzania. The program now reaches more than thirty million people in thirty-three African and Latin American countries and Yemen. It is the largest ongoing medical donation program in history, greatly improving the quality of life, as well as the economic prospects and prosperity, of many low-income communities.

Merck's role has not only been to donate free medicine. The company has also shared its management, distribution, and communications skills with its partners in order to build the capacity of public health systems and ensure that the medicine reaches the people who need it. In 1998, Merck expanded its donation of Mectizan to include the treatment of lymphatic filarias, commonly known as elephantiasis, in countries where it is coendemic with river blindness. The company entered into partnership with one of its key competitors, GlaxoSmithKline, which has led the global initiative on lymphatic filariasis; working with others, they will reach and help to ease the suffering of over 300 million people.

Since the Merck Mectizan Donation Program was first launched in the mid-1980s, the role of the pharmaceutical sector in providing essential medicines to low-income communities and helping to address global health challenges has moved from the philanthropy department to the boardroom and become a business imperative that goes to the heart of the pharmaceutical business model. The type of public–private partnership that Merck pioneered with the WHO, the World Bank, and others to tackle river blindness is increasingly seen as the only effective, efficient, and equitable way to proceed and continues to serve as a model of what is possible.

Merck itself continues to play a pioneering role. In 2000, for example, it launched the Africa Comprehensive HIV/AIDS Partnerships initiative with the Bill and Melinda Gates Foundation and the government of Botswana as key partners. This is another groundbreaking—and, some would argue, high-risk or certainly high-stakes—initiative focused on working across sectors to address a major public health issue on a nationwide and integrated basis. Lessons learned from this partnership have the potential to influence public health policy in other countries and on other diseases.

Years after the company's founding, Merck continues to act consistently with its founding values—with the belief that by serving the public interest, profits will follow. And these values also continue to help the company to navigate and adapt in an increasingly complex and demanding world.

Five: Emphasize Purpose and Values Even More in Tough Times

One of the most common critiques of corporate purpose and values statements is that even when they are implemented, they are "good only for the good times." When the going gets tough, profits fall, competitors bite, and the economy moves downward, many people feel that a company's fine aspirations and good intentions are the first thing to be jettisoned. Sadly this happens all too often, but the great companies demonstrate that it doesn't necessarily have to be the case. As Bill Ford reported to his shareholders in 2002, "We lost focus on the critical elements of products and people. It cost us dearly. But difficult times provide an opportunity to re-examine core values and to take bold action. We have done both."[13]

It *is* possible, although certainly not easy, to hang on to corporate values at the same time that a company is facing difficult economic conditions. Even when corporate survival isn't threatened, good business leaders can use tough times and difficult circumstances as an opportunity to strengthen or even implement corporate values, rather than jettison or ignore them. To illustrate this lesson, we profile Dell, which implemented an explicit set of beliefs during a tough economic period.

Dell: Implementing the "Soul of Dell" Program

Dell offers an interesting example where tough economic times have in fact helped to underpin a period of soul searching and values-driven cultural change rather than undermine them. Since its creation by nineteen-year-old Michael Dell in 1984, the company has become a legend in technology circles and beyond for having built the differentiated "Dell Direct" business model. This model has enabled it to serve customers by delivering standards-based technology more directly, more efficiently, and with greater accountability, customization, and cost-leadership than its competitors. Within a ten-year period from 1993 to 2003, the company grew from sales of $2 billion to sales of over $39 billion. Its challenge during this period was to manage phenomenal growth by hiring, building, innovating, and delivering to customers, as fast as it possibly could. As president and COO Kevin Rollins has subsequently observed, "I'd have to tell you, unfortunately, that our culture was not one of our first priorities."[14]

And then came the dot-com implosion, declining world markets, increased business uncertainty, and the public collapse of confidence in corporate leadership. Dell's senior management realized that it had a team of highly trained and successful employees, many of whom had built substantial personal wealth and had high expectations of the professional challenges and material benefits of being a Dell employee. Yet many of these employees were not all that connected or loyal to the company's long-term future. At the same time, it had to reduce its workforce by 5,700 jobs, creating another threat to employee morale and loyalty.

The challenge was to build on the cultural norms that had underpinned the company's phenomenal success, such as a strong performance culture, customer focus, excellent execution, and zero tolerance for illegal or unethical behavior, and to develop a more coherent and explicit set of values and sense of corporate purpose. A set of values that would inspire the best employees to work for and stay with Dell—not simply because of the opportunities to build personal wealth, but because it is a great company with a values-driven leadership model and sense of purpose beyond financial rewards.

This challenge led to the emergence of two complementary initiatives: "The Winning Culture," an inspirational set of operational tenets on how the business is run, and "The Soul of Dell," a statement of beliefs explicitly setting out for the first time what the company stands for and believes in. In order to make these tenets and beliefs an integral part of the way Dell conducts its business in thefuture, the company has also instituted training and employee dialogue activities, new business performance metrics and incentives, and a grassroots program called Business Process Improvements (BPIs). Based on the Six Sigma approach, this program is designed to empower employees to act as champions, show initiative, and take responsibility for finding solutions to operational and corporate responsibility challenges.

After a period of extensive employee engagement and consultation, the company is embarking on a new stage in its development. Rollins comments:

> *Make no mistake, we still want people on Wall Street and Main Street to talk about Dell as the fastest growing IT company in the world and to have strong confidence in our consistent financial performance. And we want them to recognize the power of our business model and our ability to create value for customers. But we also want those same people to admire us for the company we are becoming, not just for our financial performance. We want to inspire them with integrity and our commitment and our values.*[15]

Six: Build in Accountability Systems

While champions are needed at all levels of an organization to define, articulate, and live the company's purpose, principles, and values, ultimate stewardship rests with the board of directors. Accountability structures are needed at all levels of the company, with final responsibility for monitoring them and dealing with noncompliance resting with the board. Even before the corporate governance scandals that hit America, Europe, and parts of the Asia-Pacific region, there was growing awareness of the need for boards to take on a more proactive role in auditing the company's values as well as its financials, and in addressing the company's impact beyond simply economic considerations.

In February 2002, in response to growing public and investor mistrust of business and the capital markets, Nasdaq took out full-page newspaper advertisements entitled "The Responsibilities We *All* Share." These listed the eight beliefs that guide Nasdaq and its board of directors. Their final point was "We believe that corporate ethics take root in the corner office and with the Board of Directors. It is better to lead companies than manage earnings. Ultimately it is about character."[16] Warren Buffett, who has more experience than most in selecting executives and nonexecutive directors, puts the challenge this way: "We look at three things when we choose a CEO: intelligence, energy, and integrity. If you don't have the third, the first two will kill you."[17]

The challenge is not only about character and integrity, although these are absolutely vital; it is also about more rigorous governance and accountability structures both inside companies and in our economic and political system more generally.

We finish this chapter with the case study of BP to bring together the different elements of pursuing purpose beyond profit and to illustrate how one company is striving to meet the following challenges: aligning words with actions; engaging employees; consulting external stakeholders; demonstrating courage and conviction; building in accountability systems; and emphasizing purpose and values even in tough times.

BP
How Long-term Purpose and Shared Values Are Helping Transform BP into a Global Competitor

In October 1987, one of the largest privatization offers of its time was issued to the global capital markets. The British government was selling off its remaining state-owned shares in the British Petroleum Company. Between the opening and closing of the offer, stock markets collapsed around the world. Although not disastrous, the outcome was a disappointing setback for the company. Its global positioning and future competitive prospects looked uninspiring. It was a midsized, bureaucratic, and traditionally run entity operating in relatively few markets with mediocre performance, an unfocused business portfolio, a high-cost structure, and declining assets in its two major oil operations in Alaska and Europe's North Sea.

Today, BP is recognized as one of the oil industry's most profitable, innovative, and competitive operators—and one of its most socially and environmentally responsible. It has become America's largest supplier of oil and gas, one of its largest foreign investors, and a major retailer, with over fifteen thousand service stations, and employees and operations in almost every U.S. state. The owner of historic American brands such as Amoco, dating back to 1889, and ARCO, founded in 1866, BP is also a leader in chemicals, commercial products, and solar energy, and a major investor in information technology and knowledge management.

Worldwide, the company now operates in about a hundred countries, employs over 100,000 people, and serves over ten million consumers every day. And in terms of financial performance, as chairman Peter Sutherland commented at BP's 2003 annual general meeting, "It is a measure of our long-term performance that we delivered a higher rate of return to shareholders against the market over the past ten years than any of our direct competitors in the energy industry."[18] At the same time, the company is listed on the Dow Jones Sustainability Index and the FTSE4Good Index, both of which employ extensive analysis to track not only financial performance but also social and environmental performance, in order to identify a few hundred of the world's most successful and enlightened companies.

To achieve these results, BP has undergone a wide-ranging organizational and cultural transformation that offers useful lessons for other companies. At the heart of this transformation has been a refocusing on core competencies and an emphasis on globalization, supported by a combination of mergers, acquisitions, and investment in new locations; decentralization of the company's operating structure to over one hundred largely autonomous business units; technological innovation; and a growing emphasis on knowledge intensity and cross-boundary learning among its employees. All of this has been underpinned by an increasingly strong performance ethos. This performance ethos aims to improve management performance not only against ambitious production and financial targets, but also against a set of clearly and publicly stated business policies focused on five areas: ethical conduct; employees; relationships; health, safety, and environment; and control and finance.

The treatment of BP's five policy commitments in the same way as other business performance targets has been essential to the company's growing reputation and competitiveness. This has involved making clear public statements on what these commitments are; setting targets for achieving them; measuring, externally verifying, and reporting publicly on progress; learning from mistakes; and committing to continuous improvement in managing and accounting for them. There have been some major challenges and failures, as we will discuss, but these five policy commitments have had a growing impact on BP's corporate strategy, operating structure, and culture. This impact goes far beyond branding and public relations, to the company's corporate governance framework, its management systems, its research and development activities, and increasingly to its asset structure and product portfolio.

The Challenge of Aligning Words with Actions: The Case of Climate Change

Over the long term, BP's publicly stated purpose of being "both competitively successful and a force for good" is likely to fundamentally influence the company's business model as it strives to remain competitive in a world where the demands for energy are increasing alongside demands for this energy to be produced and consumed in ways that respect both human rights and natural environments. As BP sees it, "Confronting this paradox is our mission, but we cannot do it alone. Where others see contradiction and conflict, we see opportunities for mutual progress."[19]

Nowhere is this paradox greater, nor the leadership challenge associated with it more important, than in tackling the rising specter of global climate change. This can only be addressed by dramatically increasing the efficiency and minimizing the emissions of existing fossil fuel–based products and by switching over time to a cleaner energy mix—shifting from the world's current heavy reliance on oil to cleaner fuels such as gas and, ultimately, renewable energy sources such as solar, wind, and water energy. As governments argue over the seriousness of the challenge and the best public policy instruments for addressing it, there is a growing focus on the leadership role of industry, especially the energy and automotive sectors.

BP has played a key role in this process, moving beyond compliance with government regulations and industry norms and standards. In doing so, it has demonstrated that pursuing purpose beyond profit takes courage and conviction and often requires going against the tide, but that it is possible to be competitive and still be a force for good.

In May 1997, some twenty years after graduating, John Browne returned to his alma mater, Stanford Business School, for the first time as the CEO of one of the world's major companies. He spoke about a subject that was either ignored or dismissed in most corporate boardrooms at the time: global climate change and what a company like BP could, and should, be doing about it.

In doing so he became the first CEO in the oil industry to publicly accept that precautionary action was justified even though scientific agreement was still emerging and the data was strongly contested. After initial consultations with employees, scientists, academics, and environmental NGOs, he felt that BP should take a stand and commit to its own voluntary targets for reducing greenhouse gas emissions. He was taking a risk in breaking with the rest of the industry, but he and his management team believed that the company could deliver emission reductions in a way that was innovative, cost-effective, and leading edge. He also believed they had a responsibility to do so, even if there were major costs involved.

Having made this public commitment, Browne faced the challenge of translating his words into action and demonstrating, with measurable results, how his company was starting to address climate change.

In March 2002, five years later, John Browne returned to Stanford to report on the company's progress. He commented:

*As we've become a major participant in the US economy
we've come to understand that leadership is what people expect from
big companies. I believe the American people expect a company like
BP—the largest single supplier of oil and gas in this country, and a
company that continues to grow—to offer answers and not excuses.
People expect successful companies to take on challenges, to apply
skills and technology and to give them better choices.[20]*

He was able to demonstrate that BP had undertaken a series of concrete and voluntary actions to meet his earlier public commitment to take a leadership role on this issue. These actions touched on many aspects of the company's core business, including the following:

▪ *Setting public targets:* In 1998, BP publicly committed to reducing greenhouse gas emissions from its own operations by 10 percent by the year 2010, from a 1990 baseline. This set a clear target for employees and a public challenge for others in the industry.

▪ *Measuring progress:* An externally verified auditing system was established for greenhouse gas emissions, drawing on expertise from auditors and expert inspection companies. This has helped BP to become more publicly accountable for and transparent in its performance. It has also increased internal learning and provided useful lessons for other companies and industry sectors, and for governments.

▪ *Encouraging innovation:* Thousands of BP employees were challenged to get involved through a wide range of internal targets, brainstorming sessions, incentives, technical innovations, and awards to share good practices. Several hundred specific proposals were generated and numerous local actions taken to improve plant and equipment management, many of which saved the company money as well as reducing emissions.

▪ *Establishing internal market-driven incentives:* The company established an internal emissions trading system for greenhouse gases (GHGs), the first truly global corporate system of its kind. Piloted in twelve business units between 1998 and 1999, the system was operated throughout the entire company in 2000 and 2001. Each business unit was given an annual emissions allowance that could only be exceeded by buying permits from other units that had reduced emissions below their cap. Apart from helping to meet BP's reduction targets, this system has given the company useful "early adapter" experience in trading emissions, a process that is likely to create new business opportunities for the company as it becomes more common across different industries and countries. Having run its own internal program for a couple of years, BP is now better equipped to participate in the external emissions trading systems that are being established by governments in partnership with industry.

■ *Investing in cleaner technologies:* BP has upgraded its refining technology to the point where by 2005, 40 percent of all products sold will be cleaner fuels, an improvement that has implications for air pollution and health, as well as climate change. At the same time, it has made investments to become the largest solar energy company in the world. These have included the establishment of its own solar operations as well as equity investments in a number of innovative companies such as GreenMountain, a leading U.S. brand marketer of clean electricity. Although still a tiny part of the company's overall business portfolio, solar promises to be a profitable billion-dollar business by 2007. As government policies inevitably switch toward greater support for renewable energies, BP's experience should position the company well for what is likely to be a highly competitive sector.

Most of these achievements are still works in progress; the easy targets have been hit and the hard part is still to come, especially as the company grows. But by the time he returned to Stanford in March 2002, John Browne could report that the company had met its emissions reduction target—eight years ahead of schedule, and "at no net economic cost—because the savings from reduced energy inputs and increased efficiency have outweighed all the expenditure involved."[21] In fact, the company reports, "Rather than damaging BP's business, the four year program created over half a billion dollars of value in fuel saved."[22]

At the same time the company learned a great deal about new technologies and processes, from measuring and trading emissions, to building new R&D alliances and new businesses—all of which should position it well for the future in competitive terms and in some cases create new business opportunities, such as selling emissions expertise. The quality and efficiency of the products that BP sells have improved too, with benefits for both the company and its customers. It has also discovered that the emissions resulting from the use of its products are about ten times greater than those from its own operations, giving the company a clear rationale for focusing future efforts on delivering cleaner, lower-carbon products to its customers. Less easy to measure, except through survey results, are the energy and enthusiasm BP's programs have generated among its employees and its impact on the company's reputation among its customers, investors, and the public.

Having reached its initial target, the company has publicly set a new target of keeping the future impact of its emissions at or below 2001 levels until 2012, while growing the production of energy products at the same time.

As Browne acknowledges, "So it is a good start. But it is not a place to stop." In his speech to the business leaders of the future at Stanford Business School, he concluded, "We need to reinvent the energy business; to go beyond petroleum. Not by abandoning oil and gas—but by improving the ways in which it is used and produced so that our business is aligned with the long-term needs of the world. That is the route to creating a sustainable, profitable business."[23] In publicly sharing his aspirational vision for the future, Browne is demonstrating the courage of his convictions but at the same time working to align his words with actions by setting clear policies, explicit targets, and incentives to help the company get there.

Building Accountability Mechanisms

To have credibility in pursuing purpose beyond profit, a company needs internal and external systems for monitoring, measuring, and reporting to ensure the necessary transparency and accountability that is so vital to building trust. BP works to increase credibility in a variety of ways. Among them are:

Board-level Accountability Management accountability for ethical, social, and environmental as well as financial performance is monitored at the level of the BP board. In 1997, it adopted a written set of governance policies. Among other things, these explicitly allocate tasks to different committees including an ethics and environmental assurance committee chaired by an independent director and responsible for monitoring all nonfinancial aspects of the company's activities, among them implementation of its policy commitments. The CEO also operates under an explicit goals policy, which sets long-term and short-term targets, and an executive limitations policy, which sets out restrictions on the manner in which the CEO can achieve these results. These restrictions encompass areas including ethics, health, safety, the environment, financial distress, internal control, risk preferences, treatment of employees, and political considerations.

Linking Policy Commitments to Performance Annual performance contracts and medium-term plans are agreed on by every single business unit in conjunction with the executive committees of the company's main business streams. These agreements are designed to give each business unit considerable independence and flexibility while linking it directly to the company's progress in meeting its overall targets and standards in the areas of financial, environment, health and safety, and social performance.

Establishing External Accountability Panels During 2002, BP established external panels of independent experts to monitor and report publicly on the company's social and environmental performance in two of its most sensitive locations—Indonesia and the Caspian. U.S. senator George Mitchell chairs the Indonesian panel and has been outspoken in highlighting the economic, human rights, and environmental risks posed by BP's operations, as well as the company's potential to contribute to economic development.

Remaining Aspirational During Tough Times

Pursuing purpose beyond profit isn't easy. Not all NGOs, investors, financial analysts, business journalists, industry peers, or even employees would agree with the positive assessment we have provided of BP's financial, ethical, social, and environmental performance.

From a growth perspective, in late 2002 BP and CEO John Browne faced intense media scrutiny and investor disappointment when the company had to reduce its production targets for the third time in a year, from 5.5 percent growth to 3 percent. The fact that the original target had been ambitious and ahead of the industry average, and that some of the factors causing the drop in production were beyond the company's control, did little to mollify analysts who had become used to BP hitting this key growth indicator with apparent ease. Interestingly, several of the factors causing lower production, such as hurricanes in the Gulf of Mexico and a well explosion and other safety problems in Alaska, can be linked back to health, safety, and environmental issues, illustrating the growing relationship between these different drivers of corporate success.

The company's safety and environmental record in Alaska during 2002 also came under sharp criticism from regulators, activists, the media, and some employees and investors, resulting in fines, reputation damage, and accusations that "cost-cutting and profits have taken precedence over safety and the environment."[24] The company continues to be the focus of activist campaigns and shareholder resolutions against its investments in environmentally sensitive locations, such as Alaska's Arctic National Wildlife Refuge, and in politically sensitive or conflict-ridden countries, such as Colombia, Indonesia, Angola, and China. As a result of these concerns, some of the leaders in socially responsible investment also sold their shareholdings in BP on the basis that the company's failure to "walk the talk" represented a risk to their portfolios.

BP was also lampooned by some NGOs, business media, and industry peers for its ambitious rebranding campaign, "Beyond Petroleum." In a world still massively dependent on petroleum, critics argued that this campaign is pure public relations and hypocrisy. The U.S.-based NGO Corporate Watch labeled the campaign "Beyond Preposterous," and journalist Cait Murphy, writing in *Fortune* magazine, commented, "Well, please: If the world's second-largest oil company is beyond petroleum, *Fortune* is beyond words."[25] In its defense, the company argues that "Beyond Petroleum" is its vision for the future and a commitment to go beyond business as usual, not a promise that it will walk away from hydrocarbons immediately. CEO Browne is the first to admit that "the industry will be dominated by oil and gas for the next thirty to fifty years." But by investing in alternative technologies, he argues, "We're right up there understanding the change in the world's energy mix, and when the time is right, leading it."[26] In short, investing long term to build tomorrow's competitive advantage.

Some of BP's more courageous environmental, social, and political decisions have also been criticized by its own peers in the oil sector as being out of step with industry thinking. At the time they were initially made, for example, BP's public statements on both climate change and signature payments were criticized in government and business circles. But together with a few other major extractive industry companies, BP has led the way to greater corporate transparency and accountability by putting the issues on the table and having the courage to stand under the spotlight.

In 2003, the company announced six major new areas of development, which it predicts will be the foundation of its future growth. They are Russia, the Gulf of Mexico, Trinidad, Angola, Azerbaijan, and Indonesia—several parts of the world that face high levels of political risk and challenges in terms of governance and transparency. While these locations offer enormous long-term opportunities for the company, its implementation of responsible business policies will be more important and challenging than ever.

These challenges illustrate one of our key points throughout the book. It's not easy being socially or environmentally responsible or having a paradigm-breaking vision of your company's and industry's future. Putting purpose, principles, and values into practice, especially in highly competitive and politically sensitive industries, will always be a challenge. Criticism, skepticism, and cynicism will come from many quarters, especially when trust in business is low and economic times are tough. But as BP's experience illustrates, it *is* doable and it doesn't have to undermine commercial performance—in fact, far from it.

Courageous, purpose-driven, values-based leadership can enhance commercial performance, encourage innovation, improve brand recognition and reputation, build trust, and underpin competitive edge. Even when you can't make a "business case" for it, it is important in its own right. In a world where the private sector is a major player and people are looking to business for responsible leadership, principles, values, and a clear sense of purpose should be nonnegotiable.

Pursuing Purpose Beyond Profit

One: Align words with actions.

Two: Engage employees.

Three: Learn from outsiders.

Four: Have the courage of conviction.

Five: Emphasize purpose and values even more in tough times.

Six: Build in accountability systems.

36 Steps Toward PROFITS WITH PRINCIPLES: Summary of Principles

1. Harness INNOVATION for public good
- Embed into core business strategy.
- Be rigorous about due diligence.
- Invest in social entrepreneurs.
- Support institutional innovation.
- Implement support systems and incentives.

2. Put PEOPLE at the center
- Identify key stakeholders and what matters to them.
- Understand the emerging human rights agenda.
- Protect basic health, safety, and quality of life.
- Enable people to participate in the company's structures and success.
- Build personal potential by enhancing skills and employability.

3. Spread economic OPPORTUNITY
- Create employment opportunities.
- Invest in small enterprise development.
- Help low-income communities build their economic assets.
- Promote e-inclusion initiatives.
- Support education and youth development.

4. Engage in new ALLIANCES
- Build alliances to enhance the core business proposition.
- Harness alliances to leverage philanthropy.
- Use alliances to shape progressive public policy.
- Focus on purpose, process, and progress.

5. Be PERFORMANCE-DRIVEN in everything
- Get commitment at the top.
- Set clear targets and metrics.
- Report publicly on progress.
- Commit to continuous learning.

6. Practice superior GOVERNANCE
- Master the art of "and."
- Strengthen the board of directors.
- Implement systems to ensure integrity.
- Cooperate to raise industry standards.
- Clean up bribery and corruption.
- Engage transparently in the political process.

36 Steps Toward PROFITS WITH PRINCIPLES:
Summary of Principles (cont'd)

7. Pursue PURPOSE beyond profit
- Align words with actions.
- Engage employees.
- Learn from outsiders.
- Have the courage of conviction.
- Emphasize purpose and values even more in tough times.
- Build in accountability systems.

Conclusion

Building Wealth for Companies, Countries, and Communities

Business leaders face complex economic challenges, political uncertainty, and changing societal expectations. Regardless of their industry sector, they are under growing pressure to demonstrate outstanding performance in corporate competitiveness, governance, and responsibility.[1]

In terms of corporate competitiveness, pressure continues unabated to deliver profits and shareholder value in a period of economic downturn, high levels of competition, and greater international risk and uncertainty. This calls for business leaders and their companies to focus relentlessly on operational efficiency, cost control, productivity, quality, customer service, and innovation.

In terms of corporate governance, in the wake of scandals and public concern over accounting failures, conflicts of interest, and inadequate market oversight, there is pressure for business leaders to rebuild public trust and restore investor confidence. This calls for a much greater focus on corporate accountability, transparency, and integrity. It also calls for active engagement between private-sector leaders and public authorities to ensure that new rules and norms are suitable for protecting investors without destroying the spirit of entrepreneurship, innovation, and risk-taking that drives markets and economic progress.

As for corporate responsibility, high levels of international insecurity and poverty are combining with a mounting backlash against globalization and mistrust of big business. This calls for companies to demonstrate that they deliver wider societal value, going beyond philanthropy to encompass their overall impact on and contributions to society. It requires better communication, consultation, and collaboration with stakeholders and greater accountability and transparency on the company's ethical, economic, social, and environmental performance, as well as its financial performance. At the same time, it calls for new types of public–private partnership to address challenges that are beyond the capacity or responsibility of any individual company but are in the interests of the business community as a whole to tackle.

Beyond Business as Usual

Successful companies of the future will be led by executives who understand the strategic importance of these pressures and who recognize and harness the linkages between corporate competitiveness, corporate governance, and corporate responsibility. They will share a mind-set that takes them "beyond business as usual" in the following areas.

Beyond Shareholder Value The primary focus of leading companies is and will remain value creation, but they have a broader vision of value creation than most companies. They are focused on creating value for investors, but also on creating broader economic, social, and environmental value—what we have called societal value. They operate with a clear understanding that there are certain values and principles that are nonnegotiable in pursuit of profit.

Beyond Compliance Leading companies are rigorous about compliance. They aim to achieve conformance with legal and regulatory requirements, voluntary industry guidelines, and their own operating policies. However, they see compliance as a starting point, not an end point. When addressing ethical, social, and environmental issues, they aim beyond compliance and beyond controlling risks and costs, to a vision of value creation.

Beyond Philanthropy Leading companies all have impressive philanthropic, charitable, or social investment programs, but they see these programs as only one factor in creating societal value. They go beyond checkbook contributions to leverage their core corporate competencies, products, and services to create a better world. They recognize that their greatest impact on, and greatest contribution to, society comes from the way they run their core business activities. They aim to deliver products and services that people want in a manner that also creates wider external benefits by creating jobs, generating income and investment, paying taxes, supporting training, spreading technology, and implementing international business standards. They also acknowledge the importance of public policy and the role that business plays in influencing policy and promoting opportunity at both a national and international level.

Beyond the Zero Sum Leading companies are fiercely competitive, but on many issues they are able to go beyond a zero-sum mind-set of "I win; you lose." They look for ways to grow the size of the pie, not just to compete for what's already on the plate. They are systems thinkers and optimizers, rather than linear thinkers and minimizers. They look for win–win scenarios and consult widely with stakeholders when trade-offs, dilemmas, and tough choices cannot be avoided. On occasion, they work with their fiercest competitors in collaborative initiatives to tackle socioeconomic and environmental issues of common concern.

Beyond the Short Term Leading companies aim to deliver short-term performance but have explicit incentive and accountability systems that encourage longer-term thinking and planning. Their goal is to stay in business tomorrow, not just make a quick buck today. They focus relentlessly on competing in their current markets or getting out where they can't compete, but they also have the imagination and the management tools to anticipate change and to envision scenarios beyond today's realities. They carefully analyze social, cultural, political, and environmental trends, as well as economic trends. They look for underserved markets, either in new geographic regions or among excluded population groups. They keep their eyes constantly on the "radar screen" and their ears open, often through nontraditional forums, for new trends, technologies, and discontinuities, so that they can be better positioned to grab new opportunities and to be alerted to unforeseen risks.

Our seven principles can be used as a compass to help executives and managers navigate this new terrain "beyond business as usual." These principles will need to be applied in different ways, using the strategies and terminology most appropriate to each company, industry sector, and set of circumstances. Whatever the company, however, they will need to be explicitly adopted and deliberately implemented. Sound business principles don't happen spontaneously, and they need the support of champions and change agents.

Leadership Traits of Champions and Change Agents

In all our research and analysis, the most common lesson across every company, country, and industry sector has been the crucial importance of responsible leadership. In every case there have been champions and change agents who have implemented the principles and driven the type of performance that defines a great company. These champions and change agents can be found at all levels of the organization, especially, but not only, at the top. They exhibit superb business skills, technical competence, and awareness of their industry, but they go further to demonstrate leadership that is based on accountability and transparency, cross-boundary thinking, long-term vision, and strong values. They listen thoughtfully to, and learn from, others before making decisions.

In the wake of recent governance scandals and eroded market value, we may have seen the demise of the all-knowing, all-powerful "celebrity CEO," but the role of the chief executive as the champion of corporate values and corporate value is in fact more critical than ever. When it comes to creating a sense of common purpose, implementing transformational change, and instilling core values, not much will happen without active and public direction from the top. This is especially the case when these goals may result in trade-offs that sacrifice short-term profit. At the end of the day, the CEO, chairman, and senior management team must be both the symbol *and* the substance of the company's principles and values, not only in times of crisis but on a regular and consistent basis. At the same time, the best senior executives create the climate and opportunity to empower and inspire other leaders. In almost every company we have profiled, champions and change agents are encouraged throughout the company. In a few cases they have emerged against all odds, even when they have not been encouraged, to have a substantial influence on senior management and on the company's strategy or culture.

The leadership traits that follow characterize the champions and change agents that lead their teams, their business units, and their companies to deliver profits with principles.

Consultation: Listening to and Learning from Stakeholders

The best leaders ask for and listen to different perspectives, both inside the company and beyond. They aim to harness the ideas, energy, and aspirations of all employees by giving people a sense of ownership in the company—one that goes beyond good salaries and stock options to active employee participation in helping to shape the company's direction and strategy. They genuinely learn from their employees, rather than just paying lip service to this concept, through regular one-on-one contact; informal interaction; Internet chat rooms; employee surveys; cross-functional, cross-business, and cross-geography task forces; and learning networks. They are serious not only about harnessing fresh ideas, but also about finding out what matters to people, what motivates them, and why.

These leaders also consult with a broad group of external stakeholders, ranging from customers and suppliers to local community leaders and critics. They establish external advisory boards and undertake stakeholder dialogues on a variety of issues at both the global and the community level. Although they take responsibility for making the final decisions, they are neither too self-confident nor too timid to consult widely in order to improve the quality of the information that informs their decision-making.

Communication: Being Clear and Consistent

The best leaders recognize that clear and consistent communication is crucial for managing expectations, motivating employees, and building trust and confidence with stakeholders more generally. They achieve this through coordinated and integrated communications strategies that align corporate messages both internally and externally. While they aim for clarity and consistency of the message, they utilize a variety of communication tools or mediums. These include internal meetings and external stakeholder dialogues, executive speeches, newsletters, regular business briefings, site visits, community gatherings, the company intranet, the Internet, public reports, advertising campaigns, and cause-related marketing initiatives. They publicly communicate their company's purpose, principles, and values, and they make public commitments on social and environmental targets along with financial targets. They establish measures to drive and evaluate performance, and they report publicly and transparently on failures as well as progress.

Collaboration: Recognizing That Teamwork Pays and Making It Happen

Almost every champion and change agent we've spoken with talks about the power of partnership in leveraging resources and bringing diverse perspectives to solving problems. They are open to collaboration, often with competitors and nontraditional allies such as nongovernmental organizations, community activists, and labor leaders. They are effective bridge-builders, able to think and act across traditional boundaries, be these functional, geographic, ethnic, gender-based, or cultural.

Credibility: Delivering on Commitments

The best leaders link their personal credibility and integrity to organizational systems and incentives to ensure organizational credibility. By personal credibility and integrity we mean CEOs, senior executives, business unit managers, project managers, and team leaders who "walk the talk" and do so consistently, day in and day out. This includes acknowledging mistakes, admitting to not always knowing the answers, being honest about problems, and sharing the financial burdens in times of crisis and restructuring.

Organizatonal credibility involves implementing management systems and incentives that help to embed the company's principles and values in daily operational practice. These include internal accountability mechanisms such as board-level oversight of all aspects of the company's performance, compliance systems, help lines, and credible whistle-blowing options. They include measurable performance targets, appropriate incentive structures for "getting it right," and clear penalties and resolution mechanisms for "getting it wrong," especially when it comes to ethical behavior. Incentives include integration of nonfinancial criteria into performance appraisals and public recognition and award programs. Organizational credibility also includes leaders ensuring that there is alignment between the company's stated purpose and values and its public policy positions and lobbying activities.

As the experience of Enron and other discredited companies demonstrates, organizational credibility is necessary but insufficient without personal credibility—grand mission statements and even institutional structures and reporting systems won't make much difference if senior executives simply bypass them or don't take them seriously. The best leaders recognize that personal credibility and organizational credibility are two sides of the same coin—different but inseparable in building a great company.

Competence: Harnessing New Skills and Knowledge

Champions and change agents focus relentlessly on building their own competence and that of their teams. They invest seriously in leadership development and succession planning at every level of the company. They recognize the importance of constantly honing and improving management skills in areas such as stragegy, economics, finance, accounting, quantitative analysis, human resources, operations, sales, and marketing. At the same time, they recognize that new skills and competencies must be developed to deliver profits with principles and ensure that ethics are embedded in day-to-day operations.

This includes systematic and regular efforts to test people's understanding of and ability to manage the ethical dilemmas that most large companies face on a daily basis somewhere in their operations around the world. In leading companies, time is explicitly allocated in senior executive retreats to focus on and debate such issues. They are not simply relegated to training programs for younger managers and employees.

New skills and competencies also include the development of a broader, more global worldview among leaders at every level of the company. They must be able to assess and articulate changing political conditions, societal expectations, and economic trends, as well as what they mean for the company and industry sector. At the same time, probably as never before, business leaders need to be able to develop an understanding of and respect for diverse cultures and communities. For multinational companies in particular, global vision and expansion strategies need to be balanced with local implementation and accountability, often in hundreds of locations around the world. This calls for managers who understand global trends but are also sensitive to local issues and customs.

In today's world, the best leaders are also those who accept complexity, paradox, and ambiguity as givens but are still able to offer a sense of meaning and purpose within this context. They are leaders who have a clear sense of where their company or business unit is aiming to go over the long term, but sufficient flexibility and confidence to change the route based on changing circumstances and the lessons of experience.

Operating in this challenging environment, these leaders also recognize the need to look inward—to reflect on their personal values and how these are aligned with the business decisions that they make on a daily basis. Leaders cannot credibly uphold their organization's value system if these values are not aligned with their own personal beliefs. Offering managers the opportunity to reflect on these issues may seem a luxury in a period of relentless competitive pressures and cost cutting; yet it is an investment that some leading companies are making, and with imagination it can be done in a way that is both cost-effective and respectful of time constraints.

Courage: Moving Out of the Comfort Zone

Winston Churchill once said, "Courage is rightly esteemed the first of human qualities . . . because it is the quality which guarantees all others."[2] Today's companies and the people who lead them are in uncharted waters, and CEOs, in particular, are being asked to make decisions about and speak out on issues that are not the traditional "territory" of a business leader. Their views are being sought on issues such as trust, compassion, and hope. They are increasingly expected to take a stand on issues that are highly complex and don't have clear-cut solutions, such as global climate change, human rights, international terrorism, and HIV/AIDS. Many of them are making more decisions than usual on commercial, social, and environmental issues that have a long-term and often uncertain impact on their business while the financial markets are still focusing on short-term drivers and results.

Nonexecutive board directors need the courage to ask more searching questions, to challenge the CEO, and to break away from the deferential atmosphere of most traditional boardrooms. They are being required to monitor the CEO's performance against a growing range of nonfinancial issues that may have a material impact on their business and its future success but that are relatively new to them. Increasingly, they also have to make judgments on strategic risks and opportunities when they find their company at the forefront of difficult social and environmental issues.

Employees also need courage to bring their values and aspirations to work and make them an integral part of working life, not something that gets "checked at the door" each morning. They need courage to speak out on matters of principle, especially when they see unethical behavior or wrongdoing being condoned by their managers. They also need courage to suggest totally new ideas and approaches that represent a departure from the way their company or business unit traditionally does things.

Future success will come to those companies that encourage these leadership traits and recognize the important role of champions and change agents. We believe, based on our own research and a growing

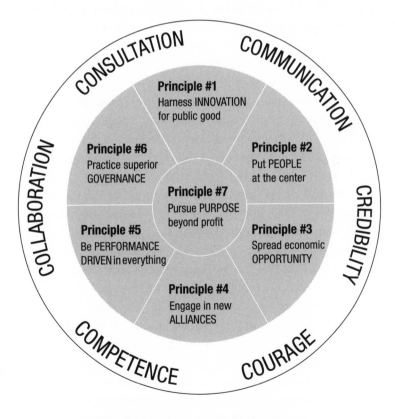

**Principles and Leadership Traits of the
Companies That Deliver Profits with Principles**

body of empirical evidence, that these are the companies most likely to deliver products and services that customers want in a manner that is both principled and responsive to the needs of other stakeholders, thereby building the trust and competitiveness that underpin long-term success. In the diagram on page 345, we summarize the seven principles and the leadership traits that we believe define and differentiate these leading companies.

The Potential of Delivering Profits with Principles

We conclude with the conviction that business is an indispensable agent for economic and social progress and that it will be profitable and beneficial for companies to embrace this role. Business, and indeed global capitalism, is being put to the test. Political and corporate leaders are being challenged to demonstrate that they can deliver prosperity and opportunity in a manner that restores public trust, tackles inequality, and promotes environmental sustainability. Companies, especially large companies, are being challenged to demonstrate that they can deliver profits with principles in a manner that is competitive, accountable, and responsible. The stakes have rarely been higher. Future generations will judge us on whether today's generation of leaders meet or fail this challenge.

Business cannot, and should not, be expected to address or resolve all the world's economic or social ills. Companies cannot eliminate international terrorism or poverty, or solve other global dilemmas. Yet there is no more powerful and promising engine for increasing prosperity and opportunity than a market system operating within effectively regulated and broadly accepted frameworks and spearheaded by principled companies and business leaders. Working in partnership with governments and civic organizations, companies have the resources, technology, creativity, ingenuity, networks, and problem-solving skills to produce products and services that can improve the quality of people's lives while decreasing the impact their operations have on the environment. Companies operating with principles can regain the energy, innovation, optimism, and dynamism that characterized the 1990s, without the greed, hubris, and arrogance that precipitated their demise. They can harness the enormous potential of business to make the world a better place, while remaining profitable and competitive.

The business practices outlined in *Profits with Principles* call for investment and conviction. There are no simple solutions when it comes to delivering profits with principles in today's complex world. Goalposts keep moving. Boundaries keep changing. Competition keeps increasing. Expectations of shareholders, customers, employees, communities, regulators, and other stakeholders keep rising. As daunting as the challenges are, it is riskier to do nothing. The long-term self-interest of corporations and the public interest are inextricably interwoven. Successful and sustainable companies need the existence of prosperous and just societies. Every person in business today can choose to build companies that support the existence of such societies. Business leaders can choose to create wealth not only for themselves and their companies but also for the countries and communities in which they operate. Our hope is that the principles and examples provided throughout this book will inspire and help people to make these choices, following the lead of those who are already paving the way. We encourage you to put these principles to work in your firm, building a great company and contributing to the creation of a good society.

Acknowledgments

There are many people in business, academia, civic groups, and government who have influenced our thinking and provided us with insights, input, and inspiration for this book. They have done so directly, for the purpose of this book, and indirectly over the years that we have known and worked with them and had the benefit of being able to learn from them. In particular, we would like to acknowledge the people who work for the companies we have profiled, both those whom we have met and spoken with and many others whose work has inspired and challenged us. We take full responsibility for the way we have interpreted their contributions, and we have endeavored to faithfully present the work they are doing to make a profit and make a difference in the world.

Thanks also to our editors Roger Scholl and Anne Cole, who have encouraged and guided us with great patience and skill, to our copyeditor, Rosalie Wieder, and to Sarah Rainone for her support. Thanks also to our talented and enthusiastic agent Helen Rees for her support.

We are grateful to our colleagues at the Prince of Wales International Business Leaders Forum and Harvard's Center for Business and Government, who have given us a combination of intellectual, logistical, technical, and moral support, all of which has been greatly appreciated. In particular, we thank Hendrika Wouters, Michael MacIntyre, Elizabeth Bulette, Helen Broderick, Jennifer Nash, Whitney Elizabeth Helms, Michele Tobie, Robert Davies, Jonas Moberg, Dave Prescott, Rebecca Dunford, Alok Singh, Peter Brew, Nancy Wildfeir, Adrian Hodges, Andrew Fiddaman, Nick Claridge, Beth Ginsburg, and Amanda Bowman. Thanks also to Alison Beanland, Tricia Woodson, Tom Herman, David Duncombe, Dena Skran, Elizabeth Riker, Diane Osgood, Simon Zadek, and Simon Winter.

Jane also owes a debt of gratitude to Chris Tuppen, Robin Pauley and her colleagues on the Stakeholder Advisory Panel at British Telecom, Jacques Petry at Suez Environment, and the socially responsible investment team at Henderson Fund Managers—three fine companies where she has served as an advisor and been inspired by their vision, integrity, and cutting-edge practices. We chose not to profile these companies in our book to avoid any conflict of interest but acknowledge their role in promoting responsible business.

Ira offers his thanks also to Lisa Prior for her initial research work and to the following students at Harvard—Toshiko Igarashi, Beth Mackenzie, Emma Smith, Kate Jackson, Sarah Cao, Milan Boran, and Laura Leon.

A special thank you to Mark Wade for his valuable insights and guidance on our title, and above all to Martha Jackson, John Elkington, and Jeff Pedde, whose advice and recommendations have helped to make this book a much better one than it would have been without their input.

And to our wonderful families—Martha, Kate, Joe, Matt, and Alex, and Tony and Libby—who have offered valuable feedback and patiently put up with countless late-night and early-morning transatlantic and transpacific trips and phone calls, our gratitude and our love.

Ira A. Jackson and Jane Nelson

Notes

Preface

1. Kofi Annan, from a speech to the World Economic Forum annual meeting, New York, February 4, 2002.

Introduction

Epigraphs. Quotes from *Newsweek,* July 8, 2002; *Economist* (cover), July 13, 2002; *Fortune,* June 24, 2002; *Business Week,* July 8, 2002; *Business Week,* August 26, 2002 and *Fortune,* June 23, 2003.

1. *Sustainability governance* is a term coined by CERES (the Coalition for Environmentally Responsible Economies) and SustainAbility Ltd. to encompass the integration of wider social and environmental risk and performance issues into traditional corporate governance structures.

1 Capitalism Rules . . . But Needs New Rules

Epigraph. Klaus Schwab (founder and president, World Economic Forum), speech, WEF annual meeting, Davos, Switzerland, January 2003.

1. "Too Much Corporate Power?" (cover story), *Business Week,* September 11, 2000.

2. Alan Greenspan (Federal Reserve Board chairman), testimony before the Committee on Banking, Housing and Urban Affairs, U.S. Senate, July 16, 2002 (Federal Reserve Board's semiannual monetary policy report to the Congress). Chairman Greenspan presented the same testimony before the Committee on Financial Services, U.S. House of Representatives, on July 17, 2002.

3. Joseph S. Nye, "Globalization's Democratic Deficit: How to Make International Institutions More Accountable," *Foreign Affairs* 80, no. 4 (July/August 2001): 2–6.

4. *Business Week,* June 24, 2002, 39.

5. Ibid.

6. "No confidence vote for British business: Company directors are untrustworthy and overpaid," *Financial Times* (editorial), June 30, 2003.

7. World Economic Forum, *Trust in Companies: Executive Summary,* global survey on trust, undertaken by Environics International, January 2003.

8. Final Report of *The Conference Board Commission on Public Trust and Private Enterprise,* the Conference Board, 2003.

9. Geoffrey Colvin, "Tapping the Trust Fund," *Fortune,* April 29, 2002.

10. "No Wonder CEOs Are So Unloved," *Business Week,* April 22, 2002; *Economist, Globalization Survey,* 2002, p. 142.

11. "Wall Street's Verdict," *Time,* July 29, 2002.

12. "No Wonder CEOs Are So Unloved."

13. Scott Klinger et al., *Executive Excess 2002: CEOs Cook the Books and Skewer the Rest of Us,* Ninth Annual CEO Compensation Survey, Institute of Policy Studies and United for a Fair Economy, August 2002.

14. Analysis of Census Bureau data by the Center for Budget and Policy Priorities and the Economic Policy Institute, quoted in Robert Jensen, "Rich America, unfair America," *New York Newsday,* May 29, 2001.

15. Analysis of Congressional Budget Office data released in September 2003, undertaken by the Center for Budget and Policy Priorities, quoted in Lynnley Browning, "U.S. rich get richer, and poor poorer, data shows," *International Herald Tribune,* September 25, 2003.

16. WorldWatch Institute, *Vital Signs 2003,* 2003.

17. Pew Research Center for the People and the Press, *What the World Thinks in 2002,* Pew Global Attitudes Project, June 2002.

18. Heather Boushey et al., *Hardships in America: The Real Story of Working Families,* Economic Policy Institute, July 2001.

19. John Sweeney (president of the AFL-CIO, which represents over 13 million American workers), statement on AFL-CIO website (www.afl-cio.org).

20. United Nations Development Programme (UNDP), *UNDP Human Development Report,* 1998. Also quoted in "The rich and poor grow further apart," *Guardian,* September 9, 1998.

21. Ibid.

22. WorldWatch Institute, *Vital Signs 2003.* Statistics on subsidies per cow in Europe and Japan quoted by speakers at World Economic Forum, Davos, 2003.

23. Vital Facts: Selected facts and story ideas from WorldWatch Institute, *Vital Signs 2003.*

24. World Wildlife Fund (renamed Worldwide Fund for Nature), "The Ecological Footprint," from *The Living Planet Report,* 2002.

25. Peter Sutherland (chairman, Goldman Sachs and BP), quoted in Jane Nelson, *The Business of Peace,* International Alert and Prince of Wales International Business Leaders Forum and Council on Economic Priorities, 2000.

26. "Good Names," *Financial Times* (editorial), April 23, 2001.

2 Building Tomorrow's Competitive Advantage Today

Epigraph. Chad Holliday (chairman and CEO, DuPont), DuPont's Sustainability Report, 2002; Jorma Ollila (chairman and CEO, Nokia), quoted in New York Stock Exchange magazine supplement on global leadership, January 2002.

1. The concept of societal value added draws on research from Jane Nelson, *Building Competitiveness and Communities: How World-Class Companies Are Creating Shareholder Value and Societal Value* (Prince of Wales Business Leaders Forum, in collaboration with the World Bank and United Nations Development Program, 1998).

2. Dow Jones Sustainability Index website and presentation materials, www.sustainability-index.com.

3. Milton Friedman, *Capitalism and Freedom* (Chicago: University of Chicago Press, 1962).

4. Kenneth Prewitt, quoted in Ford Foundation article on the 2000 U.S. Census, 2001.

5. The concepts of social, natural, human, and manmade capital have been reviewed in detail by a growing number of academic studies and initiatives. Some of the early work studied by the authors was published by Ismail Serageldin in *Sustainability and the Wealth of Nations: First Steps in an Ongoing Journey* (World Bank, 1996). Since then a number of major auditing firms and consulting firms have developed frameworks for defining and measuring intangible assets and different types of capital.

6. Alois Flatz (head of research, SAM Sustainable Asset Management), interview with author, July 8, 2003.

7. For a list of studies on the business case for responsible business, see Appendix I.

8. "When Public Trust Is Eroded," *Financial Times* (editorial), June 8, 2002.

9. Taken from description of Andersen as a partner organization, World Economic Forum annual meeting, New York, 2002.

10. Roger Parloff, "The $200 Billion Miscarriage of Justice," *Fortune,* February 17, 2002.

11. PricewaterhouseCoopers, *CEO Survey: Leadership, Responsibility, and Growth in Uncertain Times,* sixth annual Global CEO Survey, in conjunction with the World Economic Forum, January 2003.

12. Survey on "The State of Corporate Citizenship in the United States: 2003," Boston College, U.S. Chamber of Commerce and the Hitachi Foundation, July 2003.

13. Business in the Community, *FastForward Research 2002: Setting the New Agenda for Business,* survey of over two hundred corporate chief executives throughout Europe, June 2002.

14. World Economic Forum, *Global Corporate Citizenship: The Leadership Chal-*

lenge for CEOs and Boards, ACEO Statement in partnership with Prince of Wales International Business Leaders Forum, January 2002.

15. The Conference Board and the Prince of Wales International Business Leaders Forum, *The Millennium Poll,* conducted by Environics International 2000.

Principle #1: Harness Innovation for Public Good

Epigraph. Michael E. Porter and Scott Stern, "National Innovative Capacity," Chapter 2.2 in the World Economic Forum's Global Competitiveness Report, 2002.

1. Ibid.

2. U.S. Council on Competitiveness, *Going Global: The New Shape of American Innovation,* 1998.

3. "The Real Source of the Productivity Boom: It Wasn't IT That Boosted Productivity. It Was Competition and Innovation," based on a conversation with Michael Nevens, managing partner of McKinsey & Company's High Tech Practice, *Harvard Business Review,* March 2002, reprint FO203C.

4. Thomas Edison, founder of General Electric, quoted on GE corporate website.

5. World Business Council for Sustainable Development, *Eco-efficiency: Economic Growth with Reduced Ecological Impact,* South Africa, 2002.

6. World Business Council for Sustainable Development, *Eco-efficiency: Creating More Value with Less Impact,* August 2000.

7. "The Man Behind Toyota's Green Machine," interview with Hiroyuki Watanabe, *Business Week* online, November 13, 2000.

8. George Carpenter (director, sustainable development at Procter & Gamble), quoted in P&G's *2002 Sustainability Report.*

9. Executive speeches on P&G corporate website.

10. April Streeter, "Building Beyond the Box," interview with William McDonough, *Tomorrow,* December 2002.

11. William Ford Jr. (chairman, Ford Motor Company), message on corporate citizenship, company website.

12. Rick Belluzzo, *How Technology Shapes Our World* (white paper), Microsoft, 2002.

13. Kate Fish (vice president, Monsanto), "Building Dialogue into Corporate Decision-making and Communications," speech to the Conference Board conference on global corporate citizenship, New York, February 11, 2002.

14. Novartis, *Corporate Citizenship at Novartis,* 2001/2002.

15. Daniel Vasella, "Make It Meaningful," statement in "Voices: Inspiring Innovation," *Harvard Business Review,* August 2002.

16. Rosabeth Moss Kanter, paper on *Creating the Culture for Innovation,* 2001.

17. Rosabeth Moss Kanter, "From Spare Change to Real Change: The Social Sector as

Beta Site for Business Innovation," *Harvard Business Review* 77, no. 3 (May–June 1999).

18. Peter Brabeck-Letmathe (chief executive officer, Nestlé), statement in *The Nestlé Sustainability Review,* 2002.

Epigraph (DuPont profile): Gary M. Pfeiffer (chief financial officer, DuPont), "Creating Sustainable Business Assets for Today and Tomorrow," speech to the Year 2000 Conference on Environmental Innovation, New York, March 8–9, 2000.

19. Chad Holliday (chairman and CEO, DuPont), "The Challenge of Sustainable Growth," speech to the Chicago Executive Club, Chicago, March 15, 2001.

20. Investment community meeting with DuPont Senior Leadership Team, July 19, 2002.

21. D. S. Kim (president, DuPont Asia-Pacific), speech at the Sixth Annual Regional Responsible Care Conference, Singapore, November 6, 2000.

22. Paul V. Tebo (corporate vice president—safety, health and environment, DuPont), "Sustainable Growth—Do We Have a Choice?" speech, May 31, 2002.

23. Gary M. Pfeiffer, "Creating Sustainable Assets."

24. Chad Holliday (chairman and CEO, DuPont), speech at the Business Day event, World Summit on Sustainable Development, South Africa, September 2002.

25. World Business Council for Sustainable Development, *DuPont: "Zero" Targets Driving Innovation,* case study on DuPont, 2002.

26. Remarks by Chad Holliday at the Prince of Wales Business and Environment Program, Aspen Wye River, October 23, 2003.

Principle #2: Put People at the Center

Epigraph. Orlando Ayala (group vice president, Microsoft), speech on "Partnering to Realize Potential," corporate conference, July 14, 2002.

1. Adrian Levy (founder and former chairman, RLG International), speech, corporate conference, March 2001.

2. James L. Heskett, W. Earl Sasser Jr., and Leonard A. Schlesinger, *The Service Profit Chain: How Leading Companies Link Profit and Growth to Loyalty, Satisfaction, and Value.* Free Press, New York, 1997.

3. Elizabeth G. Chambers et al., *The War for Talent: Tell Me Again: Why Would Someone Really Want to Join Your Company? McKinsey Quarterly,* no. 3 (1998): 44–57.

4. WalkerInformation, *Integrity in the Workplace: 2001 National Employee Benchmark Survey,* Fact Sheet, 2001.

5. Peter F. Drucker, "They're Not Employees, They're People," *Harvard Business Review* 80, no. 2 (February 2002).

6. Based on a presentation made by Jane Nelson to the Seventy-fifth Anniversary Conference of SITA, Suez Group, Paris, April 2000.

7. Research on the business case for tackling HIV/AIDS has been carried out by the Global Business Coalition against HIV/AIDS (www.businessfightsaids.com), the International Business Leaders Forum (www.iblf.org), Business for Social Responsibility (www.bsr.org), and UNAIDS (www.unaids.org).

Epigraph GlaxoSmithKline, *Facing the Challenge: Our Contribution to Improving Healthcare in the Developing World,* 2001.

8. Quoted by Sophia Tickell, "Beyond Philanthropy," in Roger Cowe, ed., *No Scruples? Managing to be Responsible in a Turbulent World* (London: Spiro Press, 2002).

Epigraph Bill Roedy, president, MTV Networks International, quoted in Jane Nelson, *Building Partnerships: Cooperation between the United Nations System and the Private Sector,* United Nations Department for Public Information, 2002.

9. Citigroup, *This Is Diversity at Citibank,* Annual Diversity Report, 2001.

10. Sandy Smith with William Atkinson, "America's Safest Companies: Alcoa Finding True North," *Occupational Hazards,* October 21, 2002.

11. Alain J. P. Belda (chairman and CEO, Alcoa), annual letter to shareholders, 2001.

12. Sandy Smith, *America's Safest Companies.*

13. Paul O'Neill, interview in Thomas J. Neff, *Lessons from the Top.*

14. Randy Overby, "Alcoa's Strategic Direction: A Vision for Tomorrow," remarks at the World Resources Institute Sustainable Enterprise Summit, March 13, 2003.

15. Alain J. P. Belda (chairman and CEO, Alcoa), annual letter to shareholders, February 20, 2003.

16. Details provided in Alcoa, 2002 Sustainability Report.

17. Paul O'Neill (former chairman and CEO, Alcoa), interview quoted in Thomas J. Neff, *Lessons from the Top: The 50 Most Successful Business Leaders in America and What You Can Learn from Them,* 2000.

Principle #3: Spread Economic Opportunity

Epigraph Susan V. Beresford (president, Ford Foundation), "Innovative Business Strategies," foreword to *Win-Win: The Double Bottom Line—Competitive Advantage Through Community Investment,* Ford Foundation, 2001.

1. Ford Foundation, Corporate Involvement Initiative, www.winwinpartners.org.

2. Examples drawn from Ford Foundation, *Win-Win: The Double Bottom Line.*

3. Bob Dunn (CEO, Business for Social Responsibility), quoted in ibid.

4. Parts of this profile are drawn from "'Pathways to Independence': Welfare-to-Work at Marriott International," Harvard Business School case study 9–399–067, October 1998.

5. Ford Foundation, *Win-Win: The Double Bottom Line.*

6. National Minority Supplier Development Council website, 2003, www.nmsdcus.org.

7. Peter Brew (director, operational policy, International Business Leaders Forum), interview, July 2003.

8. Coca-Cola Company, *Unlocking the Power of Our Global Bottling System,* Annual Report, 2002.

9. Beijing University, Tsinghua University, and University of South Carolina, *Economic Impact of the Coca-Cola System on China,* August 2000. Also, Peter Nolan, University of Cambridge and Economic and Social Research Council, *Joint Ventures and Economic Reform in China: A Case Study of the Coca-Cola Business System, with Particular Reference to the Tianjin Coca-Cola Plant,* December 1995.

10. Beijing University, *Economic Impact of the Coca-Cola System.*

11. Alan Greenspan, "Economic Development and Financial Literacy," remarks at the Ninth Annual Economic Development Summit, the Greenlining Trust, Oakland, California, January 10, 2002.

12. Drawn from materials provided by HP's e-Inclusion program at World Summit on Sustainable Development, 2002.

13. Information on Nokia Ventures from company materials.

14. Information on stakeholder relations from company materials, Nokia.

15. Jorma Ollila (chairman and CEO, Nokia), quoted in Nokia, *Global Focus on Youth and Education,* featured company article, 2002.

16. Veli Sundbäck (executive vice president, Nokia), quoted in Nokia, *Global Focus on Youth.*

17. Nokia, vision statement, 2002.

Epigraph Business for Social Responsibility, *FleetBoston: Including the Inner City,* leadership example, February 11, 2002.

Principle #4: Engage in New Alliances

Epigraph Maria Cattaui, interview, quoted in Jane Nelson, *Building Partnerships.*

1. Accenture, *The Connected Corporation,* 2001.

2. Cap Gemini Ernst and Young Center for Business Innovation, *Measuring the Future: The Value Creation Index,* 2000.

3. Ranjay Gulati, Sarah Huffman, and Gary Neilson, "The Barista Principle: Starbucks and the Rise of Relational Capital," reprint no. 02307, *Strategy + Business,* no. 28, 2002. This article draws on research carried out in late 2001 by Booz Allen Hamilton and Northwestern University's Kellogg School of Management, which surveyed 113 executives in a representative sample of Fortune 1000 companies.

4. Interface website, http://www.interface.com

5. Ibid.

6. ST Microelectronics, 2002 Annual Report.

7. Pascale Pistorio, president's statement, in ST Microelectronics, 2002 Annual Report.

8. Rick R. Little (chair, operating council) and Carol Michaels O'Laughlin (executive director), statement, Global Alliance for Workers and Communities Annual Report, 2003.

9. John Chambers (president and CEO, Cisco Systems) statement on Internet Ecosystems, cited on Cisco website, http://www.cisco.com/.

10. David O'Reilly (chairman and CEO, Chevron Texaco), remarks, Leon H. Sullivan Awards Dinner, June 20, 2002.

11. Holly Wise (director, Global Development Alliance, USAID), quoted in Chevron-Texaco Social Responsibility report, CVX, second quarter, 2003.

12. Bill Gates (CEO, Microsoft), remarks, UNICEF breakfast on business support for children, United Nations, New York, June 2002.

13. Vernon Ellis (international chairman, Accenture), comments, CEO dialogue, 2002.

14. U.S. Environmental Protection Agency website, http://www.epa.gov/.

15. Niall FitzGerald, "Meeting Consumers' Needs in the 21st Century," address, CIAA, April 11, 2002.

16. Statistics from World Resources Institute cited on Marine Stewardship Council website, www.msc.org/.

17. Rob Bosworth (deputy commissioner, Alaska Department of Fish and Game), quoted in Unilever, *Fishing for the Future: Unilever's Sustainable Fisheries Initiative,* 2002.

18. "25 Ideas for a Changing World," *Business Week,* August 25, 2002.

19. Unilever, "The Impact of Globalization—A Perspective from Unilever," Submission to the UK House of Lords Select Committee on Economic Affairs, May 2002.

20. *Unilever Annual Review,* 2002.

21. Niall FitzGerald, address by co-chairman to Unilever PLC annual shareholder meeting, May 8, 2002.

Principle #5: Be Performance-Driven in Everything

Epigraph Ian Davis, "Learning to Grow Again: Three Key Questions as Companies Shift to Expansion Mode," *The Economist,* "The World in 2004," 2003: 106–107.

1. Lou Gerstner, *Who Says Elephants Can't Dance?* (New York: HarperCollins, 2002).

2. BT Group, *Making Our Strategy Work,* 2003.

3. Conference Board, *Communicating Corporate Performance: A Delicate Balance,* 1997.

4. KPMG, *Performance Management Study,* 2001.

5. PricewaterhouseCoopers, *2002 Sustainability Survey Report,* August 2002.

6. "Setting Measurable Goals," corporate essay in *The Next Bottom Line, Business Week,* 2000.

7. Unilever, *Listening, Learning, Making Progress,* 2002 social review of 2001 data.

8. PricewaterhouseCoopers, *2002 Sustainability Survey.*

9. Carbon Disclosure Project, www.cdproject.net.

10. KPMG, *2002 International Survey of Sustainability Reporting,* 2002.

11. Simon Zadek and Mira Merme, *Redefining Materiality: Practice and Policy for Effective Corporate Reporting,* AccountAbility and UK Social Investment Forum, July 2003.

12. KPMG, *2002 International Survey.*

13. Aspen Institute Business and Society Program, *Where Will They Lead? MBA Student Attitudes about Business and Society,* 2003.

14. Samuel Palmisano, chairman and CEO of IBM, IBM's 2002 Corporate Responsibility Report, 2003.

15. Sir Mark Moody-Stuart (former chairman, Shell Committee of Managing Directors), the Shell Report, 1999.

16. Jeroen van der Veer (former president, Royal Dutch Petroleum Company and vice chairman, committee of managing directors, Royal Dutch/Shell Group), speech to EIRMA conference, Vienna, May 29, 2002.

17. Jeff Gerth and Stephen Labaton, "Shell Withheld Reserves Data to Aid Nigeria," *New York Times,* page C-4, March 19, 2004.

18. Malcolm Brinded, Shell's head of exploration and production, quoted in the *Financial Times,* page 22. "Shell Forced to Hold Back Annual Report." March 19, 2004.

Principle #6: Practice Superior Governance

Epigraph President George W. Bush, remarks on corporate responsibility, New York, July 9, 2002.

1. *Sustainability governance* is a term coined by CERES (the Coalition for Environ-

mentally Responsible Economies) and SustainAbility Ltd. to encompass the integration of wider social and environmental risk and performance issues into traditional corporate governance structures.

2. Business Roundtable, "A Message to the American People from America's CEOs," media statement, 2002.

3. CERES, *Value at Risk: Climate Change and the Future of Governance,* by Innovest Strategic Value Advisers, 2002.

4. McKinsey & Company, *Global Investor Opinion Survey: Key Findings,* July 2002.

5. Alan Greenspan, "Corporate Governance," remarks, Stern School of Business, New York University, New York, March 26, 2002.

6. Jeffrey Immelt (chairman and CEO, GE), "Restoring Trust," remarks, New York Economic Club, November 4, 2002.

7. J. Nelson, A. Singh, and P. Zollinger, *The Power to Change: Mobilizing Board Leadership to Deliver Sustainable Value to Markets and Society,* International Business Leaders Forum and SustainAbility, 2001.

8. Arthur D. Collins (president and CEO, Medtronic), "Why Medtronic Has a Code of Conduct," statement on company website, http://www.Medtronic.com.

9. Abbott Laboratories, *Ethics in the Workplace,* Social Report, 2002.

10. General Electric, "Letter to GE's Stakeholders," GE 2002 Annual Report.

11. Jeffrey R. Immelt (chairman of the board and CEO, GE), "The Spirit and the Letter of Our Commitment," statement of integrity, January 2002.

12. General Electric, "Letter to GE's Stakeholders."

13. Jeffrey Immelt, interview transcript, "Dialogue" program, APEC (Asia Pacific Economic Council), 2001 Session, hosted by Zhang Wei, February 15, 2002.

14. Ibid.

15. Ibid.

16. Ibid.

17. "Two cheers for GE," *Business Week,* March 25, 2002.

18. General Electric, "Letter to GE's Stakeholders."

19. Larry Washington (global vice president, environment, health, and safety, Dow Chemical), keynote address, Fifth Asia Pacific Responsible Care Conference, Shanghai, November 9, 1999.

20. Ibid.

21. Kofi Annan (Secretary-General, United Nations), remarks, official launch of the UN Global Compact, UN headquarters, New York, July 2001.

22. Thomas L. Friedman, "Knight Is Right," *New York Times,* June 20, 2000.

23. Arianna Huffington, *Pigs at the Trough: How Corporate Greed and Political Corruption Are Undermining America* (New York: Crown Publishers, 2003).

24. Business for Social Responsibility, "Political Contributions," topic overview, website, 2003, http://www.bsr.org.

25. General Motors, website statement, http://www.gm.com.

26. Rick Wagoner (president and CEO, General Motors), "GM Endorses New Corporate Accountability Initiatives," statement, August 6, 2002.

27. Rick Wagoner (president and CEO, General Motors), *"GMability: Demonstrating Our Commitment to Doing It Right,"* statement on company website, http://www.gm.com.

28. For details of the Global Sullivan Principles, see www.sullivanprinciples.org.

29. For details of the CERES Principles, see www.ceres.org.

30. For details of the Global Reporting Initiative, see www.globalreporting.org.

Principle #7: Pursue Purpose Beyond Profit

Epigraph Sir John Browne (group chief exective, BP), statement in *BP in China: Partnership for Progress,* September 2000.

1. Charles A. O'Reilly III and Jeffrey Pfeffer, *Hidden Value: How Great Companies Achieve Extraordinary Results with Ordinary People* (Boston: Harvard Business School Press, 2000).

2. James C. Collins and Jerry I. Porras, *Built to Last: Successful Habits of Visionary Companies* (New York: Harper Business, 1994). See also James C. Collins and Jerry I. Porras, "Building Your Company's Vision," *Harvard Business Review,* September/October 1996.

3. James C. Collins, *From Good to Great: Why Some Companies Make the Leap . . . and Others Don't* (New York: Harper Business, 2001).

4. Research by both the Institute for Global Ethics and the GLOBE Research program has shown that the values of respect, integrity, honesty, fairness, compassion, and responsibility are the most commonly cited by managers of all ages and cultures surveyed in their various projects.

5. Robert S. Kaplan and David P. Norton, *The Strategy Focused Organization: How Balanced Scorecard Companies Thrive in the New Business Environment* (Boston: Harvard Business School Press, 2000).

6. Joshua Chaffin and Stephen Fidler, "Enron Revealed to Be Rotten to the Core," *Financial Times,* April 9, 2002.

7. Harris Interactive and the Reputation Institute, survey results published in the *Wall Street Journal,* February 12, 2003.

8. Johnson & Johnson, "Letter to Shareholders," 2002 Annual Report.

9. Ralph Larsen (former CEO, Johnson & Johnson), statement, European Corporate Responsibility Report, 2001.

10. Arun Sarin (chief executive, Vodafone), statement on company website, 2003, http://www.vodafone.com.

11. Julian Horn-Smith (chief operating officer, Vodafone), statement, Corporate Social Responsibility Report, 2002–2003.

12. Sir Geoffrey Chandler, remarks, Environment Foundation, St. Georges House, Windsor, December 2001; published as "Let's Not Fool Each Other with the Business Case," *Ethical Performance,* May 2002.

13. Ford Motor Company, "Building Our Future," chairman's message to shareholders, 2002 Annual Report.

14. Kevin Rollins (president and COO, Dell), remarks at *Business Week* CEO Summit, September 26, 2002.

15. Kevin Rollins (president and COO, Dell), in conversation with Linda Tischler, senior writer, *Fast Company* magazine, at Churchill Club & Commonwealth Club, Silicon Valley, February 6, 2003.

16. Nasdaq board of directors, media statement, February 2002.

17. Warren Buffett, remarks, Forum for Corporate Conscience meeting, Charlotte, North Carolina, March 14–16, 2003, reported on Global Futures website, http://www.globalff.org.

18. Peter Sutherland (chairman, BP), address to shareholders, Annual General Meeting, April 24, 2003.

19. BP, *What We Stand For,* business policies, August 2002.

20. John Browne (group chief executive, BP), "Beyond Petroleum: Business and the Environment in the 21st Century," speech, hosteed by Stanford Graduate School of Business, March 11, 2002.

21. Ibid.

22. BP, "Sustainable Development," BP corporate website, 2003, http://www.bp.com.

23. John Browne, "Beyond Petroleum."

24. Former BP employee quoted in "BP scarred by furor over safety issues," *Financial Times,* January 2003.

25. Cait Murphy, "Beyond Persuasion," *Fortune,* September 16, 2002.

26. "Browne battles to paint Big Oil green," interview with John Browne (group CEO, BP), *Financial Times,* August 2, 2002.

Conclusion

1. These three trends are summarized from a paper entitled "Globalization and the Challenge of Building Trust through Corporate Responsibility and Good Gover-

nance" by Jane Nelson, International Business Leader Forum, December 2002. They also draw on material in J. Nelson and C. Bergrem, *Responding to the Leadership Challenge: CEO Survey on Global Corporate Citizenship,* World Economic Forum in collaboration with the Prince of Wales International Business Leaders Forum, Davos, January 2003.

2. James C. Humes, *The Wit and Wisdom of Winston Churchill* (New York: Harper Perennial, 1995).

Appendix One

References That Make the Case
for Responsible Business

AccountAbility and Business for Social Responsibility, with Brody Weiser Burns. *Business and Economic Development: The Impact of Corporate Responsibility Standards and Practices,* June 2003.

Amnesty International and the International Business Leaders Forum. *Business and Human Rights: A Geography of Corporate Risk,* 2002.

Association of British Insurers. *Investing in Social Responsibility: Risks and Opportunities,* 2001.

Batstone, David. *Saving the Corporate Soul and (Who Knows?) Maybe Your Own.* San Francisco: Jossey-Bass, 2003.

BT Group with Forum for the Future. *Just Values: Beyond the Business Case for Sustainable Development,* 2003.

CERES. *Value at Risk: Climate Change and the Future of Governance,* Sustainable Governance Project Report. Innovest Strategic Advisors, April 2002.

Collins, J. *From Good to Great: Why Some Companies Make the Leap . . . and Others Don't.* New York: Harper Business, 2001.

Collins, J., and J. Porras. *Built to Last: Successful Habits of Visionary Companies.* New York: Harper Business, 1994.

Conference Board. *Corporate Citizenship in the New Century: Accountability, Transparency and Stakeholder Engagement,* Research Report R-1314-02-RR. Conference Board, 2002.

————. *The Link Between Corporate Citizenship and Financial Performance,* Research Report 1234-99-RR. Conference Board, 1999.

Council on Foundations and Walker Information. *Measuring the Business Value of Corporate Philanthropy,* October 2001.

Elkington, John. *Cannibals with Forks: The Triple Bottom Line of 21st Century Business.* Oxford: Capstone, 1997.

————. *The Chrysalis Economy: How Citizen CEOs and Corporations Can Fuse Values and Value Creation.* Oxford: Capstone, 2001.

Environment and Finance Enterprise. *2001 Performance Review: Profit-driven Sustainability Funds,* August 2002.

Frooman, J. "Socially Irresponsible and Illegal Behaviour and Shareholder Wealth." *Business and Society* 36, no. 3 (1997):

Garten, Jeffrey E. *The Politics of Fortune: A New Agenda for Business Leaders.* Boston: Harvard Business School Press, 2002.

Global Environment Management Initiative. *Environment: Value to Business,* 1999.

————. *Environment: Value to the Top Line,* 2001.

————. *New Paths to Business Value,* 2001.

Goyder, Mark. *Redefining CSR: From the Rhetoric of Accountability to the Reality of Earning Trust.* London: Tomorrow's Company, 2003.

Grayson, David, and Adrian Hodges. *Everybody's Business: Managing Risks and Opportunities in Today's Global Society.* London: Dorling Kindersley, 2001.

Greider, William. *The Soul of Capitalism: Opening Paths to a Moral Economy.* New York: Simon and Schuster, 2003.

Harvard Business Review. *Harvard Business Review on Corporate Responsibility.* Boston: Harvard Business School Press, 2003.

Hilton, Steve, and Giles Gibbons. *Good Business: Your World Needs You.* London: Texere, 2002.

Holliday, Charles O., Stephan Schmidheiny, and Phillip Watts. *Walking the Talk: The Business Case for Sustainable Development.* Sheffield: Greenleaf Publishing, 2002.

Innovest Strategic Value Advisers. *Research Abstracts: A Periodic Review of Research from Industry and Academics.* Innovest Strategic Value Advisers, 1993–2003.

Institute for Business Ethics. *Does Ethics Pay?* IBE, UK, 2003.

Kanter, Rosabeth Moss. "From Spare Change to Real Change: The Social Sector as Beta Site for Business Innovation." *Harvard Business Review* 77, no. 3 (May/June 1999) (reprint 99306).

KPMG. *The Business Case for Sustainability,* 2001.

Krugman, Paul. *The Great Unraveling: Losing Our Way in the New Century.* New York: Norton, 2003.

Little, Arthur D. *The Business Case for Corporate Citizenship.* Boston: Arthur D. Little, 2002.

Litvin, Daniel. *Empires of Profit: Commerce, Conquest and Corporate Reputation.* London, Texere, 2003.

Martin, Roger, L. "The Virtue Matrix: Calculating the Return on Corporate Responsibility." *Harvard Business Review* 80, no. 3 (March 2002) (reprint RO203E).

Nelson, Jane. *Building Competitiveness and Communities: How World-Class Companies Are Creating Shareholder Value and Societal Value.* Prince of Wales

Business Leaders Forum, in collaboration with the World Bank and United Nations Development Program, 1998.

―――. *Building Partnerships: Cooperation Between the United Nations System and the Private Sector.* New York: United Nations Department of Public Information, 2002.

―――. *Business as Partners in Development: Creating Wealth for Countries, Companies and Communities.* Prince of Wales International Business Leaders Forum, in collaboration with the World Bank and the United Nations Development Program, 1996.

―――. *The Business of Peace: The Private Sector as a Partner in Conflict Prevention and Resolution.* International Business Leaders Forum, International Alert, and Council on Economic Priorities, 2000.

―――. *Economic Multipliers: Revisiting the Core Responsibility and Contribution of Business to Development.* International Business Leaders Forum, policy paper 2003, no. 4.

Nelson, Jane, and C. Bergrem. *Values and Value: Communicating the Strategic Importance of Corporate Citizenship to Investors.* World Economic Forum and International Business Leaders Forum, January 2004.

Nelson, Jane, and David Prescott. *Business and the Millennium Development Goals: A Framework for Action.* International Business Leaders Forum, 2003.

Nelson, Jane, A. Singh, and P. Zollinger. *The Power to Change: Mobilising Board Leadership to Deliver Sustainable Value to Markets and Society.* Prince of Wales Business Leaders Forum and SustainAbility, 2001.

Nelson, Jane, and Simon Zadek. *Partnership Alchemy: New Social Partnerships in Europe.* Copenhagen Center, 2000.

Paine, Lynn Sharp. *Value Shift: Why Companies Must Merge Social and Financial Imperatives to Achieve Superior Performance.* New York: McGraw-Hill, 2003.

Porter, Michael E., and Mark R. Kramer. "The Competitive Advantage of Corporate Philanthropy." *Harvard Business Review* 80, no. 12 (December 2002) (reprint RO212D).

Prahalad, C. K., and Allen Hammond. "Serving the World's Poor, Profitably." *Harvard Business Review* 80, no. 9 (September 2002) (reprint RO209C).

Prahalad, C. K., and Stuart L. Hart. "The Fortune at the Bottom of the Pyramid." *Strategy + Business,* no. 26 (First Quarter 2002) (reprint 02106).

Putnam, Robert. D., and Lewis. M. Feldstein. *Better Together: Restoring the American Community.* New York: Simon & Schuster, 2003.

Reed, Donald J. *Stalking the Elusive Business Case for Corporate Sustainability.* World Resources Institute, December 2001.

Rochlin, S., and B. Christoffer. *Making the Business Case: Determining the Value of Corporate Community Involvement.* Boston College Center for Corporate Citizenship, 2000.

SustainAbility and UNEP. *Buried Treasure: Uncovering the Business Case for Corporate Sustainability,* 2001.

Tichy, Noel M., and Andrew R. McGill, eds. *The Michigan Business School Guide to the Ethical Challenge: How to Lead with Unyielding Integrity.* San Francisco: Jossey-Bass, 2003.

Verschoor, C. *Corporate Performance Is Closely Linked to a Strong Ethical Performance.* Chicago: DePaul University, 1999.

Waddock, S., and S. Graves. "Beyond Built to Last . . . Stakeholder Relations in 'Built-to-Last' Companies." *Business and Society Review* 105, no. 4 (2000): 393–418.

World Business Council for Sustainable Development. *The Business Case for Sustainable Development: Walking the Talk.* 2001.

World Resources Institute, United Nations Environment Program, and World Business Council for Sustainable Development. *Tomorrow's Markets: Global Trends and Their Implications for Business,* 2002.

Worldwide Fund for Nature (WWF-UK) and Cable and Wireless. *To Whose Profit? Building a Business Case for Sustainability,* 2002.

Zadek, Simon. *The Civil Corporation: The New Economy of Corporate Citizenship.* London: Earthscan, 2001.

———. *Doing Good and Doing Well: Making the Business Case for Corporate Citizenship.* Conference Board, 2000.

Zadek, Simon, and John Weiser. *Conversations with Disbelievers: Persuading Business to Address Social Challenges.* Ford Foundation, November 2000.

Appendix Two

Responsible Business—Useful Contacts

AccountAbility—www.accountability.org

Aspen Institute Business and Society Program—
www.aspeninstitute.org

Association of Chartered Certified Accountants (ACCA)—
www.accaglobal.com

Boston College Center for Corporate Citizenship—www.bc.edu/ccc

Brody Weiser Burns—www.brodyweiser.com

Business as an Agent of World Benefit—
www.weatherhead.cwru.edu/bawb

Business for Social Responsibility—www.bsr.org

Business in the Community—www.bitc.org.uk

Business Strengthening America—www.bsa.networkforgood.org

Center for Responsibility in Business—www.cfrib.org

The Centre for Tomorrow's Company—www.tomorrowscompany.com

Coalition for Environmentally Responsible Economies—
www.ceres.org

Committee for Economic Development—www.ced.org

Committee to Encourage Corporate Philanthropy—
www.corphilanthropy.org

Community Development Venture Capital Alliance—www.cdvca.org

The Conference Board—www.conference-board.org

Conservation International—www.ci.org

The Copenhagen Centre—www.copenhagencentre.org

Corporate Citizenship Company—
www.corporatecitizenshipcompany.com

Corporate Council on Africa—www.africancl.org

CSR Europe—www.csreurope.org

CSRWire—www.csrwire.com

Ecos Corporation—www.ecoscorporation.com

Ethical Corporation—www.ethicalcorporation.com

Ford Foundation Corporate Involvement Initiative—
www.winwinpartner.com

Forum for Corporate Conscience—
www.forumforcorporateconscience.com

Future 500 and Global Futures—www.globalff.org

Global Alliance for Workers and Communities—
www.theglobalalliance.org

Global Business Coalition Against HIV/AIDS—
www.businessfightsaids.org

Global Business Network—www.gbn.com

Global Compact—www.unglobalcompact.org

Global Reporting Initiative—www.globalreporting.org

Innovest—www.innovestgroup.com

Instituto Ethos—www.ethos.org

Interfaith Center on Corporate Responsibility—www.iccr.org

Jobs for the Future—www.jff.org

Kenan Institute—www.kenaninstitute.unc.edu

Kennedy School of Government CSR Initiative—
www.ksg.harvard.edu

Local Initiatives Support Corporation—www.liscnet.org

Milken Institute—www.milken-inst.org

National Association of Manufacturers—www.nam.org

National Business Initiative—www.nbi.org.za

National Congress for Community Economic Development—
www.ncced.org

National Minority Supplier Development Council—www.nmsdcus.org

Net Impact—www.net-impact.org

The Prince of Wales International Business Leaders Forum—
www.iblf.org

Rocky Mountain Institute—www.rmi.org

Rotary International—www.rotary.org

Social Accountability International—www.cepaa.org

Social Compact—www.socialcompact.org

Social Investment Forum—www.socialinvest.org

Social Venture Network—www.svn.org

SustainAbility—www.sustainability.com

U.S. Chamber of Commerce Center on Corporate Citizenship—
www.uschamber.com

World Business Council for Sustainable Development—
www.wbcsd.org

World Resources Institute—www.wri.org

Index